FROM THE PASTOR'S DESK

Spiritual Reflections

Msgr. Thomas M. Wells

Library of Congress
Catalog Card Number: pending

ISBN 0-9706142-1-7

Published by Our Lady of Lourdes Parish
Archdiocese of Washington, D.C.
7500 Pearl Street, Bethesda, MD 20814

Photo of Msgr. Wells by Today's Parish
Photo of stained glass window by James Ronan

Printed and bound by
CLB Printing Company
Kensington, MD
in the United States of America

Introduction

One of the greatest of all poems reminds all who reflect on God's Word and ways:

> For as the rain and the snow come down from the sky
> and do not return there but water the earth
> making it bring forth and sprout,
> giving seed to one who sows and bread to one who eats
> so shall My word be that goes forth from my mouth;
> it shall not return to me empty
> but it shall accomplish that which I intend,
> and prosper in the thing for which I sent it.
>
> —*Isaiah 55:10-11*

Since before time began, the Word of the Lord has permeated our earth and our lives. God's Word is too big and too powerful to be encompassed in the pages of all the books that have ever been written. But occasionally preachers and pastors by their words and ways provide a keyhole through which we can glimpse the larger reality of God's Word.

This book is a collection of the spiritual reflections of Msgr. Thomas Wells, called *From the Pastor's Desk,* that appeared in the Our Lady of Lourdes Parish Bulletin from March 13, 1994 to January 24, 1999. Following the tragic death of Msgr. Wells on June 8, 2000 a group of Lourdes parishioners with the assistance of Monsignor's family dedicated themselves to compiling these writings.

To prepare them for publication, the readers gave each column a title and organized them by themes. Except for minor typographical and a few punctuation changes, the writings are presented as Msgr. Wells published them in the Parish Bulletin. If the columns were republished, the original date of publication is listed under the column.

As I have read and re-read these reflections of my brother priest and predecessor as pastor of Lourdes, I felt like he was sharing his view through the keyhole and whispering in my ear about the applications of our Catholic Faith. I also felt invited: these pages invite us to go beyond Tom's reflections to listen to God's Word in prayer and action, in continued Scripture study, and in the people and world around us, and walk in God's ways.

In *From the Pastor's Desk,* Msgr. Wells offers us something to think about, something to savor, something to aspire to, something to smile at, a value to cling to, a goal to reach, a touch of humor to relax over, and a truth of faith to live by.

In our grieving, we at Lourdes are deeply indebted to all who labored to console us and all who knew him. And Tommy, we are grateful we knew you. Thank you especially for your gift of love and example, and until we meet again, your words.

May your word accomplish that which was intended and prosper in that for which you wrote it
                    GOD's GLORY . . .
        and for us remaining
                    YOUR MEMORY.

                                    Father James P. Meyers

Table of Contents

WORLDLINESS

CONCLUSION

INDEXES

How We Are Called to Live

September 3, 1995

The pace of summer is so quiet in the parish that I must confess to some regret as we move into what really is the new year in our society. It hardly seems possible, but even as we continue to pray for rain and cooler weather, those who wisely look ahead can easily see Thanksgiving and Christmas on the horizon. Since this seems to be a time for blocking off sections of the calendar year, I have decided to use this space in the bulletin for the next eight or ten weeks to develop some thoughts on the Beatitudes, those sayings of Jesus (recorded in different forms in the Gospels of Matthew and Luke) that are the beginning of the Sermon on the Mount.

Without going into too much background, it is more important to remember that Matthew, whose version of the Beatitudes is the more familiar (Mt. 5:1-12), saw Jesus as the new Moses, and saw Jesus' life as the fulfillment of the Law of Moses. So, it is no accident that Matthew tells us that the Sermon takes place "on the mount." Thus, the New Law of Jesus is linked to the mountain on which Moses received the Old Law.

However, it takes little examination to see how different are the Ten Commandments from the Beatitudes, at least on the surface. I may be able to honor my parents, for example, or refrain from stealing, but I cannot say that I hunger and thirst for righteousness in the all-consuming sense in which it is commanded by the Lord. Actually, many Scripture commentators say that even the Ten Commandments should be observed with a spiritual and interior interpretation that leads us to the heart of the Law, but there is no question that observance of the Beatitudes is impossible apart from a relationship with Him who gave them to us.

And that is the point: Jesus is the Lawgiver. He is the Law and He is the power to observe the Law. The Law is given to us so that we might achieve the blessedness that every person seeks. We are destined for God; we are made in His image and unless we live like God, we must wander through life unfulfilled. Blessedness, the life of God, is achieved through God's good grace and our choice. The Beatitudes (based on the Latin word for blessed) are reminders of the power that is given to us through God's grace and they are statements of how we are called to live.

Blessed Are the Poor in Spirit,...

September 10, 1995

C.S. Lewis has a powerful image that prepares us to look at the first Beatitude. He compares the coming of Christ to the coming of a wealthy uncle to visit his impoverished nephew who is playing in the muck of the street making mud-pies. The uncle invites the child to go off to play on the beach by the ocean, but the child refuses. God offers life to us; He offers union with Him, but our lack of faith and imagination allows us to choose the world rather than Him who is the Lord of the world.

As we look at the Beatitude, "Blessed are the poor in spirit, the Kingdom of heaven is theirs," I am struck by the difference between poverty and poverty of spirit. On the one hand who can deny our ultimate poverty? Can I really make myself all that I want to be; do I really think I am in control of my destiny; and, with the real possibility of being in the wrong place at the wrong time, do I think I can certainly defeat a sudden death? No, whether I want to face it or not, I am poor when it comes to the only possessions that really matter.

The problem, of course, is that because I am the son of Adam, my vision is limited and to use C.S. Lewis, I prefer mud-pies. I have been baptized into Christ and I have been given the Spirit that allows me to acknowledge the fullness of life that is in Him, but I hate to let go of the mud-pies. Like the small boy, I've never seen the ocean that is promised. Surely it sounds grand and with all that said, I could leave mud-pies behind and go on to castles and who-knows-what my creativity could devise. But I cannot leave the muck of the slums, with their limited, but familiar, horizons of selfishness and pride, unless I put my trust in this very kind uncle who turns out to make some pretty uncompromising demands in return for what He promises. You see, the small boy feels like he controls his puddle and the pies that come from it. This trust that he places in the rich uncle comes from a poverty of spirit that realizes that mud-pies are nothing compared to what his good uncle gladly will give him. But, can the uncle deliver?

Everyone notices how often Jesus preaches against the danger of money and human possessions. These things glitter and can buy such pretty glitter that they seem nothing like mud-pies, but compared to the Kingdom of heaven they are less than mud or glitter. If we are to enter the Kingdom, we must rejoice in the greatness of God and become detached from all that is of the world.

Blessed Are the Sorrowing,...

September 24, 1995

Sometimes, in an attempt to get a widow or a widower to look at their sorrow from a different perspective, I will say to them, when discussing their terrible pain, "That's what you get for falling in love." One thing is for sure, there will be no sorrow for the person who does not love; and likewise it is certain that one who is great in love will know great sorrow. So also it is true that He who is infinite Love knew the infinite sorrow of the Cross.

"Blessed are the sorrowing, they shall be consoled," says the third Beatitude. We try so hard to turn this world into paradise. Malls, gyms, cruises and how many other diversions hold out for us perfection in style, health or pleasure; we try so hard to deny that this is, and always will be, a "vale of tears." I am sure that all the great religions acknowledge the inevitability of suffering and sorrow; some in fact, are built around a stoic acceptance of suffering, but only Christ will so scandalously say that the sorrowing are blessed. There are a number of reasons why this is true.

First of all, the ache of sorrow, that experience of pain that comes from death or sometimes even worse, from the rejection by one who has been beloved, is one of life's most terrible reminders that we are not self-sufficient. The experience of sorrow invites me to put my trust in Him who has overcome the world. If I let my sorrow at the loss of one who is beloved lead me closer to Him whose love is everlasting, then that one who has been lost has performed, in some mysterious way, his greatest service of love.

In still another sense, the one who loves must be a person of sorrow. Can one in whom the love of Christ dwells not sorrow over the state of our world? Can I do other than be sorrowful as I see loved ones leave the sacraments; is there not real sorrow as I see a woman to whom I was once close choose to abort an unwanted baby; who could be other than sorrowful while watching children cope with grievous irresponsibility in their parents? That person is blessed because the sorrow comes from the recognition that those whom they love, in rejecting God or His way, are choosing pain either for themselves or for others. It is, in some infinitely small way, a share in the pain of rejection felt by Christ on the Cross.

Many of the great saints knew great sorrow; but interestingly enough, I read somewhere that a person will not be canonized unless there are signs of great joy in his life. Sorrow, in and of itself, is insufficient. Rather, that a person who suffers with the Lord will be consoled. As He triumphed over suffering and sorrow, so also will those who join their sorrow with His.

Blessed Are the Meek,...

One of the most frequent images used of Israel and in the New Testament, the Church, is that of the bride. Over and over again, we hear the Church referred to as the bride of Christ or the prophets speak of God taking Israel as His wife forever. Images, of course, work on several levels. Seeing ourselves as the bride of Christ allows us to meditate on the beautiful love that God has for us; but the image also implies something else. If in this image (which after all, is the inspired word of God), God is the husband of His people, then spiritually speaking, we are all feminine. Spiritual writers have recognized this for centuries. What does it mean?

Just as a woman submits to the love of her husband in intercourse, so we are called to submit to God's life and love in our lives. Now, all of a sudden, the image becomes far more difficult, especially in our age. Submission is seen as weakness; power is seen as victory, and even before we get started, spirituality is caught in contemporary sexual politics and competition. The image however, remains, and in fact, is one of the most useful ways to approach the third Beatitude, "Blessed are the meek, they shall inherit the earth."

Just as Christ who was utterly submissive to the will of the Father was not weak and just as the wife who submits to her husband is most certainly not weak as she carries and brings forth new life, so the person who possesses the virtue of meekness does not fit the equation of meekness with weakness. The person who is meek is the person who submits to God in all things; he is that person who has the humility to see every situation as God sees it and who seeks the wisdom of God in approaching a solution. The father who teaches his son not to start fights in school, but who also teaches him not to back down before a bully, may well be giving a practical lesson in meekness. The meek person may be called to teach the bully the error of his ways. Likewise, it may be the meek person who recognizes in the anger and obnoxious behavior of a fellow employee that something may be at work under the surface and who may pray for the person rather than react with anger and gossip.

It was the meekness in Christ that led him to submit to "death, death on a cross," but it is the same Christ who inherited the "new heavens and the new earth" on Easter Sunday. Likewise, the meek who submit to the will of the Father in all things will, with the Son, inherit the earth.

Blessed Are Those Who Hunger and Thirst for Holiness,...

October 1, 1995

A good friend of mine grew up in the Soviet Union during the times of Stalin's purges in the 1930's. One of the many fascinating stories that he tells concerns the wedding of his sister. That evening marked the first time he experienced two things: a religious ceremony and white bread. The wedding, held secretly in the darkest time of night for fear of the Communist secret police, was the first time his parents had dared to expose him to religion and to the beauty of the Orthodox liturgy. The white bread (which he cheerfully admits made more of an impression on him than the liturgy) was somehow obtained for a wedding dinner in their small peasant home. The bread and extra food made such an impression on this young boy because he says that he can remember that night as being the first time in his life that he went to bed without hunger pains.

Likewise, when Jesus speaks in the fourth Beatitude of "those who hunger and thirst for holiness," He knew of what He spoke. The average person of Palestine lived on the edge of survival; for such people, images in Scripture of wedding feasts to describe God's abundance rang true. Also, people who lived so near to the desert readily identified with what thirst really means and how easy it is to become desperate for life-saving water.

In a real sense, of course, we are made for God and so, there can never be complete satisfaction with this life. Even the happiest person experiences at least vague dissatisfaction with life and a sense that it could be more than it is. Our hearts are made for God. In that sense; there is a natural hunger for Him. This Beatitude, however, calls us to more than a natural yearning for happiness; it calls for an active hungering of God.

Ultimately, God is love; He is total self-giving, both within the Trinity and outside of Himself in the world. What we yearn for then, is this God who is love; who is self-giving. The great paradox of this Beatitude is that for which we hunger, God's life, can only be satisfied by giving that life away. And so, the more I give myself away, either to God or neighbor, the more my hunger for holiness will be satisfied. Jesus so much hungered to live God's life here on earth that His life was poured out on the Cross; and most completely, that hunger was satisfied on Easter Sunday.

Blessed Are the Pure of Heart,...

We are still several weeks away from November, so perhaps a thought on purgatory might seem to be rushing things a bit. However, the sixth Beatitude, "Blessed are the pure of heart, for they shall see God," reminded me of the wisdom of our teaching on judgment.

God will not force anyone to go to heaven. He does not send anyone to hell, but He certainly will respect my freedom to choose to reject Him for all eternity. In other words, I can choose hell. In fact, I believe that if God did force everyone to go to heaven, that heaven itself would be hell for those who had rejected Him. Only those who are like God can see God; only those whose hearts are pure can see His face. That purity of heart, of course, is the gift of grace (God's life within us) given in Baptism. That is why, for example, we believe that the baptized baby will be immediately in God's presence: the purity of heart, given in Baptism, is utterly untouched.

For those who do not die as infants, there is that struggle that exists as a result of a nature weakened by original sin. Truly we are graced; at the same time, there is within us an attraction to sin. A simple example: I am often surprised at Mass, when I may be holding the very Body of Christ in my hand, by a temptation to anger because of someone or something that irritates me at the time. I want to love God, especially while celebrating Mass, but my heart is torn. That purity of heart, that union with God given at Baptism is alloyed by the tendency to choose self over cooperation with grace.

Purity of heart then, is both gift and responsibility. Life is about saying "Yes" to the gift of God's life within me. Purgatory, looked at from this perspective, is not punishment in the usual sense of the word. It is confrontation with all that God has offered to me at every turn of my life and the realization of how my heart has so weakly responded to Him. Oh yes, my sins have been forgiven in life, but even then, my gratitude has been half-hearted and unfocused; so often I have fallen back into the same fault; so little did I appreciate the Blood of Jesus poured out for my sins. Purgatory is the experience of recognizing how much God has loved me and how pitiful has been my response. Will that process be painful? I suspect that it will be awful, but it surely will purify me of all that is not of God.

Does everyone go to purgatory? Certainly, I have no idea. This, however, I do know. Only those who are pure of heart will see God and either here or hereafter, we must be purified.

Blessed Are the Peacemakers,...

October 22, 1995

How ironic that we come to the seventh Beatitude, "Blessed are the peacemakers; they shall be called children of God," at this time when the lack of complete racial peace is so obvious in American life. Evidence tells us that large numbers of whites are outraged at the outcome of the Simpson trial and blame that outcome on the racial make-up of the jury. Others look at the racially charged rhetoric of Farrakhan and wonder at the future of our country as a place where many from different backgrounds can live in harmony. Blacks, of course, claim that the taped remarks of a Furman represent the attitude of many in law enforcement and from this, claim that legal justice is unlikely for them. For me, personally, the most telling remark to come out of this week's demonstration downtown was that of a man who had traveled nineteen hours driving a bus from St. Louis. He spoke of listening to his CB radio and hearing white truck drivers routinely talking about the "niggers" going to D.C. for the March. What is he supposed to feel?

Maybe we are not so bad. Canada may come apart as a country over language. The Irish have been killing themselves for hundreds of years over ways of worshiping Him who gives us His peace, and how many hundreds of thousands were slaughtered in Africa last year because of tribal differences? On the issue of peace, I suspect there have been very few "good old days." Conflict and bloodshed seems to be very much our normal state.

The Jewish greeting, "Shalom," is translated, of course, "Peace." What interests me though, is that peace, in the sense of shalom, comes from being at one with God. In other words, the life of God is peace. Our longing for peace is really a longing for God Himself. I suppose that it sounds simplistic and I know that the world goes about it in a far different way (and not too successfully, if I might say it), but a peacemaker is one who gives to each person an experience of the goodness of God. Peace is not weak: Jesus forcibly ejected those who desecrated His Father's house; but peace is that which a person, who is at one with God, chooses to give to all whom he meets.

Our racial division causes fear among some; hostility in others; stereotyping by many and frustration and hopelessness among those of secular good will. Of course, those who profess the Name of Jesus have often booted it in the past: our faith is often weak and compromised by the times; but the peace for which the world longs comes only from Him and only we who · claim to be His disciples are capable of giving that peace to the world.

Blessed Are Those Persecuted for Holiness Sake,...

November 5, 1995

I read an account recently of a homosexual parade in New York City that pointedly made St. Patrick's Cathedral its focus. The author reported activities by those marching (and deliberately did not report many such other activities) that would strain the normal imagination. The reaction of the police and city officials was one of either acceptance or in the face of individually repulsive actions directed towards the Church, indifference. On the other hand, with increasing frequency, right to life advocates who violate civic codes against blocking abortion clinic entrances report both physical attacks and degrading searches by police. Did you notice that last week the Washington Post excerpted from a book by a British author who has for years made a career of trashing, of all people, Mother Teresa? In the "Commentary" section, we are told that Mother has accepted donations from people who turned out later, for a variety of reasons, to be unsavory. Three such people, I believe, were mentioned. If I have contributed to the Missionaries of Charity, if more than a few of those who read this have so contributed, is it so great a shock that the bad as well as the not so bad have been attracted to her?

The least surprising of the Beatitudes is the last: "Blessed are those persecuted for holiness sake; the reign of God is theirs." The increasing scorn in which the Church is held by politicians and media reflects either that those who see themselves as powerful are moving farther and farther away from a religious and moral world view or that believers are doing a better job of proclaiming Christ's call to change of heart. It is probably something of both. Attempts to marginalize the Church and religious people through mockery or judicial decrees are no surprise (the Lord promised no less), but why does He call persecution blessed?

Jesus died on the Cross because in the face of hatred, He refused to stop proclaiming God's truth. Since the world's hatred is ultimate Love, conflict is inevitable. I am blessed if God gives me the opportunity to continue to love or forgive or act as Jesus would act; I am being given the opportunity to do His work in the world. I am being given the chance to do what He did: to say, in the face of sin, that God's way is more powerful; to say that the Cross has conquered the wiles and snares of the devil. On Good Friday, it was hard for Mary to see the Cross as blessedness; so will it be hard for the Church to see mockery and scorn as blessed. However, faith tells us that, just as Jesus was victorious because He did not back away, so also will His Church continue to prosper as long as she embraces with hope and joy the opportunity to share His Cross.

Self-emptying Love

December 25, 1994

There is a passage in Paul's Epistle to the Philippians which, for me best sums up the miracle of Christmas. Paul, in fact, quotes a hymn that must have been sung in the Church around the year 55. He says,

> Though he was in the form of God, He did not regard equality with God as something to be exploited, but emptied himself, taking the form of a slave, being born in human likeness.
>
> *Philippians 2:6-7*

John, in the Gospel of Christmas Day, tells us, "The Word became flesh, and dwelt among us;" but, what, exactly is that Word? This is the creative Word spoken by God that brought from nothing the majesty, the enormity and the complexity of the universe; this is the life-giving Word that gave breath to Adam and which formed Eve from his rib. This word that became flesh and dwelt among us is the Son of the eternal Father, who, with the Father and the Spirit, is eternally God.

Can you not begin to see Paul's mind "blown away" by contemplating the birth of Christ? Paul says Jesus took the form of a slave, but even that demeaning description does not touch the self-emptying of the Lord. After all, a slave is as human as his master; and so, the difference between Jesus, the Word made flesh, and us is infinitely greater than that between master and slave. It is almost as if, loving a statue that I had created, I decided to become a statue and, even more, to make myself subject to the statue.

Do not downplay original sin. Because of it, there existed a disorder in creation that no one of us, wounded and stained by that sin, could heal. We were doomed to eternity alienated from God. God's word is love; His very life is love; and it is only because of that love that He could chose to empty Himself of His divine prerogatives and live, in human form, that divine love. This He did, knowing full well that a world given over to sin would reject His love and do all it could to defeat Him, even to death on a cross.

People of Our Lady of Lourdes, Happy Christmas! May the newborn King of the Jews give us a deep understanding of the ocean of love into which we were immersed because He has come among us to share the life of God.

Christmas Sharing:
Passing on the Gift of Faith

December 31, 1995

The Holy Father has written a poem, "A Conversation with God Begins," in which are the following lines:

"Man who departs endures in those who follow. Man who follows endures in those departed. Man endures beyond all coming and going in himself and in you."

The recognition of how much we are connected with the past and the future never seems more obvious than at the Christmas season. As a young man who finds that others look at me as if I am somehow well into middle age, I do, at least, find that a certain perspective is being given to me. My grandmother who died in 1981 was born in 1878; the youngest of her great great grandchildren, now five months old, will, pray God, live until the second half of the first century of the third millennium. So well do I remember riding through the mountains of Pennsylvania to her house on Christmas night after dinner at my other grandparents' in Washington. What I received at those two homes, one Protestant and the other Catholic, was so much more important than whatever gifts were distributed. I received what had been passed on from their own parents—on one side of Yankee stock from Vermont and the other from some forgotten parts of Ireland: that what life is all about, at its deepest level, is faith and family. As I drove home from the mayhem that passes for our family Christmas dinner, I could not help but reflect that, while the style is somewhat different (a potluck dinner where the priest is expected to bring of the surplus of sweets that are dropped by the rectory), the substance is the same. God forgive us, it took so long to put the food out and to arrange and settle the young, that grace was forgotten; but, thank God, we have received and, again through God's grace only, have passed a wonderful sense that, in the Christ whose birth we celebrate, there is our deepest hope and joy.

The memorable line of Katherine Hepburn from *Lion in Winter*, "Every family has its ups and downs," reminds us that it is always possible to reject what we have been given. One of the incredible aspects of the Incarnation, that God has become one for us, is that we must cooperate in the working out of our salvation. No matter how hard those who have gone before us have worked to give us faith and family, so we must daily choose to work and pray that those who come after us know the abundant goodness of God's love.

Listening to Christmas

December 22, 1996

I had a chance to work off a little of the temporal punishment due to sin the other day by going to a mall. Among the experiences that called me to reflect on the foolishness of my sins was being third in line at an information booth. The good lady alternated by serving those standing before her and those calling. What struck me was the number of words she used to greet each of us and to tell each of us her name. Of course the holiday that occasioned both her greeting and the mob that surrounded us was not mentioned in all of those words; but she did, in a way that would have surprised her, I am sure, remind me to speak less and listen more. Hers and all of the other mindlessly cheery chatter of the mall highlight the contrast between words and the Word made flesh whose birth we celebrate.

One of the things that is striking about all of the Christmas stories is the atmosphere of quiet in which our imagination has them take place. We see the angel come to Mary while she is alone in prayer in her home in Nazareth; the shepherds watch over their flock at the quietest time of the night; the Magi search for years in the quiet desolation of the desert and Mary "ponders all these things in her heart." St. John tells of the Mystery of Christmas in the prologue to his Gospel. Those who avoid the crowds who come to Masses of Christmas Eve and actually participate in a Mass of Christmas will hear John's proclamation, "And the word became flesh and dwelt among us." Jesus, the Word, who is the Father's absolute image and self-communication, has become our brother.

One of my CCD students, when asked recently what incident from the Gospels says the most to her, responded that she is moved by the agony of Christ in the Garden because she finds it so hard to imagine His knowing the suffering that awaited Him and His choice to accept it. In other words, my student is beginning to contemplate the Mystery of Christ. And so, we see the major figures of this season from Joseph to the Simeon at the Temple as people of faith who contemplated the Word of God.

The Word became flesh but the Word speaks to the heart. The heart that is accustomed to words spoken just to fill silence will likely miss the Word so often spoken in silence. Be attentive during these days: go apart with Our Lady, with the shepherds, with Joseph and with believers of every age, and contemplate the Good News that our God has become one of us.

A Share in the Life of the Trinity

September 28, 1997

Humanity reflects the life of the Trinity. This, I think, is one of the things meant by Scripture's saying that we are made in the image and likeness of God. The better we know God, the better we know ourselves. Think about this, for example. From all eternity, it is the nature and role of the eternally begotten Son to love the Father. From all eternity, the Son responds in love to the Father whose love begot Him. The Holy Spirit, of course, is the love that eternally is exchanged between the Father and the Son.

It is the nature, then, of the Son to respond to the love of the Father. The Incarnation—the word we give to describe that God became man in the womb of Mary—is so extraordinary because it means that our brother in humanity, Jesus, not only continues to be in a relationship and intimate union with the Father, but He also enables us to participate in that same relationship. Now, St. Paul makes the crucial distinction that what belongs to Jesus by nature (His Sonship) is ours only by adoption. In other words, because of the death and Resurrection of Christ, we are the adopted sons and daughters of God. In the Spirit of Jesus, we can cry out, "Abba, Father," and know that we are heard as dearly loved children.

Our challenge is to unite ourselves with Jesus. Again, St. Paul uses images like, "Clothe yourselves in Christ," or, "Put on the armor of God," to illustrate our potential to be remade in Christ. The reality, of course, is that because our potential is to live the life of Christ, like Him we have freedom: we are not forced to live the life we were given in Baptism. Inevitably, we fall short.

This is why the Eucharist is so central to God's plan for us. The great human act of love for the Father is the sacrifice of Jesus. Until time is no more, Jesus, our brother, continues to give Himself in love to the Father for us, and the Father continues to say, "Yes," to the prayer of His Son and our brother. The incredible miracle of the Mass is that, through the sacramentality of the priesthood, we can join with Jesus in that most perfect and pleasing act of praise. Insofar as we unite ourselves with Jesus, we are caught up in the very life of the Trinity.

Real Presence of Christ in the Eucharist

April 5, 1998

"Praise, adoration and thanksgiving be to our Savior Jesus Christ, present in the Blessed Sacrament of the altar." I cannot remember whose wedding I will witness this Saturday (do not panic, I have a calendar!), but I remember the prayer that I learned as a little boy for the procession before the Eucharist on Holy Thursday. And so again this year, our children will process in honor of Christ who is really present under the signs of bread and wine and who gave Himself to us in this sacrament on the night before He died. How simply, how fervently and how beautifully those children believe; but how, also, we pray that their childlike faith will mature and develop as age and experience challenge them into adult appreciation of the Blessed Sacrament. Like children, perhaps, the Apostles may have abandoned Jesus after the Last Supper, but they did not forget the dramatic ways that He changed the focus of the Passover they had celebrated. They recognized and celebrated from the first moments of the Christian era that Jesus had made Himself the focus of that Passover and that it had anticipated both His death and His Resurrection.

It is interesting to note that it was many centuries into the history of the Church before anyone claiming to be a Christian questioned the Real Presence of Christ in the Eucharist. It was, I suppose, taken for granted that the Lord would desire to be with His people in so intimate a way. The questions about the Real Presence, when they did come, led many away from this incomparable gift, but those questions also led the Church to examine our faith and to explain how what seems to be contrary to the senses is in fact the body, blood, soul and divinity of Christ. So often, when I ask young people what they receive in Communion, they will, from rote, say, "The Body of Christ," and as far as the words go, this is true. What the Church affirms, though, is that we receive the Person of Jesus. No one questions that this is mystery. It is mystery enough when we affirm that in the Incarnation of Jesus, His divinity—His nature as God—was hidden within a visible humanity; but in the Eucharist, we affirm Jesus' Presence, even though both humanity and divinity are hidden from our sight.

So much can be said of the gift of the Eucharist. Speaking, even so briefly, of the Real Presence, does not begin to engage the dimensions of the Eucharist as worship, as sacrifice, as sacred banquet, as foretaste of heaven or as Bread of Life. As we commemorate the gift of this most Blessed Sacrament on Holy Thursday, let us beg God to give us an adult faith and love of this Mystery and to enter into the Eucharist as believing and grateful Catholics, overwhelmed that our God would draw us so close to Himself.

Sacrificial Meal
August 14, 1994

My earliest days as a priest were those of tremendous division in the Church between "liberals" and "conservatives," between those who accepted the changes in the Church and those who rejected them. And since my first assignment was in a then young parish, I suppose the differences were even more stressed and exaggerated than, perhaps, would have been the case in a more settled community. At any rate, I quickly discovered a rule of thumb for telling which "side" people were on who had invited the newly ordained priest to dinner. The so-called conservatives would serve roast beef and the liberals, lasagna. I can remember how my mom would laugh when I would share with her this distinction which was, of course, mostly in my imagination.

I share this memory with a smile because it reminds me of one of the great blessings of being a parish priest: the frequent experience of hospitality. I would be embarrassed, I am sure, at the number of family names I have forgotten with whom I have shared a meal over the years, but each one of them has offered me the privilege of sharing a bit in the heart of their family life. In that same first assignment, I made the rookie priest's mistake of telling someone what is my favorite meal. Well, it is not my favorite any-more, for reasons too obvious to state. But, again, the message: "Father, be a part of our family's life and love."

Fr. Henri Nouwen's latest book, *With Burning Hearts*, speaks of the Eucharist from that perspective of the Lord's desire to share His life and love with us. First, in the Incarnation, where God became man in Christ, God did all that he could do to communicate His love for His children. God shared His life with us completely in Jesus. But then, in the Eucharist, Jesus, in the form of a sacrificial meal, shares not just a token of His life and love (as does the family who invites a guest for dinner), but His very Self. Jesus, because His is God, has the power and the desire to be in communication with those whom He loves.

The Real Presence of Christ in the Eucharist is, of course, a difficult Mystery to understand. It is not difficult to understand—in fact, we experi-ence it all the time—that a family would seek to share its spirit through a meal. Does it not begin to make sense that this is the sign that the Lord Himself would use as He seeks to pour out His life for us?

Word Made Flesh

I had the strangest thought recently when I was celebrating Mass. Out of the clear I saw how easily I could desecrate the Blessed Sacrament. I was in no way tempted to do so, of course. In fact, I was led to a meditation on the vulnerability of the Lord in the Sacrament. Our faith tells us that we receive the Lord; bread and wine are really changed into His Body and Blood. It is the all-holy and all-powerful God whom we receive. But is it not, in some way, almost scandalous that He comes to us so easily, even in a way where He does not have to be taken seriously?

In his wonderful book, *Crossing the Threshold of Hope,* Pope John Paul speaks briefly of Islam. The Pope writes of the Muslim concept of God: "... He is ultimately a God outside of the world, a God who is only Majesty, never Emmanuel, God-with-us." Compared to the Muslim vision of God, a God majestic and omnipotent, infinitely removed from creatures who will be judged with legalistic formality, can you not begin to sense how staggering is the claim that God comes to be in intimate communion with His people under the signs of bread and wine? What we celebrate in the Eucharist, of course, is simply a sacramental living out of the miracle of the Incarnation, the Mystery of the Word made Flesh in Jesus.

One does not have to be an ESPN sports fanatic to have frequently seen the banner held aloft by fans at a sporting event that says, simply, John 3:16. Whatever group has gone to this effort over the years could not have chosen more wisely a Scripture quote to emphasize the point that I am trying to make: "God so loved the world that He gave His only Son that whoever believes in Him may not die but may have eternal life." Whether we speak about the Eucharist, the Incarnation or, really, any way in which God interacts with us, it all comes to a manifestation of God's love for the world. Is there an element of scandal in the almighty God becoming so vulnerable that our evil can cause the Cross? I am sure there is, but where does love stop? If God offers to share His life with us and, through sin, we reject the offer, would it really be love if God stopped giving in the face of our rejection?

Yes, it is possible to desecrate the Eucharist, or, perhaps even worse, to ignore the Real Presence of the Lord under signs of bread and wine. But, if even only one person accepted that gift of sharing in His life and all others rejected it the Lord would still say "Take and eat, this is my body." Love does such things.

The Enormity of It All!

December 21, 1997

The enormity of it all! It strikes me at the most surprising times. The other afternoon, I was opening the tabernacle to get a Host for a sick call and I was blown away by the reality that I was preparing to take the eternal God to someone. How could this be? How can it be that the All-Powerful allows Himself to be reduced to such apparent insignificance? As I walked the few blocks to the Communion call, my meditation led me to recognize how very like the whole mystery of Christmas were my thoughts on the Eucharist. "Emmanuel, God with us," is how we hail the Christ Child at the wonderful Mass during the night of Christmas Eve. Choirs sing of angels appearing; churches fill with the smell of incense that recalls the richness of the Orient and priests wear gold vestments hoping to honor the King of the Jews. But He was a peasant born away from even the small hovel owned by his carpenter foster father. Had a gratuitous act of violence by a drunken occupation soldier somehow ended His life that night, no one would have even bothered to investigate the death. How could this be God? Or, better, why would this be God?

China is a brutal country. Imagine the hopelessness of knowing that if you became pregnant with a second child that the government would kill the child. Could that experience of oppression have anything to do with what many commentators believe is the explosion of Christianity in that country? Jesus is God with us but He is God with us as we really are—not as we might like to see ourselves. That poor couple in China whose second child has become one of the Holy Innocents, that couple knows what it is to be completely without power. That couple, perhaps, can identify with a God whose love is so total that He takes upon Himself the experience of human powerlessness. This couple may find it easier than I to bow before a God Who is present in the muck and sadness of a shack where a small family only wants to pass on its love to another generation. They perhaps accept what I rebel against: that I am every bit as impoverished and desperate as they and that the divinity and power of Jesus, both in His Nativity in Bethlehem and under the signs of bread and wine in the Eucharist, are most easily acknowledged by the spiritually poor and hungry.

Certainly the Lord has come to save both the powerful of the earth as well as the weak; and, certainly, poor and rich alike can reject His offer of salvation. But, it is also true that "unless we become like little children," in their dependence and unless we are "poor in spirit," recognizing what we are without God, that we will never sense the wonder of these days. Because He loves us so much, He comes to us as we are—weak and without hope—and makes us like Himself, capable of living the very life of God.

His Perfect Love

May 4, 1997

I have had the great joy during the last few weeks of trying to share the Church's faith in the Eucharist with our high schoolers in CCD. The sessions have also been troubling as I discover how little they have really grasped and been challenged by, particularly, our faith in the Real Presence, but, far more, their questions and objections force me to look again at the enormity of what we believe.

"Unless you eat the flesh of the Son of Man and drink his blood, you have no life in you," Jesus says in John's Gospel. "But, that makes us barbarians," one of the students cried out after I stressed that Jesus really means what He says. Of course, Communion is not barbarism; Jesus in the Eucharist is risen from the dead; He is not diminished by our eating His Body and Blood because He is no longer subject to the limitations of space and time. Having said this, it is still overwhelming to contemplate the desire of God to be so intimately a part of our lives. The human friend or lover seeks to give himself to the other; the poet will speak of losing oneself in the beloved. While space and time, not to mention the effects of our selfishness, limit our ability to really give of ourselves to others, Jesus, who is love itself, is perfect self-giving. His desire to give is limited only by our willingness to receive Him.

Our reaction to Jesus in the Eucharist leads me to the other thing about which I have been thinking: the vulnerability of the Lord in the Eucharist. Because He loves us so much, Jesus in the Blessed Sacrament chooses to be totally accessible. So it happens that people receive for any kind of reason: from the most sublime desire to respond to His love to blasphemy or indifference. What amazes me is the message about what love really is. Jesus makes Himself totally available, even vulnerable. Terrible sins are occasionally committed against the Eucharist; but if the Lord is going to make Himself available to those who try to serve Him, He must be, inevitably, similarly available to those who hate Him. His love for us has no conditions.

The vulnerability of Jesus in the Eucharist is an important model for us as we try to live up to our commitments, especially to love our neighbor as we love ourselves; likewise, especially in marriage and family, we are called to continue to give the best for the other no matter what the response of the moment. Experienced appreciation for the Eucharist can vary according to the moments of our lives: the reality of the Eucharist never changes. May God grant us, as we receive His Son over and over again, an ever deeper willingness to share the availability and vulnerability of His perfect love.

Antidote for Mediocrity

Mediocrity. I guess that is where I most see the remains of sin in my life. Thank God, I do not sin mortally, but the quality of my response to God's goodness and His call is like the Caps early season mediocrity. I am called to so much; I give so little: mediocrity. It is not exactly a consolation to me, but I do recognize that I am not alone in this self-evaluation. Often I hear people speak about how much more they should be loving their spouses or children—and they are right. I mean, if we are called to be signs of the goodness of God to those around us, who can say, "Boy, they sure are blessed to have me as their father." We all fall short; and often we fall short simply because we do not go beyond the acceptable or the minimum: we are mediocre. And, really, is there any way out of it?

The "Yes" that is the answer to that question is one of the reasons why the Eucharist is the gift it is in Catholic life. Pay attention to some of the lines we hear Sunday after Sunday: "We thank You for counting us worthy to stand in Your presence and serve You." "Grant that we, who are nour-ished by His body and blood, may be filled with His Holy Spirit, and become one body, one spirit, in Christ." The point is that, to the extent that we open ourselves to the Eucharist, we become, as individuals and commu-nity, more than we are. We see our mediocrity—and we are right!—but God sees His people and works through us so that we might become, in His Spirit, more of what He would have us be.

On today's Feast of Corpus Christi—The Solemnity of the Body and Blood of Christ—we worship the Real Presence of the Lord in the Eucharist. It is truly the body, blood, soul and divinity of the Lord whom I receive in Communion. "My Lord and my God," we rightly pray as the Host and chalice are raised. The equally great miracle though, is that we become what we eat. The antidote to the sin and mediocrity of our lives is the Body of Christ. If we eat His Body with faith; if we recognize Him under the signs of bread and wine, His Spirit will gradually make us like Himself. Surely, we will continue to see our pitiful response to God; faith, however, reminds us that in His time and in His way, we are becoming what the Body of Christ, the Church is meant to be.

That They Be One

August 17, 1997

My sister and our whole family are gearing up for a trip next weekend to Tulsa for her son's wedding. While they met and will live in this area, the bride wants to return to her home for the celebration. My family, never reluctant to get together for a party, is happy to make the trip. While the family priest will be in the sanctuary, the couple has, in fact, received permission to have their vows witnessed in her Protestant church. In fact, the ceremony will take place in Eucharistic liturgy. This, of course, has raised the question about whether the Catholics should receive communion in the Protestant church. In fact, we have been told by the minister that we are more than welcome to receive. I discuss the question because it comes up so often today. Can Catholics receive, when invited, in other Christian Churches? Under normal circumstances, can a priest invite non-Catholic Christians to receive at a wedding or funeral mass? While in both cases the answer is no, a look at the Church's reasoning is important.

First of all, it was the prayer of Jesus that, "they be one, as you Father, are in me and I am in you." Unity is intended by God to be one of the distinctive marks of the Church. The summit, the source and the principle sign of that unity is the Eucharist. Now, thank God, we have discovered in recent decades how much we have in common with other Christians, especially when compared with those who have no faith. We can, and should, pray and study together; we should engage in common works of Christian charity and we should build each other up in our attempts to love and serve the Lord. However, the rediscovery of how much we have in common does not erase the divisions that exist within the body of those who call themselves Christian. And we must not forget that our disunity is the result of sin— and sin always has painful consequences.

The fact that next Saturday I must be at an altar at a Eucharistic celebration that looks much like our own and not receive communion, will be awkward, likewise with my nephew who cannot receive with his new bride. However, interestingly enough, that pain is a good thing. If we all went to communion, there would be no such pain, true enough; but there would be the not honest facing of the reality that real and substantial divisions exist within the Christian community. The disunity is real and it should make us uncomfortable. Perhaps that small experience of the consequences of disunity will cause us to work for and to pray for the real unity that is desired by the Lord. To pretend a unity that does not exist may feel good at the moment; but it allows us to avoid the painful truth that we are still far from the oneness in faith and action intended by the Lord.

Full Moral Communion

"You worry so much about Protestants receiving Communion. Some of them are closer to God than a lot of Catholics I see receiving." Thus spoke one of the commentators about my thoughts last week on whom the Church invites to receive Holy Communion. In fact, I had been misread on two points: first, I spend little time worrying about the matter and, secondly, I fully agree that many non-Catholic Christians who come to Communion are probably closer to God than some Catholics who receive. I am grateful for her remarks, however, because they invite me to write a bit about moral unity with the Church and the reception of Communion.

Ecclesial—church—membership is an important element in the unity symbolized and effected by the Eucharist, but it is not the same as moral unity. When St. Paul says, in First Corinthians (11:27), "Whoever eats the bread or drinks the cup of the Lord unworthily sins against the body and blood of the Lord," he is not referring to church membership; he is castigating people whose moral life disqualifies them from receiving Communion. No one can judge another's soul, but there is no question that many seem casually to receive the Body of the Lord when, at least in an objective sense, they have gravely broken their moral unity with the Church. That person knows well the Church's law, for example, on the obligation of Sunday Mass and nevertheless receives on his or her annual Christmas, Easter and Mother's Day visits to church, celebrates a unity that has been broken. Likewise the couple who does not observe the Church's law on marriage: to receive simply because it is painful not to receive does not thereby re-establish unity with the Church.

On a pastoral level, there is much that any priest has experienced that tells him that often individuals act, with good will, out of ignorance. For example, I have often seen people, on the painful process back to reunion with the Lord, who start going to Mass and Communion without going first to Confession. Not knowing the law of the Church, they respond to grace as best as they know: a sign of their good will is their response to Confession when they know the law.

The far more common and far more dangerous situation, however, is that where individuals consciously act as if the Church has no hold on their consciences. Not on God's terms, nor on the Church's terms, but on their terms do they decide whether they will receive Holy Communion. It is without doubt, painful to refrain from receiving when not in full moral communion with the Church. Almost certainly, however, the faith and the humility involved is more pleasing to God than pretending that the law of His Church does not exist.

"Do This in Memory of Me"

May 15, 1994

Memories are such a big part of this time of year. First Communion, Mothers' Day, May Procession, proms, graduations, baseball: so much that we cherish during May invites us to remember the springtimes of earlier stages in our lives. Not all memories are necessarily happy, of course. I was driving by Rollingwood field the other day and noticed a bunch of kids playing ball. As if it were yesterday, I remembered the dropped fly ball of the eighth grade season at Blessed Sacrament on that same field. I hope it was not against Lourdes. When you stop to think of it, though, so much of what we are is made up of memories. One person reacts with anger because of a childhood filled with memories of short tempers and intolerance; another person's patience reflects the memories of a parent who never quite "lost it" despite the stresses and challenges of raising children. I remember, for example, the kindness and courtesy of one of my early pastors; that memory shapes the way I try to do my job today. Memories cherished; memories suppressed; memories recalled afteryears: so much of who we are comes from our memories.

The heart of what we are as Catholic Christians, of course, is built around the command, "Do this in Memory of Me." This is not the forum to do theology, but the word memory as Jesus the Jew who was celebrating Passover, used it at the Last Supper, means so much more than just to recall a past moment. As Catholics, we believe that the recalling that takes place in the Mass is so powerful that those events, wherein our salvation was won for us, are made present in our midst. In the Eucharist, the past, where we remember God's saving deeds, the present, where Jesus continues to offer Himself to the Father for us and the future, when we will experience the fullness of what He won for us, are made present. In this memory is our life.

One final thought: in the Eucharist, we become what we eat. Therefore, the Church becomes the memory of Jesus. We, through the way we treat each other, the way we proclaim our faith, the way we forgive injuries, the way we love our enemies, through the way we live our lives as followers of Jesus, help the world to remember that He has died for us and that life is filled with hope.

A Lifetime of Communion

May 7, 1995

I must have been sick the day before my First Communion (considering the time of year, it was probably asthma from the pollen), because my outstanding memory from the day comes from when we were standing in line before the Mass began. All of a sudden, I was taken from the line and solemnly escorted into that most mysterious of buildings, the convent, where a priest had been secured to hear my first confession, which rite I had missed because of the previous day's sickness. Because those charged with my preparations for the sacrament were so vigilant, I was given the opportunity to make my first confession and was thus spared what would have been, no doubt, a sacrilegious First Communion. I think I also remember someone giving me a hard time after the Mass (does this sound a bit like an older brother or sister?) for trying to catch the eye of my parents as I was in line to receive Communion rather than looking straight ahead. These two memories, though, about exhaust my recollections of this great day.

Maybe some of our second graders who first receive the Lord in Holy Communion this weekend will retain memories far more sublime than mine of this moment, but it is not that important an issue. What really matters, of course, is the marvelous dialogue of love initiated by the Risen Jesus with these children. How he speaks to them; how they respond: these are matters that no recipient of the Eucharist can even begin to comprehend until we are in complete communion with Him in heaven. But the dialogue has begun.

As much as we pray for these children today, let us pray for their parents. Surely, there is no heart that is not moved by the simplicity, innocence and beauty of First Communion; but the Lord whom they receive is about much more than an emotional impact that may be captured as a Kodak moment. He sees these children at seventeen, twenty-seven and eighty-seven. He sees how their fidelity—or, let us be honest, their lack of fidelity—to Him in the Eucharist will allow them to make, or not to make, their way through life as hope-filled believers. I do not remember much about how I felt or what I believed on the day of my First Communion, but I remember very well my father getting up for years on end and going to 6:30 Mass on his way to work. I remember well my mother stopping at the 5:30 evening daily Mass during Lent and thus having dinner late. Their faith in the Eucharist, in the mysterious ways of the spirit, in some small way has become mine. Indeed, I, an individual, received Jesus that day forty-four years ago; but, I received Him as a member of a community of faith. May

God grant our First Communicants a supportive community of faith, especially in their homes, to help them understand what God has said to them in giving them Jesus as their Bread of Life.

Vatican II:
Church as Community of Faith

July 23, 1995

Vatican Council II seems just to have ended; but 1965, after all, is now a few years behind us. I am sure there are young adults active in the Church today to whom the words, "Vatican II," mean virtually nothing. Those older remember well the overwhelming interest of both secular and Church society in the deliberations of the world's bishops during the five years of the Council; they probably were part of parish groups that met to discuss the documents and while even from the beginning there were fears about what would come from the Council, they probably shared in the hope engendered by Pope John XXIII's attempt to reach out to the non-Catholic and even the non-Christian world. Because such great stress was placed upon the common baptismal inheritance of all believers, we were encouraged to see the Church more as a community of faith rather than as the hierarchical organization with Pope at the top and lay people on the bottom. Because we were encouraged to see the Church from this new perspective, the phrase, "the age of the laity," became very popular.

For a lot of reasons, much of the early enthusiasm generated by the Council has faded. I think that most would agree that both Church and civil society have suffered much in the years since 1965. I believe history will prove them wrong, but there are not a few who would blame much of the turmoil in today's Church on the Council itself. But what of the laity? What has been their impact in the Church since 1965?

Inside the Church, that is, within its structures and organization, the institution today could not survive without the laity. This statement is so obvious that it need not be demonstrated. Schools, parishes and social service agencies are increasingly laity run. Sisters and priests are less and less seen. Outside the Church, however, the answer is somewhat different.

One of the great tragedies of the American Catholic Church is that our approximately 22% of the population has so little impact on American life and morality. The power of the Holy Spirit allows us to be a sign of contradiction for our society, but often we follow rather than lead. The way that our lives reflect our faith; the way that we live the Cross of Jesus, could be the sign of hope that, little by little, invites people to turn to Him who is the only real sign of hope.

Serious Business

October 19, 1997

How does one explain the attitude of so many Catholics toward abortion? I mean that attitude that says, in so many words, "I would not have one, but who am I to tell someone else what is right or wrong in their life?" When asked, most will readily admit the reality of life within the womb, but there is reluctance to assert a dignity for that life that is absolute. When truth is so obvious—and still denied—what is the problem?

To come up with a solution, let us get off the abortion issue. How many Catholics believe that it is wrong to deliberately miss Mass on Sunday? How many Catholics believe that sex outside of marriage is always wrong? How many Catholics believe it is always wrong to cheat on taxes? Or for that matter, how many Catholics believe that the Church has the power to teach with an authority that binds us under the fullness of God's truth? I believe, in other words, that Catholic attitudes on abortion reflect a much wider reality, one which denies either the reality of objective truth or the nature of the Church as divinely inspired teacher of faith and morals.

Notice the attitude towards the Holy Father, for example. Of course, people acknowledge his courage, his intelligence, his charm, his faith and his role in the destruction of Communism in Eastern Europe. Despite all these qualities, his moral teaching is often dismissed as antiquated or traditional. Did you ever notice, however, how rarely Catholic scholars will argue his writings based on thought out principles? Rather, it is something like, "Well, what can you expect from someone who was formed in such an environment?" The reality of his world class education in philosophy and theology is simply dismissed. His arguments are not addressed on the basis of logic and content, they are dismissed out of hand. In other words, these arguments must be foolish; they are not in accord with what "everybody" is thinking or doing.

The greatest challenge for Catholics in our time is to take the Church on the Church's terms. Either the Church is founded by the Lord Jesus and is empowered to teach, to rule and to sanctify by the Holy Spirit, or it is not. The Church is gift, and through her sacramental life and doctrine she gives us the very life of God, but the gift of the Church must be accepted according to the intention of the giver, the Crucified and Risen Lord. To patronize the Church and not to take seriously what she claims to be is, in a real way, to patronize her Founder, and that is serious business indeed.

Archdiocesan Convocation

November 23, 1997

In speaking with the parents of our second graders who are preparing for confession, I shared with them my belief that their children may well have a better foundation for the sacraments than the parents. The reason for this is that their parents very often received a Catholic education in the seventies that was long on sentiment, but very short on content. The tragedy is that we have many Catholics in their thirties who have little understanding of the thought and tradition that is at the heart of Catholic Christianity. No weekend seminar can, by itself, rectify the twelve years of under-education, of course, but on the horizon there is an offering by the Archdiocese that I believe is going to be one of the great events in the history of the Church of Washington. It is entitled Convocation 2000.

As a way of preparing for the celebration of the start of the third millennium of Jesus' birth, this convocation will assemble some of the finest speakers in the United States to address issues fundamental to Catholic life, worship and morality. It will take place on January 15-17, at the Washington Convention Center. Because the parishes have already been assessed to pay for the event, all the talks and workshops are free to Catholics of the Archdiocese. And, of course, for those of us from Bethesda, the weekend becomes even more convenient because we can park at Lourdes and take the subway.

Registration brochures are available here in the parish and, as a matter of fact, a table will be set up in the vestibule next Sunday, where someone will be able to answer questions about the wonderful variety of choices of speakers and workshops. Each day, for example, will feature at least two keynote addresses, given by inspirational Church leaders and theologians. Francis Cardinal Arinze from Nigeria, for example, will open the Convocation 2000 on Thursday evening. Friends of mine heard him speak a few years ago at a conference in Ohio and said he was so great that they wondered if it would be OK to start an "Arinze for pope" campaign. Likewise, Fr. Michael Scanlon TOR, is famous for his transforming a small university, Steubenville, into an increasingly highly regarded university that is marked by its enthusiastic commitment to its mission to educate informed Catholics. I have heard Scott Hahn speak a couple of times. He is powerful: a convert, his Protestant background perhaps gives him his ability to rouse a crowd and educate them at the same time. In addition to the keynote speakers, there will be over a hundred workshops from which we can choose on a huge number of topics. Because of the wealth of schools here in

Washington, these workshops will be presented by top names in theology, Scripture and moral theology. In addition to all that is being presented for adults, there is also, on Saturday, a youth track to which junior and senior high students are invited.

I am personally enthusiastic and impressed by all that has gone into Convocation 2000. Nothing frustrates me more than the lack of understanding on the part of many about what Catholicism really is. I do not mind the *Washington Post* being misinformed about our faith; what I hate is that so many Catholics take the Post's ignorance as their source of knowledge. Register for Convocation 2000; it could be a big step in the right direction.

The Gift of Faith

October 20, 1996

In a recent conversation, a college student told me that he no longer goes to church because, "religion is a crutch." My chuckle was not at him but at myself, as I remembered myself at almost the same stage in my struggle with faith. At one point, I wanted to believe in God and religion, not because I needed them (I do not want to need a crutch), but only because they were true. In other words, I would believe God if God proved Himself to be true, but not because I needed God. Mercifully, having dealt with college sophomores before, the Good Lord allowed me to set the terms of the discussion and, eventually, I was able to show how firmly the Apostles believed in the Resurrection. They, who claimed to have been with Him after Easter Sunday, also cheerfully were martyred for proclaiming Him more powerful than death. Thank God, I found I did accept their witness to the divine power of Jesus.

Another line that bothered me was, "I do not know what I would do without my faith." Again, I thought that people believed only because it made life easier, not because of the truth in faith. Now, may God forgive me for saying it, I wonder how people who do not believe in the Resurrection and its promises of heaven, get through each day. How do they cope with evil? How do they cope with suffering, especially in those they love? What is the source of their hope?

These not very cheery thoughts are brought about by several recent events, but especially by the death of a woman I have known almost since ordination. Physically and emotionally, this woman really suffered. On a human level, there were certainly happy moments and events; she dearly loved her family, for example. Hers, however, was a very hard life. Did she believe? Absolutely. But, did her faith give her great consolation and peace on this earth? I cannot judge; but I surely know she did not experience the joy that many know who put their faith in Jesus. I do not know why the Lord allows such suffering in good people, but it does happen. But, crutches notwithstanding, this is no lasting kingdom. Jesus did rise from the dead and all who believe in Him will rise with Him.

Faith gives me the power to follow Jesus in this life, but faith is also the promise that the end of this life is but a passing into either eternal union or separation from God. Nothing in this life—either suffering or prosperity—is lasting. We are destined for eternity and I am sadly mistaken if I think I will walk into life without the crutch of faith.

Faith: Source of Self-Confidence

July 27, 1997

By happy chance, I caught most of the movie, "My Left Foot" on television late one night last weekend. The movie, which I believe was an academy award winner for best picture, is the story of Cristy Brown, a Dublin painter and writer who was born with cerebral palsy and is able to move only his left foot. While it is his story, it is also the story of his family (he is one of thirteen children) and especially, it is the story of a mother's passionate drive to nurture her family. I heard someone on the radio say that political reform is stymied in America because we have come to believe that only experts are capable of creating change. The mother of Cristy Brown was expert only in her conviction that her family needed everything that she could give them and that "the cripple" could create and produce in ways unique to himself. Even the father, beset by the curses of alcohol and rage, is gradually taught by her to communicate his powerful love. Great movie! Though when I was talking to one of my nephews about it the next night, he colorfully remarked, "I had to hit myself with a hammer to keep awake when I saw it."

Michel Quoist, in his wonderful book, *Christ is Alive!*, says, "As man grows richer in earthly things, he grows more and more threatened. The forces within man—those of his mind and his heart and his life—seem less under control than ever before, less unified, less balanced." What happens, I think, is that we are tricked by technology and prosperity into thinking that we should be in control of life. We transform useful and wonderful tools into the sources of our power and since they do not touch (nor were they meant to touch) the spirit, we gradually forget what we are capable of being as humans.

Faith that I am loved by God is the greatest source of self confidence. While not heavily developed in the movie "My Left Foot," there are several allusions to the mother's deep faith. She knows what Cristy and her children can be; she spends a lifetime teaching her husband how to love; she has a mother's simple confidence that she can be all that she is called to be. The fruit of her faith in God is her faith in herself. "If God is for us, who can be against us," St. Paul says. But if we do not believe He is for us, how great are the challenges and how helpless I am.

Reflections of a Father (by a Father)

June 8, 1997

The Wells are morning people. I call the homes of my family with reluctance after nine in the evening, but at seven in the morning, I can be certain of wide-awake receptions. This we get from my father. Any day, by 4:30 or 5:00, he would be at the breakfast room table reading the morning paper before he went off to 6:30 morning Mass. I often chuckle about it now.

Many mornings I would wake up early and come downstairs just to be with him. How he must have enjoyed the peace and quiet, and how he must have dreaded hearing my footsteps, since he knew the non-stop questions and comments that would break his morning quiet. But I guess, in the mysterious ways of growing up, I must have sensed this was one time I could have time alone with him.

As he grew older (and probably read the magazine articles telling him how he should have been "father") my father would sometimes say that he regretted that he rarely did the things fathers are "supposed" to do with their children: we never fished and we rarely played catch or took hikes together. He did try to help with homework; that was a disaster as he, the engineer, tried to help me, who even today cannot count beyond the number of my fingers, with math. What he tried hardest to do was to teach us how to think. The dinner table, especially as I got into junior and senior high school age, was torture. Nightly, we would be questioned (interrogated, I thought at the time) about what we learned in school and how this knowledge fit in the larger picture of life. Actually of course, my father's questions were only props to enable him to launch into a nightly session into one or another aspect of life. Since he spent most of his day in the car going from one construction site to another, I suppose he had much time to reflect on various lessons needed to be learned by his children. It was awful!

I suppose our utter lack of response to or appreciation for his lectures must have frustrated my father from time to time; but, let me assure you, he was never deterred. The marvelous joke of it all, of course, is that, ultimately, he won. Unappreciated lectures are a big part of my job. I only pray that they are delivered with some of the love and concern for his children's growth that motivated my teacher.

An Enlightening Day
with Promise Keepers

October 12, 1997

I suppose that Bethesda is not Promise Keepers country and so the Metro platform was empty last Saturday as I waited to go downtown to the rally on the Mall. About six weeks ago, a young man I have known since he was in grade school called and asked me to go with him and a couple of his friends. Frankly, I looked at my calendar kind of hoping a convenient wedding would force me to decline the invitation. As luck would have it, the day was open; and as I thought about it, I began to realize that it might be good for priests to be at that event. Also, I have long believed that since the first prayer most of us learn begins, "In the name of the Father," that there must be something critical in the role of the father of the family in the passing on of faith in our God who is Father. Thus, this gathering of husbands and fathers might be a good thing. At any rate, the platform in Bethesda may have been empty, but the dense crowd on the subway that arrived was a hint of the experience ahead of us.

First of all, the size of the crowd defies description. We never saw the stage; we never saw the Monument. We walked from about Twelfth Street down two or three blocks and then decided that our main objective should be to find a tree to sit beneath where there was a view of a huge television screen. Such a site, happily, we found. Beyond that, I can only say that there were men everywhere. Secondly, I can say that these men were there for business. During the many talks, there was not the loss of interest I would have expected (and had, I must confess); rather there was intense participation, especially when there was a call to prayer. Over and over I said to myself that much that is great in mid-western and southern Protestant America was represented on the Mall.

I had a couple of other observations that perhaps point to the future. First, this movement seems to be without traditional anti-Catholicism. With one exception that had nothing to do with prejudice, there was not one thing that should not be preached from a Catholic pulpit. It is ironic that, as the Holy Father was speaking to a crowd of a similar size in Brazil, he was saying many of the same things about family and sexual morality.

The second thing that struck me was the longing of these people for ritual. They were told to kneel; they were told to prostrate themselves on the ground as a sign of their unworthiness before God and to my shock, they were told to confess their sins to one another. Is this a new development for

Protestants? I do not know, but I could not help but see this movement heading (without their knowing, I am sure) closer and closer to an understanding of the sacramental nature of Catholicism. Are we on the threshold of reunion with this branch of Evangelical Protestantism? Certainly I do not know, but more than once last Saturday, in addition to praying for the unity "the world cannot give," I contemplated that we have come a lot farther than we suspect.

Where There Is Faith, There Is the Father's Love

March 16, 1997

A young man was hitch-hiking by the interstate just outside of Columbus. I had a three hour drive to Cincinnati in front of me so I stopped. This decision, back in 1978, turns out to be one of the few times I feel as if I was directly chosen by God to be in a particular place at a particular time. The young man, with his banjo, got into the car. Coming from near Toronto, he was making his way to Nashville where he had dreams of making it big in the Grand Old Opry. I was visiting a couple of seminaries for the Archdiocese. At any rate, it quickly developed that, while he had been baptized, he had not been raised in the faith. I was his first exposure to a priest and the next three hours were, I am certain, the most intense conversation about the things of God I have ever had. He discovered a fire within himself that was the very life of God.

This is a long, wonderful and often amusing story, but it can be summarized by saying that, even though my friend, Doug, did get a job playing with a bluegrass band in Canada, the life-style of a band conflicted with his new-found faith. He had taken instructions, been Confirmed and decided to return to college. He developed a love for and got a degree in philosophy; got his Masters in theology and has been teaching religion in a Catholic high school ever since. I was laughing with him recently about the first letter from him that I received about three weeks after our ride together. Thank God, he now has a computer and I do not have to try and read his writing, but that letter was the first of many letters and phone calls exchanged over the years.

About twelve years ago, I was privileged to witness his wedding and this past weekend, I went to Toronto to baptize their first child. That child is the reason for these thoughts. Doug and his wife have always been open to having children, but for whatever reason, there has been no pregnancy. About three years ago, they decided to do foster care and as a result of that decision, about eight months ago, a baby came to their home who is now their daughter. What is striking is that she was born of a married couple, with one other child who is apparently quite healthy. This child, Sarah, has a serious physical deformity. She was, to put it gently, abandoned by this couple because she was imperfect. Nearly a year old now, Sarah basks in, grows from and radiates love. A particular sign of her brilliance is that she laughed at all my funny faces and silly songs. Love is the air this child breathes.

Sometimes the Providence of God is blindingly obvious. From that conversation about faith on an Ohio interstate to the baptism of that dearly loved adopted child, there is a line that is drawn with God's grace. Like all such lines, pain, suffering and maybe even sin have been part of the story; but as always, where there is faith, there is eventually the revelation of the Father's love.

Faith Begins and Ends with the Family

September 8, 1996

At prayer this morning I was surprised to discover that this is a big week for me for meditation on family. I am writing on what would be my father's eighty-ninth birthday. Two days from now would be my parents' sixty-first wedding anniversary and in the realm of the present, three days from now, I will officiate at my niece's wedding. As my father grew older, he frequently would succumb to bouts of sentimentality at various family celebrations. His children, raised in a home where emotion or sentiment was not a highly developed quality, would chuckle at his undisguised joy. Now, of course, as various members of the next generation begin to make choices that reflect their families' values, the chuckles have long since given way to a sense of wonder at the good that can develop out of the daily chaos of family life. A couple of weeks ago, I had the opportunity to baptize the daughter of another nephew and his wife, and maybe even recognize in myself a touch of my father's sentimentality.

As a young priest (I mean even younger than I am now) I had many of my happiest times and longest hours working with youth. It did not dawn on me until many years later that, as a 26 year old priest, I was only a few years older than the youth for whom I was "Father." However, it did not take me long to recognize that, on the purely human level, the priest and the parish were only reinforcing and supporting what went on in the home. The parish programs were of great value, as was the willingness of the priest to "be there" for the youth, but at the deep level, most of these young people were (and are) the children of their parents. Of course, and thank God for this—it happens all the time—we can recover from a weak family life, but God's grace works most easily when it works in cooperation with nature, not when it must overcome the effects of poor formation.

A family taking its children to the first day of school here at Lourdes this morning beautifully made my point. Before going into school, the parents' and children stopped before the shrine of Our Lady of Lourdes for prayer and a first day picture. No lesson taught this year by a gifted teacher, no homily preached at Mass, will ever be able to say to those children what was said by the two most important people in their world as they led them to ask for a Mother's blessing on the new school year. That is what the expression "faith and family" is all about.

Outward Signs of Faith

August 30, 1998

On one of the tables in my room sits a Madonna and Child by Hummell that sat for years in our living room on 32nd Place. Of course, because it was venerated by five children, the Blessed Mother's head is glued in place, her hands are chipped and the Baby Jesus' halo has lost more than a bit of its luster. There was also a crucifix in the kitchen and, of course, the creche each year at Christmas (that is, the days between Dec. 24 and Epiphany—not from the day after Thanksgiving to the day after Christmas—but that's another story!) So, while I cannot say our house looked like a religious shrine, it bore—to us and to all who visited—the unmistakable signs of a Catholic home.

If a child grows up with a Budweiser poster over the bar in the family room, does not this poster say something about family values? And what does the wedding picture of Mom and Dad say to their children and to their children's children? Likewise, while rarely mentioned, or perhaps even thought about, the statue or religious picture quietly witnesses to the priority of faith.

As I visit families, I confess that I usually take note of whether or not there are religious images in view. Are they crucial to showing that the faith is loved? Probably not. But, since the heart usually makes signs of whom it loves, the Madonna or the image of the Lord probably say much about the heart of the home.

Loving Life Because God Is In It

September 4, 1994

A wise woman in my first parish told me one time, probably as we were chaperoning some teen club dance, "Father, you'll always be close to your first group of teenagers, because they grow up with you." I thought of that comment as I drove home last weekend from a party with a number from that same group. It seems that two or three of them were jointly celebrating their fortieth birthdays. This good woman, then finishing the raising of eight children, must have looked at the rookie priest and thought how close in age I was to those I was supposedly guiding spiritually into life. At any rate, she was right.

I share this because it was such a hopeful evening. I know that there were only ten or twelve of them (spouses and a couple of very young infants added to the number) and that they, in no way, could be seen, or want to be seen, as representative of their age, but they still reminded me that "God writes straight with crooked lines." They have known drug and alcohol problems, there has been at least one divorce, some have survived massive financial challenges; several have had counseling; there are PhD's and blue collar workers; a couple have not yet gotten married (but are most certainly open to it!); and they educate their children in everything from home school to public school. In other words, they are not too different from your 40 year old neighbors.

I think I went away so hopeful because I had spent the evening with a group of happy people. They know the problems they and their children are up against and they take great care about those things to which their children are exposed, but I got the sense that, in their widely different careers and environments, they love their lives.

I would like to say that the evening closed on some beautiful religious note. In fact, when I was about to pray profoundly at grace, someone called out, "Come on, F.W., we've heard it before." (F.W.—short for Fr. Wells—is what somebody started calling me on some ski slope in New Hampshire after the person next to me on a lift nearly fell off when she discovered that I was the priest being yelled at from the slopes.) In fact, they had heard it before, especially in their own homes, and now, according to their varying personalities, they are trying to live it in their communities and to pass it on to their children. Strangely enough, even in this pretty messed up world, the God in whom these dear friends of mine believe, continues to hold them in the palm of His hand.

Families of Faith Living Their Catholic Commitment

July 16, 1995

In 1981, the Cardinal appointed me to be the Director of the Office of Permanent Deacons in the Archdiocese. Since this is a Chancery position, it meant in theory, that my Sunday obligations were limited. In that mysterious way in which people sense free time in a priest, it was not long before a group of families asked me to help them with their weekend family retreat at Camp Maria in southern Maryland. It was to be, of course, "just for this year, Father." I am now beginning to prepare talks for this summer's retreat in August. After nearly fifteen years, some of the families have long since finished raising their children and have been replaced by younger families, but the opportunity to be with this group and to reflect on the Gospel with these twenty or so families is one of the highlights of every summer.

The Holy Father, as a part of the 1994 Year of the Family, wrote his, "Letter to Families." Not surprisingly, the family retreat group has asked me to focus my talks to the adults on this encyclical. What a beautiful vision of Christian family life! As is characteristic of Pope John Paul, he takes the philosophical presuppositions of the day and shows us how they affect people's daily decisions. I was particularly impressed by his comparison of the "civilization of love" with the "civilization of technology." He writes about a "civilization of things" and not of "persons," as being characteristic of our time; of an attitude where persons are used in the same way as things. Watch "Married with Children" once; pick up a copy of Playboy; or read the latest justification for euthanasia to get just a glimpse about what His Holiness is speaking. In addition, he writes of a crisis of truth where the right words continue to be used in society, (words like freedom, rights and love) but where they have lost all meaning because they are divorced from the awareness that there is no true love without recognizing that "God is love."

Because the challenges to families are so great, so also are the opportunities. As families recognize that the society in which they raise their children is so hostile to Christian values, they more and more consciously seek to evaluate their decisions in light of the Gospel. Just as the family must "hang together" to support itself, so these family retreat groups recognize that families of faith must support and challenge each other in living out their Catholic commitment.

Epiphany—Fruits of Faith

January 7, 1996

Sometimes we do not recognize the good that we do. As we celebrate the Feast of Epiphany, the day we recall the Wise Men who followed the star to Jesus, I find myself thinking about those in the RCIA program at Lourdes. As I do every year, I am meeting with the candidates individually to get a sense of how their journey to the Church progresses. Hearing their individual stories, of course, reaffirms my experience that there are many roads to Christ, but it is heartening to find how many of the stories have one element in common: that is, the faith of the Catholics in their lives.

I violate no deep personal revelations when I relate that two young women are coming to the Church because of the enthusiastic and active faith of two of their co-workers. Of her boss, one of these women said, "He makes coming to work like working in your family." Another of these candidates says that virtually all of his friends, while he was growing up, were Catholic. When he sensed the need for a Church, he remembered their pride in their Catholic identity. Still another story is both touching and sad: touching because of the memories of a grandmother's deep faith; sad because that faith was not passed on by our candidate's Catholic parent.

I am a great believer that we never know who is watching us. I suppose this truth often translates into snoopiness and prying, but it is also true that a lot of people are looking and do not even know it. The person who has been taught that he must be in control of all aspects of his life can be challenged by another who works just as hard, but who also has the sense that, ultimately, he can let go because God is in charge. Likewise, fruits of faith such as patience, forgiveness, turning the other cheek or keeping the mouth shut during office gossip can confuse those marching to the beat of a drummer other than Christ.

There are a number of people in this parish whom I could embarrass were I to tell of the wonderful effect they have on my faith. I see the star who is Christ in their lives and, therefore, find it easier to follow. Most who read this can give similar examples. We should not be surprised, then, that those who seek the peace that the world cannot give look at believers to see if, in us, there shines a light which worldly wisdom cannot explain.

Pentecost—
The Need for Childlike Simplicity

May 22, 1994

A good friend of mine coaches a CYO baseball team. Recently, he was raving about a boy on his team, who before this year, had never played organized ball. What strikes the coach is not only that the boy has shown dramatic improvement in the six weeks or so of the season, but also how anxious he is to learn the game. He used the word docile to describe his young athlete.

The Church celebrates the great Feast of Pentecost today. We recall the story of the believers who, through the signs of a loud rushing wind and tongues of fire, received the Spirit of God and became Church. We hear how those believers, under St. Peter, went out that day and converted thousands to faith in Jesus. And no doubt in homilies, we will hear that the same Spirit is active in the Church today and that the Spirit calls us, as individuals and as community, to continue the work of Christ in our world. At this point, I think, more than a few will ask themselves some honest questions about the difference between what is preached and what they experience of the Spirit in their lives as Catholics. Compared to the marvelous deeds worked by the Spirit in the early Church, our experience of the Spirit seems almost nonexistent.

Which takes me back to our seventh grade ball player. According to my friend, if I can paraphrase what he told me, the boy has love of the game, eagerness to learn and docility. One of the things we easily forget about God is that He will never violate our freedom; He will not force His way into our lives. And so, first of all, I must have a real desire to love God. If God for me is only an abstract principle or the focus of laws of morality, it is no wonder I have not yet experienced the power of His personal love for me. Secondly, like the young boy, there must be in me a real eagerness to know how God works and how He wants to use me for His good. I suppose such eagerness would be demonstrated through serious prayer, Scripture or other kinds of spiritual reading; real attention must be paid to the guidance of the Spirit. Finally, there is the virtue of docility. If I am to be led to perfection by the Spirit, the process will require humility and the realization that I will have to turn away from some things and turn towards others. I will have to drop old habits of sin and develop the new skills and habits of grace. That young ball player knew how ignorant of baseball he was; he followed directions gladly. We are as ignorant of the Spirit's plan for our lives. Will we follow with the same childlike simplicity?

Pentecost—Signs of the Spirit

May 26, 1996

I would hate to guess the number of times, in listening to couples with marriage problems, that I have heard someone say, "I had no idea." Sometimes it will be a wife who has no idea of a husband's sense of loneliness; at other times a husband will have no idea that his wife is unaware of the deep love he feels for her. Sacraments are signs; in the sacrament of marriage, the spouses have the responsibility to be signs for each other of God's love. As humans, we learn only from what the senses tell us; if partners do not look for ways to communicate through the senses, they allow the other person to assume, and often we assume the worst.

On this Feast of Pentecost, we celebrate the gift of God's Holy Spirit to the Church. Marriage, of course, and all of the sacraments are the work of the Spirit. The sacraments demonstrate the invariable movement of the Spirit to make concrete the invisible power of God. Most wonderfully, of course, is the way the Spirit worked in Our Lady: through her cooperation she conceived by the power of the Holy Spirit and the Word became flesh and dwelt among us. In today's celebration, again we recall the movement toward a concrete expression of the Spirit's power. The believers in the Upper Room receive the Holy Spirit and they become the Church, the visible presence of Christ in the world until the end of time. Because we are flesh, we depend on sensible signs to perceive the invisible Spirit at work among us.

It is the same in our personal spiritual lives. Anyone who begins to take a relationship with God seriously eventually must struggle with prayer. Am I speaking into a vacuum; is God really there; why do I not "feel" the presence of God when I pray? Creatures limited by flesh, we wonder at the power or presence of the Spirit. It is, of course, impossible to judge our relationship with God, to know either how much He loves us or how much we love Him. But the movement of the Spirit is invariable: His presence is signified in concrete signs. "The fruit of prayer is virtue," said a spiritual writer. I can make tentative judgments on my spiritual life not on the basis of how I feel when I pray, but how I treat my neighbor. I discover that, little by little, I am overcoming temptation, that I am becoming more generous with time or money, that I am more patient or that I am gradually growing stronger in the battle for chastity; then I can begin to assume that, once again, the Holy Spirit is manifesting His power in concrete ways. May we, as a parish, become an ever more powerful sign of the power of the Spirit whose Presence we celebrate today.

Pentecost—We Are the Light of Christ

May 18, 1997

Sometimes I find that, if I want to work without interruptions, it is best to do it very early in the morning. And, if I am trying to compose something, I will often find myself staring out of the window waiting for inspiration to strike. In the dark mornings of winter I have found myself preoccupied on several occasions by the office building across the street, about one third of which I can see from my desk. I find myself fascinated as, one by one, lights come on in the darkness, until finally, every window reflects the decision of whomever turned on the switch that day.

Faith tells us that in Baptism and Confirmation we are filled with the Holy Spirit, the very life of God Himself. Like the building across the street, that Spirit allows us to become lights of Christ in the darkness of the world. Perhaps my greatest satisfaction as a priest is that of knowing so many people who do so reflect the light of Christ. Just last weekend, for example, two couples, themselves best friends, both of whose weddings I had ten or so years ago, invited me to dinner. I guess I should have told them, but it really did not dawn on me until I was driving home, how inspired I was by the effects of their commitments to marriage, faith and family, and by the obvious joy that enlivens them. Financially, especially, neither of these couples has an easy time, and in different ways, each has had to struggle in their surrender to the call of faith. But their decisions to live the life of the Spirit is reflected in their love of life! (And, incidentally, how little they would recognize themselves in this "holy talk.") But, as I say, any priest can name countless numbers of such people who are obvious signs that the Holy Spirit can make us proofs of the gift of faith.

Two thoughts come to me as we celebrate this day of the Holy Spirit: Pentecost. The first is to ask the Spirit to use us so that, because of the way we live our faith, we might be the light of Christ for at least one other person. Secondly, I more and more come to understand why the Lord saved a people, not just a bunch of individuals. We need each other, if only to find encouragement in a world that so often does not believe in the apparent absurdity of the Gospel message. My prayer this Pentecost is that the Spirit will give to each of us, as He has so generously given to me, people whose lived faith in Jesus will inspire us to deeper faith in our own lives.

St. Peter—Upon This Rock
I Will Build My Church

June 29, 1997

Does anything more characterize our time than the appeal to feelings? Presidents feel our pain; those who suffer get in touch with their feelings; "if it feels good," we are told, "to do it;" and so on. Many of our most important decisions are made on the basis of how they will make ourselves or others feel. For as important as our feelings are and for as important as it is to recognize their place in our lives, we follow a Savior who certainly had and expressed feelings, but who proclaimed Himself to be Truth.

We celebrate this weekend the wonderful Feast of Sts. Peter and Paul, the two great leaders of the Apostolic Church. While the Church certainly wants us to give thanks to God for their holy and heroic lives, even more, I am sure, their feast calls us to meditate on the Mystery of the Church they were called to lead. The Gospel for the Mass on Sunday (on Saturday evening, the readings are different) is that passage on which so many of us are raised, where Jesus tells St. Peter, "You are rock, and on this rock I will build my church. . . Whatever you declare bound on earth will be bound in heaven." I am often amused at the image of rock chosen by the Lord to describe His Church. There is nothing very romantic about a rock: it's just there. They are shaped or moved only with great effort; most often, they are bland in color and except in extraordinary situations, they are taken for granted. But, of course, rocks are solid; they are used for foundations and they endure, seemingly unchanged, for all time. Thus, upon the rock—Peter, Jesus built His Church and upon the rock of the papacy the Church still presents the loving Truth of Jesus to the world. The Church is most rejected today not because she teaches doctrines like the Trinity or the Real Presence. These seem to have little to do with the world of feelings. No, it is in the realm of sexual morality, especially, where the scorn and anger of many is directed against the Church. Any objective look around us will show the devastation that has resulted from the rejection of the truth of Christian sexual morality, but this obvious truth flies in the face of feelings which crave immediate gratification.

Interestingly and importantly, Peter and Paul evangelized a world every bit as corrupt as ours. The Church they led seemed weak. That Church still seems weak, perhaps, but that Church is still led by the Spirit of God's love and truth and it will, as promised, endure forever.

The King of Love Is Victor

November 20, 1994

Jesus Christ is King, as we celebrate on this last Sunday of the Church year, not only because He is God, but because He has conquered, because He is victorious, and because to Him as victor go the spoils. Contemplate the war where He faced, alone, an enemy that had reigned unthreatened since the sin of Adam.

Contemplate that for those who despised Him, for those who ignored Him, for those whose cowardice made them turn from His call, He had no weapon but a passionate and piercing desire to embrace them with the experience of the Father's creative love. Contemplate that on the Cross, when the power of every person's hatred and sin was thrust upon Him in an experience of ugliness, pain and abandonment that weighed more than the universe itself, contemplate that then, even then, He continued to fight only with the totally self-emptying love of God Himself. Contemplate that alone, utterly, absolutely, alone, the God-man loved until He could love no more; He gave until He could give no more and then, bloodless and lifeless, He commended Himself to the Father so that our sins might be forgiven.

Where Adam and Eve and all their children blamed, defended and measured in what and how they gave, Jesus our King stood naked to His enemies and as a creature, loved God as God first loved us. This love unto death was the triumph of life. He took us to Himself and with utter purity, without any stain of self-interest, He went against the enemy and defeated Him: love is stronger than hatred; life has conquered even death itself.

Jesus Christ is King! All who are baptized are born into His kingdom, but like the King Himself, the Kingdom is one of love, decision and freedom. The Kingdom is manifest when we choose to live the life of the King. He is at the center of every heart that chooses to feed the hungry, to clothe the naked, to shelter the homeless; His reign is glimpsed when His subjects bear wrongs patiently, when they joyfully proclaim the truth in the face of indifference or hostility, when they, like their King, turn the other cheek and forgive seventy times seven times.

As in any way, the spoils go to the victor. We are the spoils that, by His sacrificial love, Christ the King has won. May the Spirit of our King allow us to recognize the victor and surrender to Him, the King of love.

The King of Kings' Holy Land

November 26, 1995

A group of eighteen of us, mostly from the parish, have just returned from the Holy Land. After eight days of visiting the sites and churches associated with Christ, Our Lady and other figures from the Bible, I confess that I am already beginning to have trouble distinguishing churches from villages from parts of the country. None of this, of course, changes the overall effect of spending these days in the land of the Bible.

Perspective, of course, is everything and this, for me, is the first blessing of being able to walk where Jesus walked. For example, Scripture classes had taught me that Jesus spent much time in and around Capernaum on the Sea of Galilee. It is, undeniably, a beautiful area: a village that is situated on what is a particularly rich fishing area of the lake. Interestingly enough, the area was probably more populated two thousand years ago than it is today. However, having said even that, Capernaum was pretty close to the end of the world. For the Romans, it was at the far end of a province that was, itself, nothing to brag about. And, even for the Jews, northern Galilee was far from the center which was Jerusalem. I mean no disrespect, but humanly speaking, Jesus was a nobody from nowhere. It is nothing short of extraordinary that, at the end of His three years of public ministry, He was acclaimed by followers as both Son of God and risen from the dead. There were many wandering rabbis; crucifixion was a common Roman form of execution; even the Scriptures tell us that there were many false messiahs. Some have said that the spread of Mohammed's doctrines was as improbable; but, almost from the beginning, that movement was accompanied by military force. With Christianity, it was almost four hundred years before it was even accorded civil legality. No, Jesus began in obscurity; He operated with no power save that of God's Spirit and, even at the time of His death, He had probably created very few waves on the sea of Jewish thought.

When He tells us that His kingdom is not of this world, I suspect that He reminds us that His followers will be most effective when they depend, as He did, on the power of the Spirit. Jewish and Roman authorities did not know how to cope with this man who loved them even as He demanded that they place their trust in Him rather than in the systems of power that seemed so immovable. They dealt with Him with the efficiency of worldly solution (with the same efficiency that abortion seems to offer us) but because He was, in addition to being weak in the world's way of measuring, the Incarnate Word of the Father's life and love, He was raised up and manifested as King of Kings and Lord of Lords.

Christe the King and Judge

November 24, 1996

The world's most populated country, China, runs a huge concentration camp system that pays for itself by forced labor. Among the things manufactured are toys, great numbers of which are exported and will be sold as Christmas presents. Does our government protest this? Do buyers reject these very reasonably priced slave labor toys? Of course not, that's business.

Parents of teen-age girls, professedly Christian, give their daughters birth control pills to keep them safe; they welcome to the Thanksgiving table the older brother and his current live-in girl friend and nothing is ever said. "After all, who are we to judge?"

People who live materially better than any in the history of humanity see the poor and give virtually nothing of time, talent, wit, wisdom or money to alleviate their pain. "If they would only get a job. . ."

The huge mosaic in the apse of the National Shrine pictures Christ coming in judgment at the end of time. As a boy, when I saw the mosaic for the first time, I was struck by the anger that appears in the face of Christ as judge. That anger was so different from the mercy and forgiveness I had associated with Him. Will Christ our King, who will come as judge at the end of time be angry? I think not. However, He will come as truth and in the face of that truth, how will a world that has lived according to falsehood and injustice perceive Him? In God, truth and love are one. As a boy, often when my parents would speak the truth in love about some aspect of my behavior, I would perceive dislike or anger on their part. The problem was not the truth they spoke or the love that motivated them; the problem was my wanting to cling to some lie about myself.

When, at the end of time, we can hide no longer from the truth of Christ the King, I suppose the fiery love that speaks that truth might seem like anger as it sears and purges the veneer of lies and pretense that is the world. But from the tree of the Cross, He was proclaimed our King and He will come to claim what is His own. Those who have recognized Him as King by faith will surely be drawn to the King of Love who is judge; but others, I suppose, will recoil in horror as lives built on lies are exposed for what they are.

God the Source of Freedom

November 2, 1997

An essay by Cardinal Lustiger, the Archbishop of Paris, and a look through a guidebook brought by a friend from Chartres Cathedral in France, permit these thoughts to be read with a French accent. At any rate, one of the great days of my life was spent in 1969 at the Cathedral of Chartres. I was in the seminary and traveled during my last free summer before ordination through Europe with two friends. That day at Chartres was wonderful both because of the Cathedral itself and because of the tours in which we participated. The guide, an Englishman who had made his life's work that cathedral, was also a university professor and a gifted teacher. So, in guiding us around Chartres, he was also teaching us how to "read" the churches of the Middle Ages which were the catechisms for an illiterate age. Looking through the book, though, reminded me of something I had forgotten about the history of Chartres.

It is thought that, from the beginnings of the basilica in the fourth century, a statue of Our Lady had been venerated. While a model of that statue is still in the church crypt, the original was burned by French revolutionaries in 1793—in the name of the liberty proclaimed by that Revolution. That sad little vignette of history struck me only because I had just finished reading a wonderful essay, in *First Things Magazine*, by Cardinal Lustiger, in which he dealt with the French Revolution's themes of liberty, fraternity and equality. About liberty—freedom—he did have some especially valuable thoughts.

The heart of Lustiger's thesis is, "Submission to God does not alienate human liberty, for the source of liberty cannot be the enemy of liberty." So often, we equate freedom with the ability to make choices, and to be sure, choice is part of the equation. Self will, however, is not the same as freedom. In some sense, obviously, our freedom is limited. I do not, for example, have the freedom to choose to be in two places at one time; I do not have the freedom to choose different biological parents. With God, of course, there is complete freedom; only He is completely free. Therefore, I am most free when I am closest to God, the source of freedom.

The task of the Christian, and I believe, especially of the parent, is to remind the world of that seeming paradox. So often, self-will, divorced from God, leads to the isolation and destruction of the French revolution and the ideologies that have followed it. The exercise of freedom that chooses the source of freedom—God—gives us the experience of freedom intended by the God in whose image we are created.

The Hidden Life

December 7, 1997

Since Scripture and tradition tell us that Jesus took for Himself Joseph's profession of carpenter during the thirty years of His hidden life, do you suppose that His divine power drove all the competition out of town because He worked so fast and with never a mistake? Or perhaps, did He as apprentice to Joseph, drive His father crazy, as He tried to talk the boss into giving poor customers (and which of them were not?) price breaks? I suppose we will never know, but these questions and a few other thoughts came to me as I was asked to give a talk this week on the hidden life of Jesus.

As always, of course, any meditation on the life of Christ yields surprising benefits. First of all, I suppose most of us would see ourselves living rather obscure—if not hidden—lives. It is fascinating to think about the things Jesus did in those years after "He returned obedient to them, from the Temple." How did the eternal Word of God cope with the vexation of customers who would spend hours haggling over the price of a door or table? Was Jesus frustrated by day after endless day of framing tiny little one-room shacks; of returning home at sunset to meals that were as predictable and ordinary as the hot, dry days and nights? Does not the hidden life of Jesus remind us that, while there is creativity in work, it often seems irritating, pressurizing and monotonous? I often note the university graduates who, upon receiving jobs with what seem like enormous salaries, are soon after bemoaning the inevitable reality that one rarely gets something for nothing in this world. Surely there is nobility in work, but that nobility is often hidden within seemingly endless weeks and years of ordinary labor. As a priest, for example, I am often asked, "How are things in your parish?" The answer to which is that I have almost no idea. I do not really know if people are growing in love of God and the desire to serve their neighbor and those are the things that should characterize a good parish. So, pray God, I hope I get up and do my work each day at least in some way as the Lord would have me.

But, of course, the hidden life of Jesus contained so much more than the things He did in home or shop. The focus of His life was to do the will of the Father: He prayed constantly; He meditated over the word of Scripture; He gave the people of Nazareth—even the most irritating—all that His Father would give them. Imagine the conversations of the adult Jesus with Mary and Joseph! The lesson, of course, is that the grace and glory of God can shine through what appears to be even the most hidden and ordinary lives. Focus on doing God's will, not on asserting our own pitiful selves and, little by little, being hidden from the notice of others does not matter so much. What does matter is that we are not hidden from the only One whose notice really does make a difference.

Like a Stream in the Hand of the Lord

A priest, you may be certain, is asked many penetrating questions about his life and lifestyle. The most frequently asked—and one to which I have no answer—is, "Why do priests always wear black?" Another question I get quite frequently (and which makes me wonder what folks are thinking as they ask it) is, "What do priests do with all their time?" Actually, this question about the use of time, is one I ask myself, in a somewhat different fashion, all the time.

On a typical weekday, I look at my calendar, and with daily Mass, there may be only six or seven hours of obligations like appointments, maybe a funeral, perhaps time in a classroom or a meeting or an appointment with someone for Confession or Marriage Preparation. As I take time for quiet prayer early in the morning, however, the problem that invariably distracts me from that prayer, is all of the other things not scheduled on a calendar that I also see as part of my job. Will I "fill up" the rest of the day sitting at my desk with administration tasks that range from planning future activities to assessment of finances; will I go on Communion calls or hospital visits; will I do a little theological or spiritual reading that every priest is supposed to do to "keep up;" or is this the time to answer the phone calls or mail that I know will take a good chunk of time? Be sure, the list is longer.

I am not complaining; I love my job. Actually, I mention this dilemma only because I suspect, according to different careers and vocations, it is quite common. Also, I mention it because of something that came to me recently in that same time of prayer that often seems so distracted. At daily Mass this week, we read from the Book of Proverbs. One of them, (Prov 21:1), says, "Like a stream is the king's heart in the hand of the Lord; wherever it pleases Him, He directs it." So many of us have so much we feel obliged to accomplish, and much of it seems never to get done. The image from Proverbs struck me as helpful: allow my heart to be like a stream that the Lord can direct wherever He will.

Submission to God's will seems like a cop-out to some. "Oh sure, God will take care of it," is said in cynical disbelief, as if the believer thinks one need only sit back and wait for divine intervention. No, there is an awful lot of hard work to be done. Submission to God's will (or being directed like a stream in the hand of the Lord) implies a prayerful willingness to do with our lives what God wants to fulfill His plan. Then we have to trust that the best we can do is, somehow, what He wants. We will never "get it all done," but if we are people of prayer, we can trust that what gets done is what really matters the most.

He Hems Me In

I am surprised at how many accidents or near accidents take place at the intersection of East-West Highway and Pearl Street. One would think, especially with East-West being one way at that point, traffic would flow smoothly. Instead, it seems to me that I am often hearing the screeching of tires that sound a near miss or, fairly often, the crunch of metal that signals a hit. It may be that folks trying to get in and out of the local fast food restaurant have something to do with it, or it may be that I am just not used to life in the fast lane and do not recognize that what I see as surprising is absolutely to be expected.

At any rate, as I see people grouped around their dents, exchanging insurance information and dealing with the police, I often think about how messed up their plans for the day have become. Small price to pay, I will grant, especially since I have never seen anyone get hurt, thank God, but still, a day carefully crafted for maximum benefit has now been exploded by a Big Mac attack.

Of course, this is simply another demonstration that we really are not in control. There was a recent report on the radio about infections coming into the country because of jet travel from exotic places. We may not have immunity to these infections and, perhaps, they may be immune to antibiotics. Strawberries from Mexico, fish from the Pocomoke, and who knows what this week will reveal there is little that is as it seems. Note the panic that besets the stock market every week or so, as the innate realization clicks in that what goes up can, indeed, come down. I have never been sick; someone a year younger than I died of a heart attack last week. We are not in control.

I sometimes think that this is the first act of faith that must be made by modern man: that plan, save and avoid fat though I will, I am not in control. The course of life is beyond me; there is a darkness of unknowing that covers every instant beyond this one. The Psalmist says, "Behind me and before me, He hems me in. Such knowledge is too wonderful for me to bear." Dear God, suppose I did have to be in control of my way through life: that I had to fend off enemies and accidents, that I was responsible for the happiness of my children and the length of my days.

Before I was formed in the womb of my mother, He knew me. Before I sinned in youthful pride, He had redeemed me. Indeed, I do have freedom, I do have the power to take charge of my life, but the greatest use of that freedom is to place all my hopes and fears, all my plans and desires into the hands of Him who seeks to draw me to Himself.

Agony (of Self-giving) in the Garden

March 29, 1998

For me, the most frightening scene in the Lord's Passion is His agony in the Garden. Of course the road to Calvary and the crucifixion are horrible, but at least then, in a certain sense, matters were underway; but at Gethsemene, Jesus makes His final acceptance of the will of the Father. While the description of the Apostles' sleep is almost amusing, their sleep reminds us that no man or woman stood beside Jesus at that moment.

Some say that our lives pass before us as we die. Was it so with the Lord? Did He review that at every moment He always did what the Father would have him do? We know so many stories from the Gospels of His serving love; how many hundreds or thousands more did He remember on that night before He died? Where were those formerly blind and deaf, where were those freed from sin on this night before He died? We heard on the First Sunday of Lent of Jesus' being tempted in the desert. If those temptations were fierce, how much worse the temptations in the Garden to bitterness. We think of love as being relationship with another. What, then, if all whom we love abandon us and if even the Father seems now to be only a concept with no reality? Having just instituted the Eucharist that He intended to be the source and symbol of unity and love, He goes into the Garden while His congregation either sleeps or disappears.

When we say that Jesus had no sin, it does not mean only that He did no bad things; it means that He was utterly free of self. In the Garden, for example, the experience of being alone and abandoned—of having no one and nothing—was absolute. His dread of continuing to love, of continuing to do the will of the Father, so consumed His person that Scripture says He perspired blood. "Out of the depths I cry to you, O Lord;" and somehow, from those depths the abandoned Jesus says, "But let it be as You would have it, not as I."

The Father's will for His Son was to love both the Father and us no matter what happened. His sacrificial gift of Himself was pleasing not simply because He had a horrible death, but because He would not back away from His self-giving. As a descendant of sinful Adam, He loved as God. Because He loved in a world under the dominion of Satan, that love cost Him not less than everything, but that love is our victory. We, the Baptized, share His victory; but we, the Baptized, also announce that victory through the way we love until the end of time.

Original Sin = Me First

June 22, 1997

Feeling just a bit like I used to when a kaleidoscope would suddenly come into focus, I heard a caller on one of the radio talk shows while driving through town last week. He was one of those typical callers, beset by guilt, but resolved to break off a "relationship" because he was not ready to give what was demanded by caring for children not his own. He found that he no longer had time for himself. Suddenly, it hit me: this is original sin. I have read the theology and can give the definitions, but never with such clarity have I understood what original sin really is. Quite simply, original sin means, "ME FIRST."

I have often quoted my friend of many years who said, in a Scripture group, that "anyone who does not believe in original sin never raised a three year old." A three year old fights for toys, struggles for attention and takes for granted love that is received. But we all know forty-year-olds who have left families to "find themselves;" thirty-somethings who are not ready to "tie themselves down;" and others who look at the poor and homeless with contempt because they will not work hard enough to pick themselves up and succeed.

I think I see the same attitude in church sometimes. As a human being, not to mention as a baptized Christian, my first privilege and obligation is to be in relationship with God. Worship, then, flows from an attitude of awe, respect and obedience. God, who created me out of nothing and who redeemed me out of love for me, deserves my worship. Since that is the case, why do I so often hear people explain their no longer going to Mass by saying, "I don't get anything out of it." Once again, if I don't like it, it is not good.

Our nature is scarred by original sin. True enough, we are forgiven in Baptism; but we cannot forget that, as a result of original sinfulness, there remains a tendency within us towards selfishness. The grace of Baptism allows us to obey the two great Commandments to get out of ourselves and to love God and neighbor, but that grace battles against a tendency toward sin.

The individual on the radio reminded me that one of the effects of sin is isolation; one of the effects of grace is commitment. Isolation so often seems easier, commitment binds us to God and to others and, therefore, leads to sacrifice of self and the Cross. The commitment of Jesus got Him into big trouble and, literally, left Him with no "life of His own;" but that, in pale imitation of His, is what love is all about.

Original Sin

I had a wonderful discussion with my high school CCD class the other night about original sin. Of course they had heard about the doctrine as children, but with their sense of adolescent questioning, this was the first time, probably, they had ever taken the doctrine seriously. I explained that Adam and Eve, because they were the entire race at the beginning, somehow spoke for all of their children in original disobedience. The result of original sin is that we were born into the world unworthy of heaven; we enter life in need of salvation. To the students this seemed so unjust: that God would condemn all of us simply because of the sin of these two people. In addition, we talked about the classic questions associated with discussions of original sin: what happens to unbaptized infants and what happens to adults who die and, through no fault of their own, never had a chance to profess faith in Jesus.

In regards to those two questions, I have no doubt that God's mercy exceeds our wildest dreams, but the point is even the unbaptized baby is conceived in need of the grace of Jesus Christ. Whether and how the grace is offered, I gladly leave to a God "whose mercy endures forever." But as to the supposed injustice of God who would condemn us to carry the sin of Adam and Eve, I think that two points are worth remembering.

First, experience argues in favor of the reality of original sin. Without a long argument, who can deny that we are prone to selfishness? We may have the highest of ideals, but how often under pressure, do we choose in favor of what we perceive to be self-interest over what is good for others? Experience shows us to be deeply flawed. Even after Baptism, we recognize that we have a tendency toward sin; that only the grace of God and hard work allows us to become more like Jesus.

Secondly, the wonderful liturgy of Holy Saturday calls original sin, "O happy fault that merited for such a Redeemer." Adam and Eve, had they never sinned, would never have experienced what we will because of the grace of Jesus our Redeemer. Theirs was what we call a natural happiness; ours, because we are graced with God's life, is supernatural.

The season of Advent is so wonderful because it signals the dawn of salvation. We are not condemned to the frustration of selfishness and conflict that flow from original sin. Jesus has come and lifts us to the freedom of living the life of dearly loved children of God.

The Grace of Conversion
March 9, 1997

I correspond quite frequently with a young man in jail whom I have known since he was in junior high school. His has been a journey, not unlike so many in our day, involving drug addiction, the inability to hold a job and finally, crime—used to finance the addiction. Always motivated more by weakness than by malice, my friend was probably doomed so long as the avenue of weakness continued to be open; and so, by the grace of God, a judge refused all pleas for leniency and gave him a substantial sentence. And so the journey began. As with the Prodigal Son, "he came to his senses at last;" but where the story told by Jesus compresses the tale, my friend lived fully the journey back to the Father.

God's grace works in funny ways. In the midst of all the chaos that is prison where, for example, hundreds of personal radios are constantly turned full blast to a variety of different stations, my friend found himself in a cell with a Christian. Thus was he reawakened to faith. Alas, the cell-mate's fundamentalist disgust with the Catholic faith challenged that basic Catholic school loyalty. My friend, only in order to get ammunition to win a fight on religion, met with the Catholic chaplain, who thank God, turns out to be a man of deep faith and commitment to the imprisoned.

What is most beautiful about the grace of conversion is how it gradually heals a person's whole being. His father is a disaster. Anyone who questions a father's power might look at how, so negatively, that power in this father damaged three sons. Gradually, my friend has seen the distinction between who he is and who his father said he is. With great reluctance, he has had to begin to try to forgive his father as he realizes that the forgiveness that he seeks, he must also give. And, finally, as it begins to dawn on him how much he is loved by God and that a loving God has given him great gifts, he begins to take college courses (until the State drops them as being unnecessary) and learns a trade.

Especially as we move toward the climax of Lent, we hear much about the journey of Israel from slavery in Egypt to freedom in the Promised Land. As Christians, we recognize that journey as prefiguring our own Passover from slavery to sin to the freedom of grace because of Jesus, our Passover sacrifice. But, what that journey was for Israel as a nation and for us as the Church, it has been for my friend, who is being led out of slavery into freedom. So, in an infinite variety of ways, will it be for anyone who will enter the promised land of heaven.

Opening Ourselves to Grace

March 26, 1995

I was giving a day of recollection years ago down at Manresa Retreat House in Annapolis. On a spring day as beautiful as we have had in the past few weeks, I asked the people to take some quiet time for prayer and to return at the end with something of nature that spoke to them of God. One person returned with nothing in his hands, but instead, asked us to follow him to the brow of the hill overlooking the Severn River. There, at the base of the hill was a rather substantial inlet from the river. What struck that retreatant, and what remains with me today, is that the water of that inlet came from the river through a little channel in the bank no more than six inches wide. To this person, this was a reminder of how little is the opening we must give to God for Him to fill our lives with His grace.

The ways in which we open ourselves to God often seem so insignificant, so incapable of being a means of His grace. In fact, however, because our nature is created by God, it is often those things which appear most ordinary that convey the greatest message. Dumb example, perhaps: my father was always there, especially when I was in a jam or in trouble—and not only when I was a kid. Now, you might say, that is only natural, a father is supposed to be there for his children. OK, but I have also recognized, with years, how much my father needed grace to fulfill his role. Most importantly for me, I probably received the best lesson I could about my Father in heaven always being there, not because I am so good, but because He so loves me. Did any one of ten thousand small decisions of my father teach that lesson? No, of course not. The decision, with his life, to cooperate with God's grace in the natural job of fathering children, (even though in many decisions he undoubtedly fell short), taught the lesson.

In what so often seems to be a small decision, we cooperate with grace. Frequent confession is another wonderful example. No doubt the person who goes to confession once a year receives God's forgiveness, but how much more does the penitent, who comes month after month with nothing particularly "big" to confess, open himself up to the power of God to gradually turn away from the propensity to selfishness within us all? We do not notice God working; we do not feel grace at work, but like the grain of wheat of which Jesus speaks in the Gospel, we gradually mature in the fight against the power of sin.

The Miracle of Family Love

February 19, 1995

I am in the midst of secret negotiations with the eldest daughter of good friends. She, with her siblings, is trying to arrange a surprise 25th celebration of her parents' wedding. You can easily imagine that Mid-East peace negotiations don't contain the intricacy of details that is contained in attempting to put together a Mass, a party, the rental of a hall and the importing of out-of-town relatives, all done, we hope, without the knowledge of an otherwise rather observant couple. O what your friendly neighborhood parish priest does not get himself involved in!

Of course, my little secret in the whole matter is that I remember, clearly, where this mature young adult was only eight or ten years ago. I remember the anger and sadness that was the daily fare of the family as she, seemingly deliberately, made decisions totally opposed to all of her parents' faith and values. Now only so few years later, she tells me as we discuss the celebration, about the Mass she went to at a chapel at the side of a ski slope. It is a miracle, but one, thank God, that many who read this have experienced in their own families.

It is a miracle, however, of grace. No one is doomed to accept grace; we can, with great enthusiasm, thoroughly reject it. However, because grace is the life of God within us, and God's life is essentially love, it is difficult to totally turn our backs on something so attractive as the experience of His love. And so, we come to the miracle of Christian family life and love. I do not know the mechanics that led this young lady to so turn against and hurt her mom and dad during those tough high school years and I surely do not pretend that she was not responsible. Her parents stood for things firmly and without compromise that were hard to accept and understand, I suppose. But they stood for them because they knew they were part of God's plan and therefore best for their children. These parents did not know the future, but they did know that, whether she rejected or accepted their vision of life, any compromise on their part was really cheating the daughter they love so much.

Love is what it is all about and God is the source of that love. Parents can do no more than love their kids as God would have them do it: with truth, with forgiveness, with sure and certain standards that come from God and the Church, and with an awful lot of patience and hope. It may not "work," since children too have free will, but in the long run, the experience of God's love is the hardest force there is to reject.

Yahweh, Close to His People

August 3, 1997

We have been reading from the Book of Exodus at daily Mass in recent days. These readings remind me again, that there are few more powerful proofs of the existence of God than the history of Israel. Exodus, of course, tells the story of the Chosen People being freed from slavery in Egypt and then wandering in the desert for forty years before, finally, being led into the Promised Land, Israel. The outline of the story is so familiar that I believe it is easy to miss the mind-blowing message it conveys.

The people had been slaves in Egypt for hundreds of years. So desperate was their situation that Pharaoh had ordered the deaths of all males because of his fear of the growth of the Hebrew people. Suddenly, this people— utterly beaten down, utterly without rights and utterly without hope—was free and found themselves at liberty in the Sinai. Now, surely Moses was a charismatic leader, but no one leader could keep together so helpless a group simply by dint of leadership skills. Look at countries today that try to move from slavery to freedom.

What is more striking is the concept of God that was formed within these people as they wandered in the desert. The Egyptians, for example, with all their scientific sophistication, had ideas of the divine that, to be polite, are laughable. Yet, this smelly tribe of wandering former slaves, by the time they enter the Promised Land, have come to believe in only one God (the first people to recognize monotheism) and to recognize that He is in personal relationship with them as His people. He cares about them.

Centuries later, both Plato and Aristotle would recognize there can be only one supreme being, but their philosophy does not come close to the insight of Israel, because Israel, in the wilderness of the desert, also came to recognize that this one God, whose Name was holy and awesome, was also a God who drew close to His people. Moses, we are told, saw God "face to face." This God, Yahweh, who is always recognized as all-powerful, is also a God who makes covenants with His people, who gives them command-ments so that they can show to Him their fidelity. To read Exodus, and to believe that the story it tells is only the work of human creativity, is to believe that Elvis is performing at Wolf Trap.

For us as Christians, of course, the intimacy of God's relationship with His people revealed in Exodus is only the start of the story. The slavery in Egypt points to the slavery of every human to sin and the care of God for those slaves only begins to lift the veil that, in Christ, allows us to see the glory and intimacy of God's love.

History of the Catholic Church

April 28, 1996

One of the things that lies before me today is to prepare a lecture on the two thousand year history of the Catholic Church. This is not as intimidating as it might seem; after all, how much detail is possible in one lecture? Looking at the broad sweep of Catholic history, whether in a talk of one hour or, preferably, by reading more extensively, does bear some valuable fruit, especially in giving perspective to anyone caught up in the temptation to see today as the only day in the life of the Church. There are so many wonderful examples of what I mean.

Those who wonder if the Church will survive the onslaughts of our world do not have to look back too far to recognize Providence in a time of agony. The results of the French Revolution in Europe were many, of course. Certainly, the Church in Europe continues to suffer from an anti-clericalism that Americans would barely recognize. The loss of properties throughout the continent threatened the very existence of the Church as it had been known since before the year 1000. Out of what appeared to be disaster, however, came a Church purified, to a great extent, of close association with the secular states in which it found itself. Because countries were no longer officially connected with the Church, bishops could now be freely appointed by the Pope. Catholics more and more saw themselves as we do today: united in faith and discipline under the visible leadership of the Holy Father. The extraordinary missionary growth of this century, especially in Africa, resulted from the work of men and women who could rise above the political maneuverings of colonial powers and lead people to a universal Church, just as able to serve even when colonial powers had been ejected.

The whole office of the papacy is another example of God's hand in history. The liturgy and spiritual tradition of the Orthodox Church in Russia has enormous depth. However, since the time of Czar Peter the Great, and especially under the Communists, the Church has been reduced to being an arm of the government. Orthodoxy produced during this century thousands of martyrs, people of deep holiness. Ultimately, though, because the state could appoint bishops, many of whom were Communist collaborators, the power of the Church to speak against evil was diminished. In the Roman Church, the Popes continued to name bishops who looked to Rome and not to the state as the source of their authority. Consequently, history rightly sees the Catholic Church as one of the major influences that brought about the fall of Soviet Communism. It is not always a pretty picture (history never is), but, as so many times before, as we look at the bumpy course of the human story, there is the Catholic Church somehow at the heart of the tale.

The Church in Early America

May 5, 1996

Considerable coverage was given recently to the tri-centenary of Prince George's County. While articles did discuss certain aspects of colonial and post-Revolutionary War history, including the Battle of Bladensburg, and while attention was paid to the plantation culture of the County prior to the Civil War, there was, regrettably, little about the religious history of the County and, especially, about the place where I was first assigned, Sacred Heart, Bowie. The Chapel, still standing, was originally a part of White Marsh Plantation and dates from 1741. It is a sight of important activity in the early history of the American Catholic Church.

John Carroll, of course, was the first American Catholic Bishop, named as Archbishop of Baltimore in 1789. What is interesting about his story is that he had been nominated by the clergy of the new United States who had met at White Marsh, a two thousand acre estate owned by priests who had been members of the Society of Jesus (which during these years had been suppressed by the Holy Father). They had received it by a bequest of a great uncle of Bishop Carroll, a native of Ireland who had done well in the colonies and who wanted to leave the land to the Jesuits, who were the only priests in Maryland. The Church in the formerly English colonies had been administered, before the Revolution, by the Vicar Apostolic in London. Obviously, with independence for the United States, the dozen or so priests in the country recognized a need for a new relationship with Rome. These priests, or representatives of theirs, met at White Marsh beginning in 1783 and devised a proposed structure for the Catholic Church in the United States.

These early meetings were to be of a great moment to the American Church for several reasons. Not only did these priests petition to Rome for permission to nominate the first bishop, a permission which was granted, but they also were the initiators of "The School—to be erected at Georgetown on Potomac," which became, of course, Georgetown University.

After the Ordination of Bishop Carroll, American Church structure took on a more traditional form, but White Marsh remained prominent for the Jesuits until 1832. It served as the location for the first novitiate for the Society in America and in fact, the first novices for the Missouri Province began their formation there. One of these men was Pere de Smet, the famous Indian missionary in the West.

Eventually the Jesuits moved their novitiate to other locations and Bowie became a small country parish. During this century, White Marsh became a mission of Ascension in "old Bowie," as it is called, because of the location of the railroad near that church. In 1960, the parish became independent, under diocesan priests, but the Chapel and much associated with the earliest days of our Catholic history is waiting for your visit. Certainly Sacred Heart, White Marsh, represents one of the finest pages in Prince George's history.

Visiting the Shrine and Monastery

June 11, 1995

Last weekend's wonderfully successful parish picnic was spared by the Good Lord from the effects of several summer storms. The picnic was also a reminder of how many young families there are in the parish, as large numbers of children joined parishioners of every age for sports and picnic food. Thanks to all who so carefully planned out the day.

The number of young families also reminded me that vacation time will soon be upon us. I wonder how many of these families have taken advantage of the many wonderful day trips in our area that can enhance a sense of Catholic Tradition, especially in children. For them, often Catholic means Lourdes; they have little sense of the universality of the Church or of its history or its variety of expressions. There are some interesting and fun destinations within an hour and a half that can help give that wider perspective. Allow, this week, a couple of local examples.

I was surprised, recently, when I discovered how many of our second graders have never been to the National Shrine of the Immaculate Conception on the campus of Catholic University. Not only is this one of the largest churches in the world, but in its many chapels there is a chance for each visitor to be exposed to the wonderful variety of devotions to the Blessed Mother. Few aspects of Catholic tradition are more appealing to children than the story of the Virgin Mother and her Son, Jesus. The National Shrine has dozens of chapels that beautifully invite not only children to come to a deeper confidence in Mary as our Mother.

For some reason my mother used to love to go to confession at the Franciscan Monastery, which is only 10 or so blocks from the National Shrine. Since they had confessions on Sunday, we would often go there for both Mass and confession. The Monastery today is as beautiful as it was in the fifties. It is run by the Friars who run the Shrines in the Holy Land and, quite frankly, it was built early in this century, to be the center of fundraising for those churches. So, on their large amount of land, the Franciscans have developed gardens and shrines that are meant to put one in mind of the Holy Land. (I'll let you know after the trip in November whether they succeed). However, for a kid, the best part of the Monastery is the catacombs under the Church, where an attempt is made to simulate the catacombs in Rome. When I visited recently with a group of children, I got a kick out of seeing how the effect is the same today on children as they wander in the semi-darkness from shrine to shrine, picturing for the first time, the persecution of the early Christians.

Both churches are worth a day trip. Most importantly, however, is a stop on the way home at Ledo's on University Boulevard in Hyattsville, where people from Bethesda can find out what pizza really tastes like!

Visiting Emmitsburg and the Trappists

June 25, 1995

Allow me a final column on summer travel hints. I give them because I remember how much I was impressed by these places when my parents took us to them when we were children. Our Catholic faith is based on sacraments (signs) that point to deeper realities. Thus, these places that remind us of heroic expressions of faith can challenge us to a bit of heroism in our own Catholic lives.

Emmitsburg, Maryland, is only about an hour away, but in this little town there is a wealth of Catholic history. Much of it is connected with the life of St. Elizabeth Seton, the first American born saint. "Mother" Seton (called this because she was the foundress of the American Sisters of Charity) was a New York born daughter of a prominent Episcopal family. She married, had five children, and upon the death of her husband, she entered—after a long journey of thought and prayer—the Catholic Church. Eventually, the widow and mother felt the call to religious life and seeing the need for Catholic education, began her work first in Baltimore and then in Emmitsburg. Her tomb is in the chapel of the mother house of the Daughters of Charity in the town, and the "White House" where she and her sisters lived can also be visited. Growing up in New York, Mother Seton met many of the great heroes of the Revolution, whose homes we respectfully visited. Certainly the places of her pioneering and saintly work are as worthy of pilgrimage by any American Catholic.

Also, while in Emmitsburg, on the campus of Mt. St. Mary's, the second oldest American Catholic college, visit the beautiful grotto in honor of Our Lady of Lourdes. This beautiful area, deep in the woods of a hill behind the college, was a place of prayer for Mother Seton. The combination of quiet with the shrines along the path make it very easy to appreciate the holiness of the place.

One final, brief suggestion. The Trappist Monastery in Berryville, Virginia (about two hours away) is an active reminder that the traditional monastic way of life is alive and doing very well. There is a guest house on the grounds for private retreats where one can pray throughout the day with the monks, but even a visit for Mass or for one of the times when the monks gather to chant the psalms of the Divine Office give a glimpse of a way of life that reminds us that life lived for God alone is the highest calling. The land of the monastery, where the monks raise cattle and run their bakery, is along the Shenandoah River and is as beautiful as it gets in that wonderful part of Virginia.

The Perfect Prayer

July 10, 1994

The core of my spiritual life has always been the Mass. Even as a small boy, I figured that if the Host really is the Lord, it would be hard to find a better way to be close to God than by going to Communion. Therefore, I would hear, for example, that the Mass is the perfect prayer or the perfect sacrifice or that, because the Mass is, fundamentally, the prayer of Jesus Himself, that is the only act of praise that is worthy of God and I would accept all this as making good sense. But, it is funny how you can repeat something all your life before you really hear it.

I really do try to pray. I do not try hard enough, I readily admit, but I believe I have an obligation to go apart each day and spend some time with the Lord. After all, since everything that is good comes from Him, it makes perfect sense to me that I should give at least part of my day back to God. The problem is that, for the most part, I experience my prayer as very imperfect, filled with distractions, and rarely, if ever, yielding insights into the nature of God and life. However, I certainly do recognize the fruit of prayer in my life and so, as poorly as I go about it, I am committed to at least trying to pray.

All of this leads to the Mass. I was celebrating Mass one morning, using the Third Eucharistic Prayer, when all of a sudden some of the lines spoke to me as I had never heard them before. "See the victim whose death has reconciled us to yourself." "May He make us an everlasting gift to you." "May this sacrifice, which has made our peace with you..." Of course my prayer is flawed, but the prayer of Jesus, the sinless son of God, is not; of course, because of my sinfulness, I sense a lack of unity with God, but Jesus, when He prays, is completely one with the Father.

The Mass is such an awesome gift because Jesus allows His prayer to become our prayer, too. "Do this in memory of me," He tells us. Do this (celebrate the Eucharist), and I will gather all your hopes, prayers, and needs, distorted as they are by the effects of sin, and I will unite them with one perfect sacrifice of thanksgiving and praise and I will present them to the Father. In the Eucharist, there is no need to focus on our very real limitations; they are nothing compared to the offering of Jesus, the great High Priest, who intercedes with the Father on our behalf.

Mass Links the Living to the Dead

June 28, 1998

In writing on loneliness, Dom Hubert van Zeller, OSB, writes, 'It is easier to escape from a presence than from an absence." How often I think of that line as I watch people begin being widowed. All of us know the loneliness of being homesick, for example: but, usually, this pain fades as we either make new friends or return home. How hard it must be when for forty or fifty years this chair or that place at table or even that creak on the stairs has been associated with this now absent person. As a priest there are few things I more enjoy than marriage preparation; these young couples would be surprised, I suspect, if they knew how often I imagine the pain one or another of them will have to go through in, pray God, fifty or so years when one of them goes to God. If I think I know a widow or widower well enough, I will sometimes say, in a weak attempt at humor, "That's what you get for falling in love." There is truth in it, though. Life offers few pains that are deeper than the loss of a loved one.

Marriage, or any true friendship, for that matter, is so sacred because it points to the joy that finds its fulfillment in God. We rarely think about it, especially when we are young, but we are in exile on this earth: the home to which we are called is in heaven with God. Understandably, though, even a believing couple can make what seems a permanent home out of the companionship and achievements of marriage and family life. We are pilgrims, though; and the ache and depth of loneliness has in it the call to focus on companionship with Jesus.

Years ago, I was closely involved with a family whose eight year old son died overnight from a rare heart virus. You can easily imagine the grief; but, out of that grief came a group—that still functions—of families who meet each month. Their common bond is the loss of a child to death. From the beginning, my friends who started this group wanted the Mass to be a part of each month's get-together. Eventually, as non-Catholic families began to join this "First Sunday" group as it was called, the question was raised as to whether another form of non-denominational prayer might be more suitable for the meetings. This little boy's mother was adamant that Mass be included because, as she said, "I am as close to him at Mass as I will be in heaven."

Every priest has the experience that a great number of people at daily Mass are widowed. I am sure that part of this is because often, being retired, they have the time for Mass. As I grow (ever so slowly) older, I come to suspect there is more to it than simply time. As they go through this painful stage in life, people seek to develop that union with Jesus from whom we will never be parted; but, also, they recognize that the union of love, even with the dead, is most fully present as the whole communion of saints joins in the great act of worship that is the Mass.

Signs to Be Remembered

January 21, 1996

On the Sunday of the snowstorm, about five minutes after Mass began, a family with three or four children ranging from, I guess, seven to thirteen, came into the church through the side door. In theory, I was listening to the readings from Scripture; in fact, I was remembering a winter Sunday in the mid-fifties when my father piled us into the back of the chevy station wagon to make it through the unplowed streets of Chevy Chase (what has changed?) to Mass. The trip involved pushing the car part of the way and walking the rest, but, at some point during the Mass, we made it.

I know that many, especially the elderly, could not have made it to Mass during this storm; I know that the Cardinal dispensed us from the obligation. I know that, apart from the priests, everyone would have been at least a little inconvenienced getting to mass. Having said all of this—and with my thoughts on the future rather than the past—I think a lot of parents missed a God-given opportunity to make a faith statement to their families; a statement that would have been remembered for years.

The Catholic religion is sacramental. We believe that, because of the make-up of human nature, God communicates with us and we with God, through the use of signs. Words, bread and wine, oil are used by the Church to convey the actions of God in our lives. Likewise, the fact that we worship as a community, kneeling and standing, our common prayers, the sign of peace and so much else, speak to us in easily understood signs about our relationship with God and with each other. Marriage is a sacrament, for example, precisely because it points to—and makes present—the creative power of God's love. For Catholics, signs are everything.

Last week, I pray God, our children spent hours getting frozen and soaked with the never-to-be-forgotten chance to play in more than two feet of snow. Others, I hope, got sore from shoveling and making good money (and helping those who couldn't pay). I feel so badly, though, that so many of their parents who could have, did not give to their children a sign to be remembered for a lifetime: that our responsibility to God must come first in life. Two hours of walking in snow-drifts and worshiping as a family could have untold dividends.

Eucharist on Vacations

January 8, 1995

For virtually all of the first 20 years of my priesthood, my custom during one of the first weeks after the New Year was to take a group of young people skiing, either in New England or (as some of them got a little older or as plane fares became more reasonable) to the West. Many a get-together even now is enlivened by stories from those weeks. One, which, even now, is not especially beloved by my own brother, concerns the time his station wagon which I had borrowed, caught fire and was destroyed in a snow storm in New Hampshire, loaded down with eight passengers, their skis and baggage—and my dog! Another year we made it to our mountain top condo in Utah and then did not move for the week as it proceeded to snow for three straight days and nights. Happily, we could ski right out the back door.

Our routine was invariably the same. We would ski all day, come home and shower and then have Mass. Perhaps because so many really important friendships have come from those trips, I especially remember those simple celebrations of Mass. Because either the first or second week of the year was convenient for me and my collegians on vacation, this meant that every year we would hear the same readings at these Masses. I mention this because the first reading in the week after New Year is taken from the first letter of John, the great celebration and description of the life of love to be lived by the Christian community. While, God knows they never would have wanted or encouraged a homily, there were times over the years when, after Mass (before the TV had warmed up), one or another comment would be made about such powerful lines as, "No one has ever seen God; if we love one another, God lives in us and His love is perfected in us."

My favorite line from that letter comes from the 2nd chapter where John (and I always see him writing this letter after sixty or so years of reflecting on the Mystery of Christ) says, "See what love the Father has for us in letting us be called children of God." All that Christian life is about, from obeying commandments to feeding the hungry to being Confirmed proceeds from the incredible truth that the infinite, all-powerful God has formed us in His image and called us his dearly loved children. Perhaps for those young people over the years there was some little experience of the love that is supposed to characterize the people of God: I know there was for me. And, pray God, perhaps they grew in an understanding that the nourishment of that life is found in the Eucharist.

Changes in Ritual

October 9, 1994

I suppose everyone has heard by now that the Holy Father has allowed for a change in the discipline regarding those who are permitted to serve at Mass. The tradition, of course, has been to allow only boys and men to serve at the altar. The thinking behind the change in discipline, as I understand it, has at least two sources. First of all, in many parts of Europe and North America, young ladies have been serving for years and there is an old Roman saying, "Custom becomes law." Secondly, even while, in older times, one who served at Mass might be seen as headed toward priesthood, there is nothing about serving that is inherently of either a priestly or diaconal character. In other words, bringing wine and water to the priest, holding the book or carrying a cross or candles are not liturgical actions that are normally performed by ordained persons. Not surprisingly, Rome has made efforts to differentiate between those who are preparing for priesthood and those who serve at Mass. For example, in many parishes (not ours) where servers still wear cassock and surplice, that custom must be changed if girls are to serve. They will wear a gown like those used in this parish. Seminarians who are preparing for priesthood will continue to wear cassock and surplice.

People will greet this change, which will go into effect here at Our Lady of Lourdes on the first Sunday of Advent, in various ways. Probably the greater number will take note of it, pretty much shrug their shoulders, and continue to live their lives. Others will be happy; especially those with daughters who have wanted to serve. Others will find the change difficult to accept. To these, I think, something should be said because their difficulty in accepting this change probably says good things about their life of faith.

Thanksgiving was my favorite family ritual of the year, partly because, well into my college years, the good things took place, in the same way, year after year. As my brother and sisters began to get married and my grandmother died, inevitably, things changed; and, even though I was, by then, a young adult, I found the change difficult. I associated the unchanging family ritual with the goodness of Thanksgiving. Happily, I was wrong. The form of the celebration had to change, but the holiday is as much fun, and as unifying, as ever. So it is with the many changes we have experienced in the Liturgy over the last thirty years. A lot of externals have changed—and those externals often gave us deep satisfaction—but the heart of Liturgy, where God's people give Him glory and praise, is utterly untouched. The Church allows externals to change in order to draw more deeply into the center of our faith, but it is the sacred core of worship, and not the surroundings, to which we give our faith.

"Uh Oh, Lent is Coming"

February 25, 1996

When trivia games were so popular a few years ago, there were, inevitably, several Catholic Trivia Pursuit spin-offs. I wonder if they included questions about the three Sundays before Ash Wednesday. These Sundays, each given a long Latin name denoting the number of days before Easter, were warning signals to Catholics that Lent was on its way. The priest wore purple vestments at Mass, but no Lenten practice was observed. The person in the pew saw the purple and said, "Uh oh, Lent is coming. What am I going to do this year?"

Now, of course, the season is suddenly upon us. Every year, we receive phone calls on Ash Wednesday from people asking for Mass times because they have seen people with ashes on the street and realized what day it was. It is a shame that Lent does now kind of sneak up on us because there is great wisdom in preparing for this spiritually and psychologically important time of year.

In some ways, the Church year mirrors life. There are times of celebration (Christmas and Easter), but most of life is living from day to day, something like what the Church calls ordinary time of the year. Inevitably, though, in differing ways throughout our lives, we are forced to step back and look at where we are, where we are going and what really is important to us. In the Church year, of course, Lent invites us to that same kind of self-examination.

The three traditional practices of Lent (prayer, fasting and almsgiving) challenge us to remember our place in the world and how easily we lose focus. The added prayer of Lent, and especially the struggle to focus on God and to give Him time that He deserves, reminds us that while we are commanded to love God with our whole being, we fall incredibly short. Likewise the challenge of fasting and, by extension, all our Lenten self-denial, give witness to the self-gratification that we so take for granted. Whether it is time before the TV or eating between meals that we "give up," we recognize, especially as we fail after the enthusiasm of the first few Lenten days that, talk aside, our love for God must not be so strong if we have such a hard time giving up such trivial things for love of Him.

Finally, Lent invites us to give to the poor, traditionally called almsgiving. As we consider our gift to the Cardinal's Appeal, for example, we can examine whether we really do consider the poor, the dirty, the homeless, the mentally ill—all of the weak ones of the earth—to be our brothers and sisters. St. Paul says, "Where your heart is, there will your treasure be." Lent is that time of the year where, especially, the Church asks us to see if our hearts recognize a brother or a sister in that wretched person who seems so different from me.

Lent: An Opportunity for Reflection

March 13, 1994

Where does the junk come from? I have been here for almost ten days and only now can I begin to see small, spring-like buds of order emerge from the bags and boxes that came from Hyattsville. If I ever get transferred again, I will simply nail the door shut, put wall board over it, paint it so that it looks like a wall and leave. Then, a hundred years from now, someone will discover all these artifacts from a priest of the 1990s and make a lot of money. But, I never want to pack again.

Of course, the whole process does have some value. I have a third grade school picture that I rescued from my parents' house after they died. It, my 8th grade graduation picture and diploma from Blessed Sacrament, and a lot of family pictures are carefully put away and, regrettably, only see the light of day when I pack them up again. This is also the time when I look through high school and college yearbooks and when albums of memories from my first assignment as a priest come, briefly, again into sight.

I do not know whether such times for reflective memories are either necessary or important, but they certainly are enjoyable, especially for someone who, far from taking time for such quiet musing, spends most of his time trying to cope with the demands of the last hour.

Maybe there is some small lesson here. What I have been doing with these pictures and letters over the last week or so, is much like what happens, in a more spiritual sense, on my annual retreat. I try to review my life in terms of my vocation and to dedicate myself anew to responding to the call to serve God and neighbor as a priest. I will no doubt write in the future about the good a weekend retreat can be in someone's life, but I also recognize that, for many, such times away are very infrequent. That is why we cannot waste the season of Lent.

Anyone who takes their faith at all seriously knows that one of the fruits of Lent is that of reflection on how well one has been living the spiritual life. As I try to take more time for prayer, or as I try some form of self-denial or service to the poor, I cannot but reflect on how much or how little these things are normally part of my life. In my Lenten prayer I think the Lord shows me small snapshots of moral weaknesses or refusals to take up my daily cross in pursuit of Him. One need not unpack after a move across town in order to reflect on the past; only respond to the season of Lent.

Lent: "This Joyful Season"

March 3, 1996

One of the prefaces used in Lenten Masses has the line, "Each year you give us this joyful season..." The first time I used that Preface this year, I chuckled to myself as I recalled my early Lents as a priest. Ordained in 1971, I saw the Church coming through the liturgical changes of Vatican II. I grew up in an environment where the life and traditions of the "old" Church were pretty much understood and loved; consequently the changes, in mood as well as language were difficult for me to accept. There may have been even a bit of, dare I write it, immaturity in my response. At any rate, the first time as a priest that I read in this Preface about Lent being "this joyful season," I reacted with disgust.

Say what you will about the Lent of the fifties, joy is not what was emphasized in prayer or practice—at least in the understanding of a child encouraged to give up anything that smacked of pleasure. At any rate, as a young priest, I saw the connection of joy with Lent as a way in which the Church was trying to water down the good old fashioned misery and suffering of these six weeks. Imagine this: I may have been wrong.

My favorite line in all of Scripture is in John's Gospel (Jn 15:11), spoken by Jesus at the Last Supper, the night before He was to die: not, for Him, a joyful time in the usual sense of that word. He said, "All this I tell you that my joy may be yours and your joy may be complete." What is "my joy," of which Jesus speaks? All that I can think is that Jesus is speaking of the joy that is the life of the Father, Son and Holy Spirit; that He desires that we know the joy that is God's eternal life.

He wants us to know that joy, but because it is interior and spiritual, it is incredibly easy for us to miss it. Prayer, of course, is the first way to put us in contact with the source of our joy, but fasting, self-denial and almsgiving also have the effect of challenging us to go beyond surface pleasure or convenience in an effort to be in communion with deeper spiritual realities. Man is a marvelous mix of flesh and spirit, but it is the spirit that gives to the flesh vitality. Our spirit has been enlivened by Christ who is our joy. As we die to the legitimate desires of the flesh during these Lenten days, we are enabled to know more surely the Lord who lives within.

Joyful, in the sense of fun: I guess not. But, joyful in terms of coming to know Him who is the heart of our being, surely this is a season of joy.

From the Darkness of Sin into Light

April 9, 1995

There is a passage in the thirteenth chapter of John's Gospel that speaks of the betrayal of Jesus by Judas. John tells us that immediately after Judas had shared a bit of food with the Lord, he left the Upper Room on his mission of betrayal. John writes simply, "It was night." (Jn 13:30) Those three words, to me, speak of the sadness and the blackness of our sin, as we, through Judas, respond to the light of the world.

We cannot adequately respond to the celebration of Holy Week if there is not substantial time given to the bleak power of sin—both personally and in our world. I doubt very much, for example, if any priest in the Archdiocese will be able to recall the gift of his own priesthood, given by the Lord on the first Holy Thursday, without shame as he remembers his four brothers who so abused that priestly office. As a pastor, I know something of the responsibility that is mine to lead, in the name of Christ and His Church, the people of this parish. That being true, how much scandal is given by my selfishness, my pride and my laziness? Instead of showing light, am I ever a way into the night?

As I get to know our children, how often and how deeply I grieve over how many of them are being misled by those parents given to them by God to show them the light of Christ. How much greater darkness can there be than that shown to a child who asks to go to Mass on Sunday only to be told "we have more important things to do today" and this happens over and over again in homes in our parish family.

And the wretched, awful darkness of abortion, which ever so gradually, seeps in our national consciousness into a tolerance for the killing of the weak and terminally ill. Dear God, how your Son from that Cross must have been tempted to despair as He saw millions, created in your image and likeness, slaughtered because they were inconveniences on the road to success and prosperity. Could any but your Son have endured the grief as he beheld politicians, judges, and even clergy, baptized in His name, complicit in the crime?

"It was night." How powerful, how corroding is the dark power of sin and I am part of it. It was I who walked out of that room, after having received the Eucharist, and betrayed the Lord of life. It was I who nailed Him onto a Cross and it was I who mocked Him and pierced Him with a lance. Oh, what kind of love is it that still can look at me and invite me to come to Him, just as I am, so that He might lead me from night into day?

Attacking Our Weakness

February 15, 1998

I know some people who look forward to the coming of Lent with a sense of anticipation-even of joy. They look forward to the Church's invitation to prayer, fasting and almsgiving to give them a spiritual shot in the arm. Not me! I see that Lent begins in ten days, on Ash Wednesday, and I groan within. Not for me the call to penance and self-denial. However, whether received with joy or dread, this great season of grace is upon us. In the days before Vatican II, there were three weeks of preparation for Lent, where Catholics were encouraged to decide how they were going to observe the season. The Church, wisely, wanted to encourage people to take advantage of these six weeks in the desert with the Lord.

Lent is of greatest value when it attacks our weakness. Hence, a few suggestions based on my limited observations of life in Bethesda. First of all, in what might seem to turn the call to fasting upside down, let our families resolve to eat together each day, with the television off! Few things more rip my heart out than asking our 2nd graders how they eat dinner and hear how many of them eat alone, in their rooms, in front of individual televisions. How are faith and family passed on; how do we combat the isolation of our society, if not at the dinner table? I surely am a great believer in fasting (much as I do not like it), but many, I believe, must fast from the TV dinners that, literally, live up to their names.

Following Jesus is hard! Picking up a cross and carrying it toward a share in crucifixion goes against the grain. Even the Lord Himself dropped his Cross three times. The crosses we choose for ourselves during Lent should remind us of how weak is our commitment; they should attempt to attack with some vigor areas of weakness in our lives. The person who sees a possible addiction to work that affects family relationships should attack that addiction; the person who is tight with money, using any excuse to avoid giving it away, should dramatically commit to fighting that self-sufficiency that we think money can guarantee. The person who has heard friends and family make the comment, "You've always got to be right," should begin the painful process of examining pride and a competitive spirit and recognize that it is tough to need God if I am always right.

Finally, we must resolve to take seriously the call to prayer. For many of us, the things of God are not first in our lives. I knew God was important to my parents because they taught me to pray and because they often talked about the things of God. If only an Our Father and a Hail Mary at the time of grace, we must begin to pray as families. Individually, many of us can participate in the only perfect prayer, daily Mass. We can take the first ten minutes of our daily commute to say the Rosary. We can open the Bible and meet Jesus in the Gospels. And, most especially, in this season of repentance, we must plan to take advantage of the Sacrament of Penance and Reconciliation and go to confession.

Easter and the Cross:
Two Sides of the Same Coin

March 31, 1996

The Apostle John several times in his Gospel quotes Jesus as He speaks of being "lifted up." In John 8:28, for example, Jesus says, "When you have lifted up the Son of Man, then you will realize that I am He." Of course, we hear Jesus speak of being lifted up and think, rightly, of His looking forward to the Cross; but with John, so often the words mean so much more than they seem. Those couple of words point to much in John's unique way of looking at the Cross of Christ.

Traditionally—and rightly—we see the Cross as the result of our sin. Our prayer this Holy Week should call us to reflect on the power of our evil choices that caused the suffering and death of the Lord. Saint John, though, calls us also to shift our attention to Jesus' free choice of the Cross. When he uses that phrase "lift up," he is making a play on words. We hear lifted up as referring to the Cross; John's readers would have heard the same thing, but they also would hear a phrase that spoke of a man being "lifted up" or exalted as a king. In other words, John tells us that the Cross is not the sign of disgrace, but of victory. Jesus is proclaimed as King from the "tree of the Cross."

To back up what I am trying to say, pay close attention as you hear John's version of the Passion read at the service on Good Friday. In contrast to the other three Gospels, which do place emphasis on the Cross as the result of our sin, John does not see Jesus so much as the victim, as the one who freely chooses to lay His life down for those He loves. Listen carefully: when He is interrogated by Pilate, does not Jesus come across as the one who is "in charge"? Again, it is John who places the emphasis on the sign over the head of the Crucified, "Jesus of Nazareth, King of the Jews." Finally, when Jesus dies, again John emphasizes the kingly power of Christ with the words, "He gave up his spirit." John does not emphasize the execution of the Lord, rather the free choice of the high priest, Jesus, who lays down His life for us.

The relevance for us in all of this is the connection between the Cross and the Kingdom of God. We all recognize and want to be a part of the reign of the Risen Christ. John recognizes that the Cross and Easter are two sides of the same coin. It was the choice of Jesus to love, even to the shedding of the last drop of His blood that was the proclamation of his kingship. We all desire the victory over death that is Easter; John reminds us that, unless we freely choose to "go up to Jerusalem" with Him, "to die with him," and to love those who hate us as did Jesus, we can have no part in that Kingdom proclaimed from the Cross that has become our "tree of victory."

Christ's Love of All, Even Haters

March 23, 1997

I do not believe that I have ever really been hated by anyone. I fear that I am sometimes the focus of anger, but never, I believe, of hatred. Likewise, while I sometimes get mad at folks or situations, I am sure I have never hated anyone. As a priest, I am pretty sure that I have been involved in situations where there have been hateful attempts to do evil to others, but even that kind of hatred, for an outsider, is seen more than felt. However mercifully limited is my experience of hatred, a cursory glance at our world indicates that an abundance of hatred does exist.

Jesus says in Scripture that, "Whatever you do to my brethren you do to me." I usually think of this in the good way; for example when I am good to the dying, I am consoling the dying Jesus, but I am sure the saying works in the opposite way also. For example, to take advantage of the helpless is to take advantage of Jesus. But think of hatred; think of that attitude that truly seeks evil for another person. Our theology tells us that Jesus, in His Passion, experienced the pain due to each sinner for each sin ever committed. He experienced that pain, of course, because of His love. The thing that I have been thinking about recently is His love in the face of all the hatred of all time. No, not so much the hatred—the haters, the individuals who have hated and who will hate until the end of time. Jesus on the Cross felt the venom and contempt of their individual hatred. It was directed at Him; and since He was completely without sin, He felt the power of that evil even more than those who, throughout history, are the conscious targets of that evil. Words fail: the onslaught, the gale, the wave after wave of malice felt by the Savior is, mercifully, beyond us. And in the face of it, is only His passionate love for each individual hate-filled person.

Dear God, how little we understand when we kiss the feet of the Crucified on Good Friday; how little we understand about the depth of what He suffered; how little we understand when we confess our faith that we are loved by You. Bless us, Father; make us grateful, Father; for without His love, we are nothing.

The Messianic Banquet

April 16, 1995

I write these lines during Holy Week, so maybe I am just tired of Lenten fasting; but, as I look through the Scriptural stories of Easter and the appearances of Christ after Easter, I am struck by how often Jesus eats with the Apostles. As always, of course, the writers recall a story because they wish to teach a lesson and these post-Resurrection meals teach several. First, in the story of Jesus with the disciples whom He meets on the road to Emmaus, there is clear reference to the meal which is the Eucharist. "They recognized him in the breaking of the bread," St. Luke tells us. Also in these stories, we are reminded of all those references in the Old Testament where, when the Messiah comes, there will be an abundance of every food. Jesus, the Messiah, shares the Messianic Banquet with believers.

For us, I think, there is something else. Jesus in His human birth took on our nature. That was wonderful humility, hard even to imagine—that God would become a creature. But what is even harder to comprehend, is that after His work was completed, after He had offered Himself to the Father on the Cross, Jesus rose in His human flesh. Of course, because He had conquered death and was no longer subject to mortal limitations, He no longer had ordinary hunger, but He did eat. That eating demonstrates that Jesus did not reject His assumed human nature and return to being, so to speak, "just God." No, it is as a human that the Son of God reigns until the end of time. Our humanity, in the Spirit of Jesus, is capable of divine life.

This is not just a pious thought to comfort us about a relative who has died—though such comfort is there. Rather, it concerns all who have been given that divine life in the waters of Baptism. We are called, now, to live in our humanity, the life of the God-man. Notice how often, in secular advice, we are told that we cannot control our emotions or sexual desires; that we will be less than human if we struggle to discipline ourselves according to the standards of Christ. But that is just the point, in Christ all things are possible. He is Risen; our brother has conquered death and has gone before us and we, with the power of His Risen life are able to go where He has gone. We are human, yes; but in Him, our humanity is capable of divine life. Happy Easter!

Lourdes Parishioners Touch a Heart

April 26, 1998

Because, so often, we do not understand all that is happening, I share this letter with our parishioners:

"Dear Monsignor Wells:

Two weeks ago, I began a new job in Bethesda, across the street from Our Lady of Lourdes. Prior to this, I'd been going through some very difficult times which had been with me for a year. My mother had been diagnosed with cancer and then after 11 months, she passed away. But, there were also many other diffculties and circumstances that just seemed to keep coming at me from all directions. I felt as if the storms were going to completely overwhelm me and that I was being swept away into total despair. I feared that my faith was in jeopardy and it seemed that I simply couldn't carry the Crosses another moment. As well, I knew that the new job wouldn't work for me, that I'd have to leave the position and begin all over again trying to find a position where I could use the skills I'd built up over 22 years of a working life. I felt a desolation overwhelm me.

"But, something quite miraculous happened to me that first day. As I went for a walk at noontime, I passed in front of your church. I couldn't believe my eyes and I remember saying out loud, 'My God, You've placed Holy Church right here for me!' I practically ran inside and once inside, I felt a peace overcome me and I attended Mass and received our Lord. Something very profound happened to me that one day in all my life. I remembered that it was Holy Week, and that perhaps the sufferings I was feeling and had been feeling most keenly during all of Lent, was a participation in Christ's sufferings. That week was an agony for me, but as I kept going back to that little church, something else happened to me in that sacred place: I was very drawn to that church and I began to watch the people. I began to see a beautiful people who were in love with Jesus Christ. I watched them at Communion, and I watched them in front of the Blessed Sacrament. I began to 'see' the presence of Christ in each of those lovely, humble souls. I remember thinking that these were uncomplicated people, hard-working people, who loved God deeply and a people who were, unbeknownst to them, in that church at that time of their lives to help me with one of the most difficult times of my life, for you see, they touched me with their love for God. It's something I can't quite explain, Monsignor, but it happened to me.

"I left the job and thanks to God, was directed to another position in D.C., which I am very grateful for. Yet, something continues to stir in my heart and for some reason, I can't stop thinking of those people at Our Lady of Lourdes. I'd never seen such love come from anyone for God as I saw in those people. They will never know how much they touched a hurting soul simply by my being near them in that church. Therefore, it is because of them that I wanted to write to you and to thank you for your lovely parishioners and your lovely church and for serving God so humbly and faithfully. You also touched my life, Monsignor, as did your other priests."

The Resurrection: Center of Our Faith

April 10, 1994

Some Catholic Churches today have images of the Risen Lord where once they would have had a traditional crucifix. The image of Christ Resurrected tries to portray Him as triumphant over death and invites us to reflect on our destiny to share in His victory. However, even though the Resurrection is the center of our faith, I think it is safe to say that most Catholics still feel more comfortable with the traditional image of Christ's crucifix.

Part of the reason for this, I think, has to do with the fact that it is easier for us to identify with the Cross than with the Resurrection. Most of us have experienced that life can be quite hard—even cruel—and that the promise of the Lord that we will be invited to share in His Cross is one that He will surely keep. In preparing couples for marriage, for example, I find it easy to think of possible ways in which their love and commitment will bind them closely to the suffering love of Christ, but it is harder to give concrete examples that describe the Resurrection life that is also at the heart of every Christ-centered marriage. Did you ever notice, as another example, how fervently Catholics observe the Lenten season and how quietly we celebrate the equally long season of Easter? Lent looks forward for forty days to Easter and then, after one day, Easter is forgotten. Yes, for whatever reason, we seem more comfortable meditating on the Cross than on the Resurrection that followed it.

The main reason for this, I suppose, has to do with the simple question of experience. I have an idea what the pain that will lead to death is all about, but I have virtually no concept of what it means to rise from death. Also, it is comforting to know that where I will go in the experience of pain and suffering, Christ has already gone. But, after all is said and done, the point of life is not the Cross and death, but union with the Risen Lord and the life He has won for us. All of the Church's symbols—the flowers, the gold and white vestments, the light of the Easter candle, the new water of the baptismal font—speak during this season of the promise of life that belongs to those who believe.

The experience of the Resurrection is not one that necessarily must wait until death, but it is one, I suspect, that can only come to that person who has embraced the Lord Jesus in whatever way He comes to us. Christianity seems foolishness to the world, and it most surely involves the Cross, but the person who follows Him, no matter where He leads, must surely know at least a bit of the joy and triumph that the Apostles knew on that first Easter.

The Dawn From on High Shall Break Upon Us

April 3, 1994

I studied for the priesthood at St. Bonaventure University in Western New York. I was well pleased with the education given by the Franciscans, but let me quickly assure you, one would only go to Allegany, New York, for something like education—never for the weather. One of my favorite Easter stories concerns the weather one Easter morning in the seminary. The rule in those years (the late 60's) was beginning to ease up just a bit. That meant that, while we had to be in the seminary for all the ceremonies of Holy Week, we could go home for Easter week. But, even though the Easter Vigil was over by 1:00 a.m. or so, we could not leave until 5:00 a.m.. They did not want us to go long distances without sleep. Anyway, when we got up that Easter morning, it was pouring down snow. Well, after having been in that place since Christmas, you had better believe that another day of snow was not going to stop us, so off we went. I was driving and, whether because they were so close to God or so crazy, everyone else in the car quickly fell asleep. As I remember the drive, we went south over a couple of groups of mountains until we finally came out of the worst of the drive somewhere in central Pennsylvania. Gradually, as we went south, the snow ended; but, what I will never forget is the sudden burst of light at dawn as the sun came up in an Eastern sky that was completely clear. That bright, clear spring sunrise after the windy, snowy, winter black of just a couple of hours earlier has, since then, served as one of my favorite Easter images.

That sun was glorious and in no way do I wish to downplay the power of nature; but the brilliance of that morning does nothing more than hint at what we celebrate today. On Good Friday, Jesus took upon Himself the sins of the world. Ours is an age that likes to explain away or soften spiritual reality, but we had best be careful lest we soften to the point of non-existence the truth that we would have died in our sins if Jesus had not died for us. The punishment for sin is eternal damnation, but the Lord Jesus, because He loves me so much, has offered Himself for me so that I might share in His life. Jesus means life more brilliant than one thousand sunrises for those who believe in Him. Not to accept Him, or to cease following Him, means death that is more barren and more bleak than the deepest gloom of human experience. To accept and to follow Jesus is to accept life; to reject Him is to choose death.

May the grace of this Easter day and season be one that leads each of us into a deeper experience of that power that flows from the Resurrection of the Lord. Happy Easter!

Be Not Afraid

April 7, 1996

The Holy Father and Cardinal Hickey both celebrate fifty years of priesthood this year. Pope John Paul's story is, of course, one of the most dramatic of the century. He studied for the priesthood in secret because of the Nazi occupation of Poland; he was ordained just in time for the Communists to take over when the Germans were defeated and then spent most of his priesthood and episcopacy doing battle on behalf of the people and Church of Poland against the completely anti-religious Marxist puppet regime of his country. It has been said so many times that it becomes almost trite, but surely the Holy Spirit could not have given to the Church a more perfect instrument of hope to be Holy Father than he did when he gave us Pope John Paul II. This man—brilliant philosopher, compassionate listener, political genius and spiritual giant—has personally experienced the world at its worst. And yet, despite all he has seen of the power of evil, virtually the first words he spoke as Pope, words he has repeated over and over again, were, "Be not afraid!"

Our Holy Father can tell us not to be afraid for the same reason that the angel tells the women at the empty tomb of Jesus the same thing: Jesus Christ is Risen from the dead! His resurrection is the proclamation of God's victory over sin, evil and death itself. "Fear is useless, what is needed is trust," Jesus told those who wept over the dead daughter of Jairus. Trust Jesus, we are told, because all that really matters in life He will freely give to those who put their trust in Him. Of course, it is hard to believe: we crave control; we want to be in charge; we want the assured outcome. How could there be an infinite God who cares about me who, as the Psalm says, "holds me in the palm of his hand"? The world is so big, the obstacles against me and my family are so overwhelming, how is anyone supposed to be able to place trust in God, especially when He asks things so alien to all that the world teaches. But the Resurrection is the Father's response to the trust of Jesus who believed that no evil could prevail over His Father's love.

May the Spirit of the Risen Lord Jesus conquer the fear in our lives; may that Spirit fill us with the joy of the women at the tomb; and may that Spirit give us the zeal that drove the disciples to the ends of the earth with the Good News. May God bless each of us this Easter Day.

The Risen Christ

March 30, 1997

I suppose that C.S. Lewis put it best when he said, "In the face of the foolishness that contends that Jesus was a good man or a prophet or a wise moral guide, but that He was only a man, that Jesus is either God or a blasphemous liar." Those who see Jesus as a kindly teacher of gentle wisdom use as their authority the Bible, but Lewis, and our whole tradition, points out that that same Bible reveals Jesus as if He is God: He forgives sin; He "teaches with authority"; He even raises the dead to life. That same New Testament is written around the event we celebrate today: that Jesus Christ is Risen from the dead.

For many, faith is a challenge. The world appears so material, so physical. Can we believe there is an eternal spiritual reality that underlies what our senses perceive? When evil is so brutally obvious, is it other than a fairy tale to confess a God whose goodness has already defeated the power of evil? A priest told me one time of a child who confessed that he no longer believed in the Easter bunny. Was the child simply on the right track, disposing of simple myths before the more complex?

I cannot prove the Resurrection. I can refer you to the Scriptures and show you that the jumble of Resurrection accounts, which do not match each other in details—as those involved in a conspiracy would have attempted—reflect the excitement of finding an empty tomb and the recollection of experiencing their Risen Lord. I can remind you that virtually all of those who claimed to have seen Jesus after the Resurrection were later martyred for their faith, and that they went joyfully to their deaths, believing that now, for them, death had lost its meaning because they shared the life of the Risen Lord. Likewise I can invite you to look at history and see how this powerless group of early believers went from denial and abandonment of Jesus on Good Friday to travel all over the world in an attempt to invite others to believe in His victory over sin and death.

What we celebrate today is the claim that God, in Christ, has offered us salvation. Our Christian faith says that the death of Jesus on the Cross and His victory over that death on Easter Sunday is the only event in history that really matters (save, I suppose, the original disobedience of Adam and Eve). Either I believe that Jesus is Lord of history or I do not. Let us play no games of trying to make Him into a teacher of unforgettable sayings. He is either the God who will judge me or a liar.

Unity of Mind and Heart

April 17, 1994

You will notice during these weeks of the Easter season that we will hear much at Mass, both on Sunday and during the week, from the Acts of the Apostles. This book, written by St. Luke, was very probably one complete work with his Gospel; the separation that we see in our Bibles probably was something that took place in the early Church. The reason we read so much from the Acts during these weeks is because the book tells the story of how the Church, filled with the Holy Spirit, took the Good News of the crucified and Risen Lord from Jerusalem to the ends of the earth. Jesus promised, before He died, to send the Spirit; the Acts is the story of how that Spirit, living in the body of believers, the Church, began the work of converting the world—a work that will continue until the end of time. While we might read the many stories of Peter or Paul or the other leaders of the infant Christian community and be fascinated with their individual histories, a close attention to the Acts never allows us to forget that this book is really "The Gospel of the Holy Spirit," as it is sometimes called. It is the Spirit who is, and who always will be, the hero of the Church's story.

As we listen to and read the Acts of the Apostles, we are recalling the first days of our family history. To an extent, we are no doubt being told the best of that story (does not every family do the same?), but Acts reminds us of what we as Church, as God's family, are called to be. In particular I have meditated quite a bit on Acts 4:32. "The community of believers were of one mind and one heart." Two or three things strike me about that line.

First of all, it reminds me that head and heart were as one in these early believers. With their heads, they heard the Good News. To some extent, they understood what God had revealed in Christ. They believed that He had risen from the dead and that, only in Him, was there salvation. Therefore they understood that they must choose to follow Him, even to the Cross, if necessary. The great thing, though, was that they not only understood with their heads, they also gave their hearts to what they understood the Good News to be. So often, I understand the Church's message, but instead of giving my heart to that message (or some part of it, like forgiveness or chastity or charity in speech) I love, I choose the message of the world. Because in so many of us mind and heart are not united, we experience, individually and in family and community, the chaos and disunity characteristic of sin. Only when the individuals and the community of faith are characterized by unity of mind and heart can the Church be an effective sign of the unity that is within God Himself.

God's Love—More Powerful Than Evil

May 19, 1996

Most will remember the murder, just over one year ago, of a Prince George's County Police officer, who was sitting in his patrol car outside a shopping center where he was working a part-time security job. For no reason, save perhaps drug-induced malice, the life of a young man was taken from him and from those who loved him. Because he worked with and was close to another policeman whom I have known for years, I was honored to be asked to be a part of a memorial service at Sgt. Novabilski's precinct that marked the first year anniversary of his murder. The widow of the officer was present, as were all the "higher-ups" of the County Police, but the ceremony took place at what is the daily "roll call" at the start of the afternoon shift. The routine that starts each day was changed because of this awful anniversary; but each of these officers had to reflect on what can happen on any otherwise routine day because of the reality of the evil in our world.

We come close to the end of the Easter Season. Next Sunday, the great feast of Pentecost will remind us that the Holy Spirit of the Risen Lord is present among us until the end of time. But for one last time this year, it is good for us to be reminded that Easter is, first and foremost, about Jesus' victory over sin and death. In my prayer at that ceremony, I prayed for the repose of the policeman's soul. I also prayed that those officers in that room who engage in this important job for us live each day as if it were their last. Few things illustrate the power of evil more than a murder like this one; but daily faith in the Risen Lord is the way to victory over that evil: it is the only way to victory.

Evil, of course, takes many forms; and often, we sense our powerlessness against it. We take precautions, as do these officers, but ultimately the vicious comment, the mindless vandal or an evil can cause terrible harm. In the face of evil we have, finally, only the power of Jesus, who took all the pain and punishment of evil unto Himself and offered it to the Father. Our Easter faith affirms that, in the face of the evil that will be in the world until He comes again, there is only the power of God's love that flows from His Cross and Resurrection that is more powerful. May God deepen our faith in Him who has conquered sin and even death itself.

Potential for Good

I guess I first heard the word potential applied to me from my seventh grade nun. I was standing in the hall outside of class, where I had been sent—probably because the other children were being a bad influence on me—when Sister came out, and among a few other warm words of support, she shook her finger at me and said, "Tom Wells, you have great potential either for good or for evil!" Whether there was any potential, or whether it was for good or for evil, I do not know; but I do know that I find myself frequently using the word, especially when working with the young.

The ten days between Ascension Thursday and Pentecost Sunday were days spent in prayer by the Apostles, Our Lady and the early believers as they waited for the Spirit, whom Jesus had promised to send upon His return to heaven. They already had faith. After all, they had seen, spoken with and eaten with the Risen Lord after His Resurrection. What they awaited was His Spirit that would empower them to do the work of Jesus, to be His Church, until the end of time. In other words, the Holy Spirit was the source of the potential that would allow that simple group of Jewish peasants to begin the proclamation of the Good News. Sister was probably speaking about a natural potential on that day in seventh grade, and as I say, she may or may not have been correct, but a couple of things are beyond question: the Church derives its power for good (its potential) not from natural gifts only, but from the very presence of the Spirit of God at the core of its being. Secondly, any member of the Church, especially when confirmed, possesses that same potential to dramatically communicate the goodness of God to the world.

No potential can be developed unless the decision is made to make it develop. God will place no limits on my ability to show His goodness as a priest, but I must choose daily to cooperate with His grace and to do the hard work involved. God will never say to a married couple, "You have experienced too much love, you must wait for heaven for the rest." But, likewise, He will not force them to make decisions of forgiveness, patience, self-denial and faith in Him, as well as the partner, that are the essence of love. And so it is, in workplace and ball field, the Spirit of God gives us the potential to be powerful signs of the presence of God in our midst, but we must decide to develop that potential. In this week before the Feast of the Holy Spirit, let us pray as a parish that God will deepen our faith and our courage so that we might ever more sincerely pray:

"Come, O Holy Spirit, and fill the hearts of the faithful. Kindle in us the fire of your love. Send forth your Spirit and we shall be created and you will renew the face of the earth."

Is There Someone You Can Invite to RCIA?

June 5, 1994

Several weeks ago, I was invited back to St. Mark's for a reunion of all who had been involved in the RCIA in the six years since its beginning there. All of those who have been received into the Church, their sponsors, those involved in the teaching and those involved in preparing the liturgical ceremonies for the RCIA were invited. Even though many were unable to be present, there were still about seventy-five people in the Church. The program attempts to thoroughly prepare those who are coming into the Church by making them familiar with the teachings, traditions, morals and prayer life by which a Catholic is called to live his or her life. What struck me that night a few weeks ago is that, after these six years, a significant number in that parish have been exposed to the program either for formation for the non-Catholics, or for renewal for those Catholics who serve as sponsors. It is impossible, obviously, to measure the effect on the faith life of the parish because of the RCIA, but I know that many of those who serve as sponsors talk about the RCIA being a great boost for their spiritual lives.

All of this, of course, is written because we are beginning to gear up our own RCIA program for the new year. The title of the program, The Rite of Christian Initiation for Adults, begins to describe its goals. We seek to prepare those who have never been baptized or who have been baptized in another Christian community for the sacraments of initiation: Baptism, Confirmation and Eucharist. Planning has already begun and I am certain that Our Lady of Lourdes will lead candidates into a Catholicism that is complete, enthusiastic and prayerful.

It is the role of our laity to invite possible candidates for the RCIA. Most practicing Catholics derive tremendous satisfaction from their faith. While they may not talk about it very much, they recognize that their relationship with Christ and His Church allows them to approach life with a hope that many around us do not have. Catholics, however, are very slow to share their faith and, consequently, many whom we may know quite well wander through life unaware of the Rock that is our anchor. During these next weeks, ask the Lord if there is someone to whom, perhaps, He wants you to suggest the RCIA. All they can do is say "no"; they probably will not laugh in your face; and, who knows, you may be the voice used by God to call someone to Him.

Confirmation Empowers Us to Proclaim the Good News

April 30, 1995

We at Lourdes are delighted to welcome Bishop Corrada today as he comes to administer the Sacrament of Confirmation to twenty-two of our teenagers. After spending some little bit of the last month or so interviewing them to make sure they have some concept of what the sacrament is, and more importantly, to see if they have begun to take their faith seriously, I can say that I believe they are at least open to committing themselves to live as adult Catholics.

The gist of what I try to get across in these interviews might be of some interest. As I see it, Confirmation is the sacrament where we are given the fullness of the Holy Spirit so that we are enabled to proclaim, with our lives, the Good News of the death and resurrection of Christ. The model of the sacrament is Pentecost, where the believers received the Holy Spirit and went out and converted five thousand people that same day. At any rate, in these interviews, if they have managed to memorize a definition about the "Good News," I will then ask them what the Good News is. Eventually, often after considerable effort, they manage to say that the death and resurrection of the Lord is the Good News. Then the real problems begin, because at this point I ask them, as individual believers, why it is good news to them that Jesus died on the Cross and rose from the dead. Almost, but not always, that question is answered with a blank stare.

What followed with one young man illustrates the challenge and opportunity of parents and the Church in working with our youth. As I struggled to try and get him to understand how the death of Christ was good news for him as a person, I asked him if he were ever selfish. With honesty, he answered in the afffirmative. I then asked if he were pleased with the situation. "No," was the response. Could he work really hard and overcome his selfishness? He doubted it because, he so wisely perceived, often he is selfish without thinking about it. "Is there any way out of it?" I asked. He seemed to think not. Until that moment, it had never occurred to this young man that Jesus the Savior (he knew this word applies to Jesus) could save him from the selfishness that he recognizes and does not like in his life.

Each of us who is confirmed is commissioned to proclaim the Good News that Jesus is the Savior, MY Savior. Until I accept the grace that allows me to recognize how much I need His salvation, to see how unable I am to save myself, His death and resurrection will be no more than words. When in seeing my weakness, I turn to Him and experience the strength flowing from His resurrection, then I will recognize that He is Good News and then, believe me, I will with the Apostles go out and share that Good News.

The Grace of Ordinary Time

May 25, 1997

Last Sunday's celebration of Pentecost marked the end of the Easter Season. Though I am sure few took note of it, on Monday morning, the Church returned to what is called the ordinary time of the year. Since Advent, the weeks that precede Christmas, we have been commemorating the events of the life of Christ: from Christmas and the feasts of that cycle and then, after only a short break, Lent and the Easter season. Until that cycle begins again in December, the Church celebrates its life in what is called ordinary time. I have to admit that I am always glad for the wearing of the green vestments that signal ordinary time.

Everyone experiences family and childhood differently. I know that, at least in the commercial imagination that seeks to fuel our spending, the holidays are supposed to be the high points of life; for many, I am sure they are. Of course, I liked the holidays as a child (I was as greedy for gifts as the next person), but I look back on the ordinary as the source of deepest good. Our nightly dinner table conversations, for example, seemed torture as my father grilled us about how what we learned at school applied to life—but what an influence they have had on me! In eighth grade, I would have to walk to the "big tree," half way between home and school where I would meet my mom and Kindergarten sister and walk her to her afternoon session. (This unusual practice was instituted in consultation with the eighth grade nun in the hopes of teaching Tommy self-discipline.) But is that one of the reasons my sister and I are so close today? Likewise, our screen porch furniture was a bright, cheery, summer yellow; it was also made of a fake leather which, if you spent a hot afternoon on it trying to read, would induce sweat like a sauna. And yet I wonder, were not those ordinary summer afternoons valuable in giving me time to do nothing but think and read and learn to be alone?

The festivals of life are important, whether in Church or family. Baptisms, weddings, graduations and awards received marked important events and moments. Yet, after all is said and done, it is in the apparently ordinary flow of life, where one year becomes another without our even noticing, that makes or breaks us as individuals. It is in the ordinary, I believe, that we accept the grace of God and where the grace of God is able to transform us into extraordinary signs of His presence in the world.

St. Therese of Lisieux—Do Ordinary Things Extraordinarily Well

June 12, 1994

St. Therese of Lisieux, often called "The Little Flower," was a Carmelite sister of the late 19th century who, even though she lived only twenty-four years, has had tremendous influence on the Church of this century. She was unheard of during her lifetime, but her autobiography, which she was encouraged to write by a very wise spiritual guide, contains a spiritual wisdom which reflects extraordinary spiritual gifts. I think of her for two reasons.

First of all, there is a pious belief that "The Little Flower" will sometimes show her intercession before God on behalf of those who turn to her in a very simple way: by giving roses to them. Last week, the wife of a couple who are good friends called to tell of her husband's unexpected heart problem. He went to the doctor's office at two in the afternoon of feeling faint, and by seven that evening he was undergoing quadruple bypass surgery. At any rate, as his wife tells the story, she turned to St. Therese, asking her prayers for the husband during the surgery, and within moments, a neighbor arrived at the door with, as you have guessed, an arrangement of roses from her garden. The husband, thank God, has already come home.

I think of St. Therese for another reason, however. She is most famous, I suppose, for what is known as her "little way." By this she meant that the Christian should do "ordinary things extraordinarily well." You may have noticed at Mass today that the priest wore green vestments. These are a sign that we are in the ordinary time of the Church year. Almost since Advent (with the exception of a few weeks after Christmas) we have celebrated the principle events of the life of Christ. The cycle that includes Advent, Christmas, Lent, Easter, Pentecost and the beautiful Sundays of the Trinity and the Body of Christ is one that invites us to particular types of prayer or celebration. I believe, however, and I think that St. Therese and the Church agree, that it is in the ordinary times of life that most of us work out our salvation. The day of my ordination was, emotionally and spiritually, beyond belief; but my salvation is won or lost in the way that I live out my priesthood by serving people (especially those I may not feel like serving), by praying daily, by putting myself into sacramental celebrations and so on. Most of us, I think, see our lives as very ordinary—and we are probably right. But, I assure you, no life can be as ordinary (on the surface) as that of a Carmelite sister. Any life, lived extraordinarily well, by God's grace, can be the source of great goodness to others.

"Gotta Do" and "Get To Do"

January 12, 1997

Even though this story is several years old, it still serves to remind me of the importance of generosity in my life. As happens sometimes, all of a sudden I was awake. There were still thirty minutes or so before the alarm, so l lay in bed looking forward to the day. With a kind of early morning dread, I found myself saying, "I've got to do this. . . and this. . . and this. . . and this," until the day stretched before me like a highway of classes, appointments, Masses, wakes, and God knows what else. I found myself looking forward to that moment, sixteen hours later, when I would be able to sit down in front of a TV and relax before bed and before starting the same routine over again. Gradually, I looked at the days that had just past and those that were ahead and I saw a stream of fourteen or sixteen hour days, broken only by a single day off each week, where every moment was taken, most often by demands placed on me rather than by activities of my choosing. I found myself looking for ways I could cut out chunks of time from where I would be serving others, so that I could have free time for myself. This attitude of looking at all that "I gotta do," was not new; what followed was.

I suppose I was just about to kick myself in the rear end and to tell myself to stop feeling sorry for myself, when all of a sudden the distinction between "gotta do" and "get to do," came to mind. I do not know whether the distinction has changed the way that I do my work; it certainly has changed the way I think about it.

I share this because I suspect that many Catholics have a "gotta do" mentality toward faith and religion. "I've gotta go to Mass; I've gotta help the kids with homework; I've gotta write thank you notes for gifts not wanted in the first place; I've gotta spend a few minutes today with my spouse." In this attitude, there is a necessary first step. We recognize the obligation of responsibility. The next step, I believe, is the recognition that "I get to. . . " give the goodness of God to others. For me as a priest, for example, it means that instead of focusing on obligation, I try to look at the privilege it is to represent Christ and His Church in the countless situations of parish life.

Even in tough things, we Christians "get to" be Christ in our world: Jesus who forgives; Jesus who is patient; Jesus who tries one more time with a stubborn spouse or Jesus who simply waits for the prodigal. Perhaps this is a meaningless distinction; but for me, the attempt to shift my focus from what I am obligated to do because I am His priest has been a very important distinction. My Christian vocation is not a burden; it is a gift.

A Pilgrimage of Love

July 31, 1994

The beach, especially the Outer Banks, is made for reading. Most of the houses have roof-level decks that catch whatever breeze that comes from whatever direction. For me, the essence of an Outer Banks week is to get a book, cold drink and chair, tell all that I have gone to the beach and then, quietly sneak onto the deck and read.

Alas, the group with whom I traveled this June was, while an awful lot of fun, far too active. One of the books I took with me, an under $3.00 selection from Crown, was untouched. By Chilton Williamson Jr., the book is titled *The Homestead* and is about a family's ability to deal with a crime of violence committed by one of its members. As a matter of fact, even though the book is short, I am only half way through it since I do not have the time here that I do at the beach, and also because, except for one strange reason, I do not especially like the book. I suppose it is a tribute to the author's skill, but as I read about these people, I have kind of a vague sadness, the kind I sometimes have when I work with people who seem to have stopped caring about each other.

Christianity often seems a futile exercise. At a certain stage, most of us consciously chose to live our lives as followers of Christ. Perhaps the decision is forgotten more often than remembered; perhaps we have fallen short more frequently than we would ever have dreamed possible and, perhaps, our ideals have been often and easily compromised. But still, the faith is kept; decisions for love of God and neighbor are made, however routinely, and somehow, another year passes in living out a youthful word of commitment.

I guess what I am reminded of by this novel is the alternative to following Christ. Yes, my Christian commitment does, often, seem futile and pitifully unimportant—especially in the face of much that sees that commitment as an out-of-date relic. But the alternative is selfishness and selfishness means isolated loneliness. Yes, I sometime wonder if it all matters or if I really make a difference, but I never wonder if I am loved or if the best course for me is to be there for others. The grace of God makes this a pilgrimage of love, not of isolation and emptiness. It is often a journey that seems utterly ordinary, but it is also one where I have the power to show to others just a hint of what God's love is all about.

Our Holy Father

September 7, 1997

During the hot Sunday afternoons of September, TV commentators will often remark at how high the temperature must be on the NFL playing fields. And, indeed, our hearts go out to these men, in perfect physical shape, who struggle to earn their day's wages, sometimes exceeding one half million dollars for the hour's effort.

Two weeks ago, in Paris, the great spiritual athlete of our time, Pope John Paul, took the field before a crowd of far better than one million, on a day with heat and humidity like our worst summer days, and celebrated Mass. Physically, far from being in the prime of his life, but rather, showing ever more obviously the effects of his years and of the physical ravages he has undergone, the Holy Father let himself be poured out once again so that million—and all of us—might be reminded of the love of God for His children. I am told that, at one point, the Holy Father paused in the celebration of Mass and that TV viewers wondered if he would be able to continue. A wave of applause rose from the crowd which seemed to revive him and the Mass was finished. Certainly Pope John Paul must be a man of great physical strength to push himself so powerfully. But knowing as he must the toll it will take, how much faith he must have in the Gospel he proclaims and how much love he must have for us.

Theologically, the Holy Father has taught me much, especially about the individual dignity of each human person. So much of what he writes reminds me that God encounters each person with a grace that is individually theirs. On the gut level, however, what most challenges me as priest and believer is how hard the Pope works. The work of Christians is to show the world how much God loves us and that is very hard work, because love is not a word, it is actions. I believe in God's love for me because Baptism allows me to believe, surely; but the love of my parents, day after day, in sickness or health, whether to a cute three year old or a snotty adolescent, brought God's love to life for me. And so it is meant to be, no matter who we are or what our vocation. God gives us the grace to work hard to let others know what the goodness of God is all about.

The cross of Jesus is many things, of course. One of them is the sign of a Man who gave and gave until He had no more to give, to the last drop of His blood. Jesus' life was hard work. Thank God, that among the many other things Pope John Paul has done for us, he continues to remind us that followers of Jesus are called to work hard in living out their faith.

First Friday Group—
Faith in the Marketplace

February 8, 1998

About fifteen years ago, a group of men started meeting in the rectory after the 7:00 a.m. Mass on the first Friday of the month. The format of their meetings, which continue to this day, is very simple: the Scripture readings from the following Sunday are read and then, until exactly 8:30, a discussion of what those readings say to the individuals takes place. The coffee and the big, fat, immoral doughnuts are added blessings of the hour. This group has no structure and its membership varies from month to month, though, in recent months it does seem to be growing a bit—sometimes to fifteen or so.

I write about this group, not because I am recruiting new members, but because of how the meetings help me. While the discussions are on Scripture readings, they invariably move into the ways in which these men are challenged to live their faith in the marketplace. Those who come run the gamut from single, young adults to retirees and so their reflections give me a glimpse into the ways Catholics make decisions in law office, construction site or business place. I first started participating with this group when I was at Lourdes as an assistant in 1987, and from that time, the thing that has most impressed me is the tremendous struggle it is to live an integrated Christian life.

The temptation is to compartmentalize our lives. This part of my life is affected by religion: I will be faithful to my spouse; I will go to church on Sunday and I will help the elderly neighbors across the street shovel their walks in the winter. On the other hand, when I go to work and the pressure for sales is so great, maybe I do have to fudge the truth a little bit in order to make a quota. After all, people should have the sense to read fine print. How much insurance is too much for this customer? They have the money; they should know what they need. I know, for example, that when I came to Montgomery County as a pastor, bids I received for major repairs were much higher than those to which I was accustomed at St. Mark's. For example, a local car dealer gave me a bid of $750 for repairs to air conditioning in a parish car. A dealer I trusted replaced the freon for $50 and the car would still chill an Eskimo.

Recent public opinion polls seem to say that Americans believe that a person can be effective in one area of life and immoral in another. In one sense, I guess that can be true: Is a greedy bus driver less effective than one who is generous? Ultimately, though, faith tells us that the Spirit of Jesus penetrates every dimension of our being. In fact, I believe that (mechanical skills being equal) the moral bus driver will be the better. The men who participate in our first Friday group show me what a struggle it is to live morally in the marketplace; but I also recognize that, tough as is their path, their attempts at honesty and integrity allow those who deal with them to get just a hint of the truth that is God's Word. That is what each of us is called to do as we take the Gospel into the world.

We Are All the Gospel There Is

October 4, 1998

"Abandonment to Divine Providence," by Jean-Pierre de Caussade, a 17th century Jesuit, is a gem of spiritual writing. Fr. de Caussade had no idea he was writing a book, and we would know nothing of him or his spiritual insights except that a convent of Visitation Sisters in Nancy, France, kept his letters and notes of retreats he gave to them when he was their chaplain. At any rate, de Caussade, in one of his letters, tells the sisters, "The Holy Spirit writes no more Gospels except in our hearts." The lives of the saints give us an idea of what the author means: St. Theresa, the Little Flower, shows us the purity and simplicity of the Gospel; St. Ignatius of Loyola hints at its dynamism; St. Francis at its power to triumph with nothing of material power. But what of my heart?

Jesus Christ came into the same world in which we live. Even apart from the text of the Bible, one does not have to be an astute reader of history to see that the powerful held all the cards. Family life even among the Jews (not to mention the pagans of Rome and elsewhere!) was in disarray; political corruption was a given, as we see from the esteem in which tax collectors were held; and the entertainments in the Roman Coliseum tell us exactly in what value was held human life. Jesus, in that world and in His humanity, spoke the Good News. He spoke the Good News as a man because, among other reasons, He wanted us to recognize what we are capable of being and doing as men and women.

We believers have got to understand that, for many, we are all the Gospel there is. Do we find it hard to see God and therefore shrink from acting on faith? How dark do you think it was in the Garden the night before He died? Do we fear the scorn of the powerful in the professions? The Pharisees hated Jesus because He dared question their place as interpreters of what really matters. Do we look around and see, among our fellow believers, lack of talent, creativity and zeal? Check out the talent pool of the Apostles. Folks, the Gospel, as we allow the Spirit to write it on our hearts, is all the Good News our world is going to hear.

Catholics, all believers, are somewhat shell-shocked by the state of the world as we have come to know it. However, what we "on the streets" experience is only the fruit of several centuries of terrible philosophical thought. However, through Vatican II and the pontificate of John Paul II, the Church—in its intellectual response—has gotten to its feet again. We, as Catholics, cannot give in to either complacency (I'm okay, let everyone else take care of themselves) or despair at the corruption around us. When the

Holy Father says, over and over again, "Be not afraid!" he is talking to us. May the Gospel be written large on our hearts and may all of our words and deeds announce what is in our hearts.

Living with Faith Not Fear

November 22, 1998

I do not know why the Lord puts me in these situations, but He surely does and I might just as well stop asking why. I was at a wedding last Saturday of a nephew. It was a particularly wonderful time for me because it was out of town and I did not have to worry about having to get back for any parish obligations. Anyway, I was making my way through the reception and came across two couples, the men of whom had been friends of my nephew's from grade and high school days, and whom I had sort of known as he was growing up. Of course they are not married; of course they were taking a few extra days in Florida to see the sights, and of course their living arrangements on the trip were totally contrary to God's law. I did not find this out by prying, but simply by listening to the usual travelers' stories of motels, reservations and so forth. Now I know I should have kept my mouth shut, but. . . oh well, I'll try again next time.

Actually, the conversation was valuable for me because I think I saw in them what happens when faith is abandoned. They call themselves Catholic, of course, and take great pride in their Catholic education and heritage, but moral decisions that count are not made on the basis of what Christ, Church or Scripture teach. But what has replaced faith, I believe, is fear. There is a fear of commitment; fear of divorce; fear of not having enough money; fear of bringing children into a messed up world and on and on and on and it all makes perfect sense! I respect their fear. If God is not an active Father whose Spirit is with me, if I must control life and destiny by myself, then fear makes all the sense in the world. It is a funny thing, but the one fear they seem not to have is the fear of mortal sin and dying and going to hell. But, of course, a good and loving God would never send anyone to hell, blah, blah, blah. . .

The example of people living together is common, of course, but the fear that motivates it is a danger in every believer's life. What will neighbors think? Do I dare stand up for the person being mocked in the work place? Will I open my mouth when "everyone" assumes that abortion is fine. Of course, we all fall short; but as I flew home on Sunday I was both sad for these increasingly not so young people whose potential is little by little being drained away because of fear; but I was also a little bit happy because I felt like I had learned just a bit about what life is without faith.

Parish Community

April 20, 1997

The Washington Post Magazine is spending two issues discussing the history of the Mother of God Community, a large group of Catholics who established a prayer group in the Montgomery Village area in the 60's and 70's. I know very little about the Mother of God group and am unable to comment on the accuracy of the story, but the comments the issue has evoked has led me to think much about parish community.

First of all, the people—mainly families—who joined Mother of God are like so many of their Catholic peers in their desire to experience Christian community. It is an ironic thing, but just as Vatican II was writing so beautifully about the Church as community (in the early and middle 60's), American Catholics were moving by the millions out of the neighborhoods based around parish churches where they had experienced the Church as community even though no one ever used the word. Catholics had always joined groups to support various dimensions of Catholic life, but, for the most part, such groups were attached to parish or diocesan structures. Suddenly, as Catholics moved into the suburbs, and as society as a whole was losing faith in organized groups (example: more people bowl today than ever before but fewer people belong to bowling teams than ever before), spontaneous groups began to form where people bonded together for various spiritual purposes. The goals were good; the people were good, but often there was little, if any, formal association with the Church, whose experience over two millennia, could guide, correct and form. In retrospect (one of the best teachers), I suppose it is no surprise that problems have arisen.

Finally, this leads me—a pastor—back to thinking about the parish as community. First of all, I know that I have an obligation to try to help people experience that community means we find the Lord Jesus in other people who are willing to love and serve in His name. From Sodality to Helping Hand, from CYO basketball to Scripture study and in one hundred ways, we seek to share faith, to find Jesus in others and to give Him to others. To facilitate community is one of my most important jobs.

But, and here is the glory of Catholicism, the reality of community is that membership comes through Baptism. That means that those people who so frustrate me when they show up only on Christmas and Easter are as Catholic as I. Not only Lourdes, but the whole Church, is kind of an ugly duckling of a community, but it is who we are. Somehow, and this becomes more true depending on how much individuals cooperate with God's grace, that ugly duckling moves through the centuries as the best expression the world has of what Jesus intended His Church to be. Because each of us falls so short in living the Gospel, the whole Church suffers, but the temptation to withdraw into exclusive groups of like-minded people is always to be regarded with caution.

Our Parish Family

January 11, 1998

As we come to the end of the holiday season and after I have met so many people at social functions who no longer practice the faith, I find myself over and over again asking what has gone wrong over the last thirty years or so. I know there are a lot of answers and most of them have validity. Some speak of the breakdown in religious education during the seventies, which means that many Catholics in their thirties today have little knowledge of basic Catholic doctrine (some surveys say, for example, that fewer than 50% have a Catholic understanding of the Real Presence of Christ in the Eucharist). Others rightly point out that the attitude in morality that says that right or wrong is determined by personal feeling rather than by objective moral principles has meant that many determine the course of their lives without any reference to the teaching voice of the Church. Also, of course, the Church stands as an institution—with all of the inevitable human weakness of any institution—in a society that is fiercely individualistic. To all of these answers I submit another.

Frankly, I think we are doing a rotten job in conveying the joy that comes from following Jesus. St. John says in his First Letter, "Love, then, consists in this: not that we have loved God, but that He has loved us and has sent His Son as an offering for our sins." (1 John 4:10) Think about it: the God who created the farthest away star; the God who knows every fish in the sea; that God loves me. Anyone who has had the experience of human love has a hint of what this means. First of all, it means that I do not earn love (any more than I earned the love of my parents) and secondly, that the closer I am to the lover, the deeper my joy. If God does so love us, why do we treat Him as no more than a law-giver?

I do not excuse those who have left the Church. Whether from reasons of laziness or fear of living the Cross of Jesus, they have culpability for their choices. However, I do have to wonder how many have experienced the joy of Christianity in believers they have known? Have they encountered people who hunger to receive Jesus in the Eucharist? Have Catholics they have known talked honestly about their love for God and their desire to relate to God in prayer? How many friends have they who want to love Jesus as He is found in the poor or the weak of the earth?

A young woman, just this morning, came to the rectory to talk about joining the Church. The reason she came here was her attraction to the faith of the Catholic family that lives on the floor above her and their willingness to be with her in a recent time of loneliness. She wants to have in her life something of the joy that is within that family. It is that joy, a gift that comes from being friends with the Source of all joy, that will draw others to the Church.

Source of Joy

September 6, 1998

For a variety of reasons, we often receive calls from out of the parish from parents who desire Baptism for a child. Generally, we are happy to oblige once we receive a letter from their pastor giving them permission to have their baby baptized outside their own parish. This we require for a couple of reasons: to make sure the family is actually practicing the faith and that they actually are registered in a parish. A recent call made me think about this requirement. This particular couple showed every sign of going to Mass each week. However, despite having lived in their up-county home for over five years, they do not belong to a parish and go to Mass at several different churches—not including Lourdes. The call made me ask myself why belonging to a parish really does matter. Is a parish a filling station where we go each week to receive spiritual gas for another week, or should the phrase "community of faith" mean something?

I remember so well a seminary theology professor saying that the image of gift and response was central to describing the Christian mystery and it is an image that touches every dimension of life. So a woman loves a man; unless he responds to that love the relationship goes nowhere. Children naturally love their parents, but if the parents do not maturely and generously respond to that love, the children will pay an awful price through life. God's love is freely given; it cannot change me unless I respond to it by the way I live my life.

And so, in a subtle but real way, is it in the Church. In Baptism, God gives me His life, but He does so through the Church—His people—and through this particular parish community. Likewise with the Eucharist: He feeds me with the Body and Blood of his Son, but this happens in this particular local Church community. (Did you know, for example, that a private Mass at the beach with a priest friend on Sunday does not, strictly speaking, satisfy the Sunday obligation? We are supposed to celebrate with a parish community.)

The point is that, as with any family, individuals in a parish not only receive, but they respond to what they have received. Granted, the most important response takes place outside what is, strictly speaking, parish life. But the sign of peace at Mass (which I used to so dislike) does point to an important reality: before I can receive the Lord in Communion worthily, I must recognize my bond with those who will also receive. Now obviously, going to a different church each week to get the shortest sermon or the most convenient time does in some sense fulfill the Sunday obligation, but how about that deeper human need to be a part of a spiritual family where members who have received God's love and mercy and have listened to His Word respond to what they have received? Are there concrete ramifications to belonging to a parish? Come back next Sunday to find out!

RENEW: The Parish Responds

September 13, 1998

I wrote last week about the image of gift and response as being a suitable way to see the relationship between ourselves and God. God offers us Himself, but we must respond to that gift with faith and love in order for the gift to bear fruit. In Catholic life, the local parish is the focal point where the gifts of God are regularly made present and celebrated, especially in the sacramental life of the Church. The gift is presented, but again, the gift demands personal and community response. I can go to Communion every Sunday of my life, but if I do not, at some point, begin to respond to the Lord who comes to me in the Eucharist, I probably should not receive. Part of that response takes place in the context of the parish community, in that most local experience of the Body of Christ. At the most basic level, the response involves simply being known! Registering in a parish is not the most personal act of commitment we will ever make, but it does, in some small way, allow me to step away from the isolation and anonymity characteristic of our time. Secondly, we remember Jesus telling us that, "Where your heart is, there will your treasure be." Suppose the first hour of the work week was given to God through a donation of its income to the parish; such a response would revolutionize the ability of the Church to serve the world. Instead, so many see the basket coming and look for the smallest bill they have.

RENEW 2000 will begin with sign-up Sunday next week. This will provide an opportunity to join with individuals in small groups for six weeks, about one and one half hours per week, to share thoughts on living the faith in our world. The materials for the discussion are well prepared and are designed to challenge participants to deeper response to the call of God in their lives. So many talk about finding Him in prayer and community. Especially to those who are on the edges of parish involvement, I invite your participation in RENEW. It could be a life-changing decision. May the Holy Spirit lead this parish to a deeper response to God's call through our participation in RENEW.

Balanced Spirituality

September 20, 1998

As we look at these new office or apartment buildings going up in Bethesda, there is a sameness in their construction. Foundations are dug, shoring is put in the hole, concrete is poured, structural steel is erected and so on. Obviously, every phase of the job is integrated with the others. We will never see the northeast corner be raised to roof level while on the southeast concrete is laid at the lobby level. The landscaping does not go in while trucks are still delivering scaffolding to be used by bricklayers. Like the construction of a building, life, too, should be integrated.

So much has happened in Church and society in these last 30 years. In the Church, Vatican II, with its invitations to look at aspects of the faith from different perspectives; the sexual revolution within the larger society (and the ramifications of that which so absorb us today); and the ramifications of philosophical subjectivism that encourage us to look at decisions from the point of view of how I feel about them and how they affect me, rather than from a point of view of objective and unchanging truth. People of good will trying to cope with these and other developments have understandably lost perspective in trying to erect, if you will, the moral and spiritual building of life.

Some hear the Church speak of an option for the poor and take this so seriously that much effort is expended denouncing the rich; others fear that the Church is abandoning devotion to the Mother of God and they go about measuring priests by their supposed faithfulness to apparitions of Our Lady. People come into a new area and go on shopping expeditions for just the right parish, where either the liturgy is "relevant" or sermons are "orthodox." All of these pursuits spring from valid perceptions of some aspect of Catholic life, but sometimes, the perspective becomes skewed and the spiritual life is lived and judged much too narrowly. Where lies right or wrong on each issue? It is awfully hard to say. But one thing is for sure: where there is anger in an individual there is danger.

Listen to the Church and listen to Scripture, the book of the Church and try, as best we can, to listen to all that is said, not only those things with which I am most comfortable. The human body, like those new buildings, grows with balance—everything developing according to its natural schedule. So, with the spiritual life, we must beg the Holy Spirit to grow within us according to the plan of God and not according to our shortsighted vision that sees only small parts at one time.

It Ain't About Money, Folks

December 10, 1995

Because I so much enjoy helping with marriage preparation, I committed myself quite a few years ago to helping with the weekend retreat experience, Engaged Encounter. Two married couples and a priest give a series of presentations on marriage and the Christian concept of the sacrament. These are followed by the couples individually going apart, writing answers to questions based on the talks and then discussing their answers with each other. Because the topics covered are so diverse, the weekend offers these couples the opportunity to look at areas of marriage they may not have previously examined.

On Saturday evening, there is an activity that offers a little variety to the routine of the weekend. At that time, the engaged couples have the opportunity to share their ideas on various questions presented by the other engageds. Since I have worked on a number of these weekends, I thought I knew what to expect: discussion of things like when to have children, communication in marriage, problems with mixed marriages and (I hesitate to mention it) problems with in-laws. With only a couple of exceptions, none of these topics was raised. Instead, I would say that three quarters of the time was spent discussing money in marriage.

The Advent season we have entered is not only a preparation for the feast of Christmas, but it is also (and maybe even more importantly) a reminder that He will come again. He will come in glory at the end of time; but also, He will come into the lives of those who believe in Him. As believers, we are constantly on the watch for Him. We recognize that the people and events of life often disguise His attempts to come to us. The improbability of God's birth in Bethlehem reminds us that we cannot predict or control the ways in which He will show Himself.

Though sadness is not a frequent emotion of mine; I was somewhat saddened by the fascination of those engaged couples with the topic of money. Of course, I know about practicality; but I think I am also able to recognize a desire to control when I see it. The unspoken presupposition was that, if we have enough money, we will have conquered marriage's greatest challenge. Our Christian belief says that if two people work hard, pray hard, and trust God and each other, that somehow marriage works. Jesus does come into those families that welcome Him. Did I spend the weekend with engaged couples who consider such faith to be naive?

"Come, Lord Jesus," is the prayer of Advent. May He grant us the faith to look forward to, and expect, His coming.

Whose Life Is It Anyway?

By coincidence, I had meetings one recent evening with two engaged couples. I have known one of each of the couples from previous assignments and was asked to perform the ceremonies because of associations going back to their days in either grade school or a teen club. This is, obviously, a frequent experience for priests. I enjoy marriage preparation because I have a chance to work with people at a time when they are as open as they have ever been to the message of the Church. But, it can be discouraging.

To put it quite simply, neither of the two Catholics in the couples goes to Mass; neither has been to confession in years and both of the couples live together. In my shy and retiring way, I spoke with them about the old saying, "actions speak louder than words." None of them would ever say, directly, to God, "I know what your laws are; I know what your Church teaches; I know what the Bible says, but, frankly, dear Lord, we know better than you what is good for us." No, these couples claim to believe in God; they feel as if "they are good people;" and they most certainly do not feel that their lives are, in a sense, in direct rebellion against God's explicit word. But, actions speak more eloquently than words or feelings.

Now, mind you, I have engaged in almost the same dialogue many times over the past years, so I am able to do it in such a way that the couples do not stalk out in anger and, in fact, they listen with fixed attention. For many, it is the first time that they have either heard or listened to the message of the Church on these dimensions of the moral life. The sad thing, often (but not always), is the looks I receive. It is, often as if they are saying, "We like you, Fr. Wells, so it is nothing personal, but you are so naive to think that the future success of our marriage has anything to do with our following what you say, or the Church says, are God's rules." I always end these encounters by saying that the decision is theirs: if, after talking, praying and thinking, they decide that they are going to try to change their lives so as to try to live in accord with God's law, then call me back: I would love to witness their marriage, but according to God's standards, not the world's.

My point in all of this is to talk about the difficulty of faith, especially when the demands of faith require a complete change of life. The fruits of faith, it seems to me, are only tasted after the decision to live the faith. Before the decision is made, faith seems either foolish or too great a share in the Cross of Christ. Pray for the young, the very young, and for their parents, that from the earliest stages of life, they make small decisions in faith that will prepare them for the greater.

It's a Hard Life - But a Great One

May 21, 1995

Life is hard. Making a marriage work for forty or fifty years is hard; raising children is hard; being widowed is hard; working fifty or sixty hours a week is hard; being disappointed by people you have trusted is hard; sickness is hard; even the life of your friendly neighborhood parish priest is not always easy. Life is hard.

Nowhere do I say that life is not good because, indeed, life can be very good; but, again, life is hard. In the preface of the Mass of the Ascension which we celebrate on Thursday, the Church reminds us, "Where He has gone, we hope to follow." How much time do you give to thinking about heaven, or even judgment, for that matter? Quite a few years ago, I was chairing an adult discussion group. One of the questions was simply that: "How often do you think about going to heaven?" What most interested me was my own response that indicated how rarely the thought of heaven crossed my mind. Of course, it is not a question of faith. My faith in eternal union with God "for those who hold out to the end" was not the issue. It was simply that my preoccupation with the everyday and the challenges and joys of life allowed me not to spend that much time thinking about the afterlife. A number of things have forced me to change.

I guess what most troubles me is the whole marriage situation. I admit that, as a priest, I only see the bad cases; but some of them seem so very sad and unnecessary. I am not talking about fidelity or alcohol or physical abuse: these really are hellish things about which any outsider is foolish to judge. I also do not want to diminish selfishness, communication problems, the demands of children, the distribution and sharing of household tasks, the needs for free time and a hundred other really tough questions. But, daggone it, life is hard and this is not where we are expected to find the fullness of happiness. Everyone would like to think that they will find the perfect spouse, but how many do? Marriage is a sacrament because, among other reasons, it is a call to show the other the goodness of God, and among His qualities are patience, forgiveness, trust and a lot of other things that are best communicated over the very long run.

I do not mean to seem pessimistic, because I really do love the life to which God has called me. Life is hard, though, and "there ain't no heaven this side of heaven." Foolish is the person who thinks life can give lasting satisfaction and, also, foolish is that person who thinks that heaven is guaranteed.

Loving When the Going Gets Tough

January 14, 1996

I recently was asked to officiate at the twenty-fifth anniversary celebration of a couple with whom I have become rather close over the last dozen years. Such celebrations are always enjoyable, but this one perhaps a bit more than others because I have known, fairly well, some of the challenges in their marriage. For them, in truth, it can perhaps be said that these most recent days have been the best of their marriage.

Their success as a couple—and, of course, this is true in any good marriage—can be attributed to many factors, but one of these is their recognition that once a word is given, it must be kept. An active faith in God, regretfully, has been late in developing, but there has always been a kind of gritty determination to stick to a commitment once made because, really, there was no other choice.

More and more I believe that life was meant to be both tough and good, and that the experience of the good, for adults, often is dependent upon acceptance of the tough. A couple who decides that the best for their children is a mom at home also may have to make tough decisions about overtime and second jobs for the husband. A spouse who perceives selfishness in the other may for years have to forgive, to challenge and to resolve (with God's help) to get up and to try again. Every family knows the tough love, administered over and over again, that makes children do homework, learn to share, get to bed at a regular time and say prayers when young bodies are ready to drop.

All of this reflects, of course, the Paschal Mystery of Christ's death and resurrection. He chose the toughness of love even to the last drop of His blood: that love yielded the fruit of His Rising from death. One of our greatest dignities is that, through His Spirit, we can participate in His commitment and His decision to love—even when love means choosing to suffer. Likewise through that same Spirit, we learn that, even when it is tough, commitment in Christ leads to the experience that life is good.

Mary: the First and Perfect Disciple

December 17, 1995

"Blessed are you among women." How often we address these words to Mary, the mother of the Lord—and rightly so. But, did you ever look at her blessedness as she experienced it? Her life reminds me of the famous comment of St. Teresa of Avila, "It's no wonder you have so few friends, Lord; look at the way you treat them." Mary's holiness first was seen in her faith-filled agreement to conceive the baby Jesus; but her submission to God's will meant appearing to others to be unfaithful to the sexual laws of Israel. Likewise, Mary's blessedness led to her agreement with Joseph to forego the privileges of marriage so that they might be totally given to devotion and service to her Son. Her blessedness allowed her to see Jesus rejected by the people and nation He loved and, finally, she, "blessed among women," stood at the foot of the Cross as the "fruit of her womb, Jesus," was mocked, scourged and killed. This she had to watch almost alone because all but one of the men He had trained and called His friends for three years had run away in fear.

The sorrows of Our Lady remind us that, so often, blessedness and suffering are connected. There is a certain brutal honesty in Christianity that cannot forget that blessedness means sharing in the life of Jesus and that sharing in His life means sharing in His Cross. Mary chose to love God and neither the gossip of neighbors nor the scorn of Jewish community leaders would budge her from that willingness to unite her life to that of her Son. Sometimes, non-Catholics wonder why we pray to Mary, but as we consider her perfect love and loyalty to Jesus, is it any wonder that we recognize that He will hear her prayers before any others? How deeply she suffered because of her love; but that love never allowed her to give in to anger with His persecutors or self-pity at what the mother of this Son had to endure. She was the first and most perfect disciple.

The poverty and humility of Mary at Bethlehem remind us of our attitude before the Creche. He did not need comfortable bedding; what He needed was faith, loyalty and love. What He asks for is believers, like His mother, who so believe in His Gospel, that they will endure any suffering so that His name might be known and loved.

Fear Is Useless; What Is Needed Is Trust
December 18, 1994

Isaias Powers, C.P., in his book, *Quiet Places with Mary*, (Twenty-third Publications, 1987), has a phrase itself worth the price of the book: "holding on to the right to worry." Who can deny the sense that lies beneath fear, anxiety and worry? Our children, our communities, our Church, our marriages, our schools, our jobs: the opportunities for hand-wringing and "ain't it terrible" meditations are unlimited. In the face of this absolutely legitimate pastime, we have the angel's greeting to Mary (and, for that matter, to the shepherds, too), "Do not be afraid." The next time I teach a Scripture course to high school students, I think I will reserve as a punishment an assignment making a student go through the Gospels in search of the number of times we are admonished against fear and anxiety. Everybody is different, of course, but I strongly believe that, for many, the first great challenge to spiritual growth is overcoming the fear that keeps us from believing that God's promises are true in the face of the attractive and seemingly sensible message of the world.

Now, of course, there is a difference between worry and questioning— even when sometimes the line is hard to draw. Mary, when greeted by Gabriel and told that she was to conceive and bring forth a son, legitimately questioned how this was since she "did not know man." But, and I think this is important, the answer she received was basically to trust God. She had no idea what being overshadowed by the Holy Spirit meant. She knew what it would be to shame her parents; she knew that Joseph could walk out on her; she certainly knew the tongues of a small village. But, being overshadowed by the Holy Spirit: that must have been a tough one to figure out. Mary's heart, of course, was one that totally accepted God's love for her; she rejoiced that the God who so loved His people could never lead them astray and so, she responded, "Let it be done to me according to your word."

Faith, very often, means acting against fear. I know a woman who, when raising, disciplining and trusting her high school children says she often stands at the kitchen sink just repeating the line from Scripture, "Fear is useless; what is needed is trust." The world tells us that we must be in control. Folks, it is a great big world that we must control; no wonder we are prone to anxiety and fear. May we learn from the Mother of Jesus and our mother too, to submit ourselves to His will and His plan for our lives. It surely beats the heck out of worrying ourselves through life.

Mary: Model of Trust

December 13, 1998

I will tell you what I most love about Our Lady. Here is this fifteen year old girl. We know more about her, in so many ways, than she knew about herself. Certainly, for example, she did not wake up mornings and meditate on being free from original sin, and it never occurred to her that she was to be the Mother of God. Rather, obedient to her parents (and what great souls they must have been!), she accepted their faith in the promises that God had made to Israel. Mary went about her daily tasks at home in the village as a woman of faith. Everything she did, every choice of hers was made with God's will for her in mind. The beatitudes speak of purity of heart, a habit of being that is at peace, because it is confident in the presence of God. I often imagine what joy that purity of heart must have brought to family and neighbors as Mary went about Nazareth. Imagine knowing a person who treated you only as God would treat you! That's Mary.

St. Luke tells us that she was troubled at the greeting of the angel Gabriel. A bit later, hearing that she was called to conceive and bear a son, she even questioned how this could be since she was still a virgin. But, and here is the key to Mary's decision, she asked her questions from an attitude that expected God to act. Of course she was troubled; of course she could not understand conceiving as a virgin; but, valid as were these human questions, Mary also knew that God can and will intervene on behalf of those whom He loves. Hers was an attitude of faith and trust that was the high point of the expectant longing of Israel. Mary expected God to speak His redeeming Word to His people; if, as part of His plan, she was involved in a dramatic way, she could only respond as the servant of the Lord. God is good, Mary believed, and serving His goodness is our greatest dignity.

And so, because Mary trusted in the promises of God, she put her life on the line; and because of that faith, she gave the world its Savior. Therefore, I guess before we contemplate the things God could possibly ask of us, we might more profitably ask whether, as Mary, we really believe in the promises He has made and whether we really believe that He will act on behalf of those who trust in Him. In obedience to Gabriel's command, "Do not fear," Mary continued to live in her habitual trust of God. As I look at Mary, Joseph, John the Baptist and the rest of those whose trust prepared for the Lord's coming, I must examine my faith in the light of theirs.

Annunciation Faith

March 24, 1996

On Monday, March 25th, the Church will celebrate the Feast of Our Lady's Annunciation. Even though we come close to the climax of Lent, we are, so to speak, interrupted by this feast that reminds us of the Birth of Jesus. The reason, of course, is because the Annunciation, when Mary said "Yes," to the invitation of the Angel Gabriel to be the Mother of God, is exactly nine months before Christmas. Have you begun your shopping?

As different as Lent, with its emphasis on penance, and the joyful faith of Mary that is celebrated at the Annunciation might seem to be, their focus on the mission of Jesus gives them themes in common. Particularly am I struck by the faith that allows both Our Lady and her Son to assent to the plan of the Father, when such faith was expressed with no knowledge of where it would lead.

"How can this be since I do not know man," Mary asks the angel. Her Son, from the Cross, cries out, "My God, my God, why have you abandoned me," as He prays the psalm that laments the apparent absence of God as the innocent suffer.

At the beginning of life, where Mary's faith and cooperation in the divine plan of salvation were essential, and at the end, where alone, Jesus hangs between heaven and earth bearing the intensity of the punishment deserved for every sin that has been and will ever be committed, it is faith in what cannot be seen or understood that empowers first the Mother, then the Son, to say, "Thy will be done."

Contemporary Catholics are noted for their willingness to "pick and choose" among the doctrines of the Church. The Holy Father is one of the world's most popular figures, yet we cheerfully see him as "out of date," when he restates positions that are both traditionally Catholic and tough to live. Many wonder why they derive so little satisfaction from religion, but fail to understand that the satisfactions from religion have to do with the experience of finding that God is as good as His word; that when we entrust our decisions to His direction and that of His Church (no matter how ridiculed such faith seems to be in the world) we open ourselves to the "peace the world cannot give."

Mary's Annunciation faith opened her to the scorn of her neighbors; despite what they saw, Mary's Annunciation faith also was the seed of her salvation.

The Maidservant of the Lord

May 12, 1996

Virtually the first thing Scripture tells us about ourselves is that we are made in the image and likeness of God. I have long believed that this, our greatest dignity, is also at the heart of our troubles. The serpent tempts Eve by saying, "You will be like God, knowing good from evil." I am sure that knowing good from evil did not interest Eve—after all, could she have even imagined what the word evil meant—but being like God, having His power: this she could at least imagine.

One of the great obstacles to faith is our perceived insignificance. Oh sure, there are probably people in our parish considered important by the world, but how about five years after a debilitating stroke takes the power to influence others by the use of mental or physical talents? Priests have a saying, to illustrate how fleeting is the influence of a priest in a worldly sense, "There is nobody deader than a dead priest," or another saying, "I'll never forget good old Father what's-his-name." So many of us crave being like God in the sense that He is the key, that He is central to existence. We want others to notice us; we want to "matter." In the face of all the problems and opportunities of the world, what difference do I make?

I think it can be argued that, apart from her Son's obedience to the Father, the most important decision in human history was the "Yes," of Mary to the angel Gabriel. Her "Yes," though, was that of a servant: "I am the maidservant of the Lord, let it be done to me according to his word." Mary's life, because she saw it as that of a servant, was lived in total obscurity. It is really extraordinary when you think of it, but the greatest human ever born was hardly noticed by her contemporaries. Where Eve desired to be god-like, Mary would say, "My being proclaims the greatness of the Lord; my spirit rejoices in God my savior."

The submissiveness of Our Lady to the plan of God was not the cowering of a beaten slave; rather it was the clear-sighted recognition that cooperation with Him who is the source of our being is the only way to fulfill our greatest potential. She knew, and her Son demonstrated to the point of His death, that our greatest dignity is to live the self-giving love of the triune God in whose image we are made.

Mary: So Sensitive to Our Needs

May 29, 1994

I have in my bedroom a Currier and Ives print entitled "Virgin and Child," given to me by my good friend who is also an antique dealer. She told me that if the print was not of a religious subject it would be quite valuable, but that Currier and Ives' religious subjects just do not do well. I am still meditating on what that says about the value of our friendship, but I still highly value this gift. Because it is nineteenth century and reflective of the Protestant culture of the day, the print is romantic in style and gives no emphasis to the holiness of Our Lady. But on the other hand, what the picture does do, in my opinion, is to emphasize the human warmth of Mary's motherhood. I am also reminded of Our Lady's motherhood many times each day as I look out my office window onto her statue beside the Church and watch numbers of people stop, however briefly, before her image to greet their mother or to take to her some need. I am moved as I watch high school students from B-CC, business people walking to or from the subway and strollers from the neighborhood simply acknowledge that the Mother of Jesus is truly our mother too.

No incident from Scripture speaks to me more wonderfully of Mary as our mother than the wedding feast at Cana. The incident, of course, is one where a mother would be alert and sensitive. The Mother of Jesus was there and Jesus and His disciples were also invited; but, since six of His disciples had been called by Him only two days before the wedding, could either the hosts or Mary have guessed how many would come with Jesus? Could these extra guests have contributed to the sudden shortage of wine? No matter how the crisis developed, we note in the few lines about her, the qualities of her maternity. First, as a mother, she senses the shame of the parents of the bride and groom. Secondly, she knows the solution will come, not from talking about the problem, but from going to her Son. Also, notice that she does not tell Him the solution, as we often do in our prayer, she simply puts the problem before Him ("they have no more wine"). Her faith is total. Finally then, she directs all attention to Him as the solution to the problem ("Do whatever He tells you"). After this, we hear no more of her: after all, she is only a guest who has seen a problem, known the solution, and then stepped back into the background so that no glory would be taken from those who deserved it on their wedding day.

Mary, our Mother, you are so sensitive to our needs. Watch over us; take our problems to Jesus and teach us to trust Him in all things. Amen.

Mary Our Mother

May 11, 1997

I gave convert instructions years ago to a woman from Dublin who, strangely enough, was raised Protestant in that most Catholic of cities. She became interested in the Church when, as a young girl walking home from school, she would see people going in and out of the church on the route to her home. Since her own church was locked during the week, she would go sometimes into the Catholic church and simply sit, both watching the people and absorbing the warmth of their faith. This woman also absorbed something of Catholic devotion to the Blessed Mother.

One evening, I was giving a presentation on Mary; I was trying to be theologically accurate and, getting more deeply into theology than I should have, everyone was nodding gently off to sleep. Suddenly, my friend interjected, "Father," she said, "I think I can explain why Catholics love Mary." She then spoke of her trips into the quiet Dublin parish church, but especially she spoke of women she saw sitting in the last pews of the church. She said these women were humbly dressed; they had hands and fingers that were thick and cracked from hard work and, invariably, the rosary was being passed through those fingers. Even though the crucifix was in front of them at the altar, the eyes of these women were on the image of the Blessed Mother. My convert friend speculated that these were women who only knew life as hard. They believed that Jesus was King, Lord and God; but, mother to Mother, they could go to Mary knowing she would understand them, even though their lives were so insignificant in the eyes of the world.

Technically, the theology of these women was wrong, of course. Jesus is our brother; He became one of us precisely to demonstrate His union with us in our human struggle. But, despite theology that may have been flawed, these women in the back of a Dublin church knew something in their hearts that must bring great joy to the Son of Mary. They understood that, faced with the struggle of believing and hoping while trying to raise families in poverty, they could turn to their Mother, Mary, for support, wisdom, guidance and access to the source of all grace.

Mary, full of grace, is as united with her divine Son today as ever she was. As a Mother, she wants only the best for us, and that best is union with Jesus. May she intercede for us now and at the hour of our death.

Lessons of Mary's Assumption

August 11, 1996

I confess that I do not think about death as much as, probably, I should. It has occurred to me that, apart from the wonderful asthma medications today, a couple of the very severe attacks I have had could have been even more dangerous and that my lifestyle could be less active than it is. Also, as a priest who celebrates three or four funerals most months, I obviously am acquainted with death and dying. On the other hand, compared to the Spanish monks of the sixteenth century who used to keep a skull available to remind them of the "certain, sad, sentence of death," I find my meditations much more concerned with the here and now. All things considered, I suppose the primary focus on living as a Christian today is better than living in fear of the judgment to come.

However, it is easy today to forget that, ultimately, our goal is union with God and heaven. That is one reason why this week's feast of Our Lady's Assumption is such a blessing. The Church reminds us that just as Mary, a creature like us, is body and soul in heaven, so also are we destined to the "resurrection of the body and life everlasting." No, there is no reason for my being preoccupied with death, but I should be concerned with living the life of Jesus that only becomes more glorious with physical death.

The doctrine of the Assumption, of course, teaches that Mary's body was not corrupted by death. (Whether or not she actually died or, rather, was raised to heaven without experiencing death, has never been defined. Most theologians speculate that she did die but that her incorrupt body was assumed into heaven). Her bodily assumption separates her from us in that our body and soul will not be reunited until the Last Judgment at the end of time. This difference may seem not too important (after all, if I get to heaven, I do not think I will mind waiting a couple of thousand years to be reunited with this body!), but as always, doctrine has practical lessons.

First of all, the doctrine of Mary's and our bodily resurrection reminds us of the sacredness of the body. It is not just the soul that is redeemed by Jesus: our whole being is redeemed and, in fact, the way we show our faith is most often through the actions of our bodies. Secondly, we remember that Mary's bodily Assumption is a privilege of her sinlessness. We are made for eternal life; but the effects of original sin will be with us until the final victory of the Son of Mary is proclaimed at the end of time. One of the great horrors of sin is death and bodily corruption. Mary's Assumption reminds us of the beauty of her sinless motherhood, but it also reminds us of what we are apt to forget: that apart from her Son, we would be subject to eternal death and corruption. Mary is the first fruit of Jesus' victory; but, surely, those who hope in Him will be with Him and His Blessed Mother in heaven.

Mary and St. Bernadette; Holiness You Can Touch

February 11, 1996

The grotto at Lourdes, France is one of those places where even the most cynical "feel" the presence of the holy. Even the town itself, with its buying and selling of statues, pictures and bottles for the water of the spring, has a joy about it as people from all over the world mingle in restaurants and stores, sharing common faith and tips on where to find the best prices. The holiness, throughout, is something that can almost be touched. For example, a friend, a psychiatrist, gave into his wife's pleas to go to Lourdes and, contrary to all of his expectations, experienced a conversion in his life that has led him back again and again.

And yet, that atmosphere is not what Bernadette knew. Even today, the shrine is virtually closed in the winter. Lourdes is high in the Pyrenees and the winter features heavy snow and rain. Bernadette was desperately poor. We would see her as emaciated; her lack of size was probably the result of being undernourished. In modern terms, the family structure was weak and her mother had to cope as best as she could with the irresponsibility and joblessness of her husband. As we experience a fairly hard winter, I find myself wondering what Bernadette was wearing to protect herself from the damp and cold that February 11, 1858, when she received the first of eighteen visions from the "Beautiful Lady from heaven."

Over and over again, of course, the Scriptures remind us that the powerless who put their trust in God will find the Kingdom of heaven. Mary chooses in Bernadette one whom the world considers unimportant to demonstrate the radical difference between the standards of God and those of the world. "Without thinking what I was doing," Bernadette tells us, "I took my Rosary in my hands and went on my knees." This poor child has no one to trust in time of crisis but God; as always, such trust is rewarded.

The hundreds of sick, and those volunteers who serve them, are among the great experiences of Lourdes. In wheelchairs and stretchers, they come each afternoon to be blessed by the Eucharist (for Mary always leads us to her Son). There are occasional miraculous cures, but it takes a very hard heart indeed not to be personally healed by the vision of faith where the weakest of the weak beg their Mother's intercession with Jesus that they might submit to God's will for them.

Our Lady of Lourdes, our patroness, pray for us.

Forgive Us Our Trespasses
As We Forgive...

October 8, 1995

A man came by the rectory one recent afternoon to pay back fifteen dollars that we had given him for gas earlier. Since it was obvious that his financial condition had changed very little, I told him to keep the money; I forgave his debt. In some way, I guess I showed him mercy; but, of course, it was not my money and I did not have to replace the fifteen dollars out of my pocket. Real mercy is costly. When Pope John Paul went into that jail in Rome years ago and embraced the man who nearly killed him, the cost must have been tremendous. Not only did the Pope have to overcome his own anger, but he also had to risk that his assailant might reject the overture of forgiveness. I have often thought that as the Pope prayed the Our Father while he was recuperating, he must have been prodded as he prayed "forgive us our trespasses as we forgive those who trespass against us." He recognized that if he wanted to experience the mercy of God in his own life, he must be willing to extend that same mercy to one who had hated him enough to try to kill him.

The ancient Hebrew language had only two thousand words in its vocabulary. However, in that small number of words, there were four different ones that we would translate with our word mercy. There is no way around it: from the time of Adam until this day, we stand before God in need of that mercy. I will sometimes hear a person in Confession say, "I am a good person, Father, but. . . ," almost as if what they are about to confess has nothing to do with the sins for which Jesus died. We want to see ourselves as good; we want others to see us in the same way. It is most uncomfortable for us to recognize that the only way we will slip into heaven is because of the mercy of God.

Only the person who sees the need for mercy in his own life can really be merciful. I do not mean the attitude that says from a position of strength, "Yes, I know what a pitiful person you are, but because I am so good, I deign to show my power by being merciful." Rather, must our attitude be that of Christ who, when He read the heart of the woman caught in adultery, said nothing to her about her evil or His mercy, but simply told her to go and to sin no more. That merciful person, who accepts the wisdom to read hearts as Jesus read them and to treat people as mercifully as did He, will obtain mercy both here and hereafter.

The Mark of a Believer

November 9, 1997

I used to say of some dear friends of mine: "they learn only by experience." And so, as their children went through school, they got into every kind of trouble. I have bailed them out of jail; talked parents into letting them come back home after this or that disaster; tried to calm them down when they were angry and lent them money to repair the effects of imprudent purchases. Happily, most of this large family is grown and doing well in adulthood, but, as I say, they learned only by experience. The wisdom of parents that could see future consequences had no value; only the sensation of the foot in the rear end could convince that a kick was a bad thing. Experience may well be the best teacher, but it is not the only teacher and it certainly is not the easiest.

I was walking down East-West Highway with someone else the other day. He is a recovering alcoholic. When we came upon one of the homeless looking for a hand-out, he immediately reached for something to give the person. I noted the generosity and my friend replied, "Father, after you have been there, you understand." Again, experience teaches. The problem for believers is that Jesus calls us to reach out to others, particularly the suffering, even though we may not have had the experience of a particular kind of suffering. If we have not known depression, for example, it is easy for us to grow frustrated with a depressed person's inability to motivate himself or to function in a practical way. I may work in an office with someone who has experienced virtually nothing of what I take for granted in terms of family support or affirmation and then I grow angry because that person's neediness expresses itself in obnoxious behavior.

The mark of the believer is that he or she treats the suffering with compassion, even if they have not experienced the suffering. St. Paul says that we must "put on Christ." We stand in awe of Mother Teresa and her sisters and their love of the suffering, but in looking at them, we perhaps forget that they put in two hours a day before the Blessed Sacrament in prayer, in addition to Mass and prayers they say in common. We cannot "be compassionate as your heavenly Father is compassionate" unless the Spirit of the Father is alive within us. Yes, experience is a good teacher and great is the fool that is not taught by it; but the far greater teacher is God Himself and He will surely teach us to act like His Son and in the Spirit of His Son if we will but go to Him in prayer and ask.

Living for Heaven

October 25, 1998

It occurs to me that there is some little bit of difference between staying out of hell and going to heaven. If the focus is on avoiding the punishments of eternal damnation, the chances are that I will approach religion a bit differently than if the goal is to be united with the God who so delights in me that He created me in His image. Now, let us make no mistake about it, God respects my freedom enough to allow me to reject Him and to choose hell. He will not force me to go to heaven. All have heard the dumb comment, "A loving God would not send anyone to hell." True enough, but that same God loves me enough to give me the awesome freedom with which I can reject Him for all eternity. It is a start toward wisdom that recognizes the real possibility that my choices can merit me a damnation that has no limit. Quite frankly, I thank God for my adolescent faith that kept me aware of my sins and close to Confession. Pray God, it will have kept me out of hell.

Going to heaven is, I think, quite another thing. Oh sure, the person who spends his whole life avoiding mortal sin and fulfilling the obligations of religion will avoid hell and will go to heaven. That is no small thing. I do believe, however, that in this life, God invites us to something more in our spiritual journey. I believe He wants us to experience, certainly in a veiled way, but really to experience on this earth a hint of how much He loves us.

An example may demonstrate my point. One of our priests on a recent Sunday was startled at Mass and thought he had lost his place in the liturgy when he invited people to pray the Our Father and the response was almost inaudible. He had not lost his place, it was only what may have been the response of a large group of people intent on staying out of hell rather than on being with the Lord Jesus as He leads us to closer union with the Father of mercy and love.

I believe the answer has to do with generosity of heart. Do I really believe God personally loves me? How do I show my gratitude; how do I express that gratitude in the way I treat my neighbor, my enemy, my boss, my fellow parishioner or, for that matter, my God? I believe the great suffering of purgatory will involve my kicking myself for my stinginess in self-giving when I realize how much God has loved me. Yes, it was a great start for me as a twenty year old to realize that I really could go to hell and to be afraid of that, but I hope to God that I have taken my eyes off of hell, and have begun to focus on living right now the life that God wants for me for all eternity.

Our Ringleader: Gail Gardes
May 8, 1994

People are often surprised to learn that, in a normal week, Sunday is often the quietest day for a priest. In that same normal week, life in a rectory often resembles a barely managed three ring circus. As those who spend any time in a rectory know, the ringmaster (despite what he may think) is not the pastor. It is the parish secretary. And, if any pastor is foolish enough not to believe this obvious truth, let his secretary resign. Well, this pastor has enough experience to know how central is the secretary, but he—and all of us—have to cope with the resignation of Gail Gardes. Gail has been at Lourdes for better than thirteen years and so, after this length of time, she knows where every file, book, certificate and parish memory is stored. Her successor will spend, I am sure, the first couple of months just trying to figure out what is what.

Of course, I knew Gail when I was stationed here as an assistant in 1987, but the last couple of months have shown me how her loyalty, efficiency and organization skills can make life so easy for the one in charge. In addition to this, I am so grateful (and I speak for Msgr. O'Donnell, too) for the way Gail deals with the public. The parish secretary is usually the first person that one meets when he or she knocks on the rectory door. Both the parishioner of fifty years and the stranger coming to the church for an extraordinary need are made to feel (or not to feel) welcome by the greeting received at the door or on the phone. Thank you, Gail, for your goodness to so many people over these past years. May God grant you long and happy years in your new home in the West. Believe me, we will miss you.

Speaking of leaving, this Thursday is the Feast of the Lord's Ascension into heaven, the fortieth day after Easter. Masses on this holy day of obligation will be celebrated on Wednesday evening at 6:00 p.m., and on Thursday at 7:00, 8:00, noon and 6:00 p.m. There is a line in the Preface for Mass of that day that sums up the Ascension for me: "Where He has gone we hope to follow." The Ascension reminds us that, despite all of our goals here on earth, the believer has an ultimate goal which is heaven. This is no lasting kingdom and, to some extent, the decisions that I make today should be made with at least some reference to how they will lead me either toward or away from my ultimate goal.

The Heart of a Servant: Ellen Mann

March 19, 1995

In His teaching, Jesus constantly gave images of how total is the commitment to turn from the world's values and to follow Him. "Take up your cross" . . . "Whoever loves his own life will lose it" . . . "Turn the other cheek" . . . "Love your enemy." The Gospels are full of striking demands by the Lord that illustrate that following Him means making a complete break with the world. The image that has always most challenged me is that of Christ who came to serve and not to be served. I believe that in a world that thrives on power which often defines success in terms of authority, that the person who seeks to serve the needs of others is one of the most authentic signs of what St. Paul means when he says that we must "put on Christ."

Happily, as a priest, I have come to know and, quite often, to bury, many extraordinary individuals. And, only in the most unusual of circumstances is a column such as this an appropriate place to speak of any particular person. With the death of Ellen Mann, however, the person and the situation are matched. I write about her not because she worked in the parish as organist and teacher since (we think) 1939, and not because she has come to know so many who have lived in Lourdes over the years. Rather, I write about her because she seemed to me to have what I call the heart of a servant. One of the tough things about a contemporary priesthood is that we seem to be transferred more frequently than in the past, but my limited experience in this parish as well as stories of many whose memories extend far back in parish history, all point to the same quality in Ellen. Her joy in making life for others more beautiful; and so her craft, making music, was almost a sacrament, an outward sign of her inner reality.

God has given to each of us different gifts. Ellen Mann had a cheerfulness that was probably as much a part of her personality as a result of virtue. We all cannot have that personality. What she also had, though, was a disposition to always put others first. That is a result of a lifetime of cooperating with grace, of saying "no" to her own convenience and "yes" to God's will. This parish community has been extraordinarily blessed because of Ellen Mann's disposition of serving love. May God allow her to rest in the fullness of the love she so generously lived with us.

The Gift of Self: Rene Whyte

April 21, 1996

"Don't ever single out a parishioner from the pulpit," the homiletics professor told us. By extension, his advice would apply to this weekly column, I
suppose. As with most rules, this one too, is made to be occasionally broken.
Rene Whyte first began working in Lourdes during the Second World War.
How many thousands of children have passed through the school and have
known her as she managed lunch-time in the school cafeteria? How many of
those same children benefited from the CYO program she served (with her
beloved husband, Babe) during the strong and not-so-strong years of youth
sports at Lourdes? This Easter, for the first time almost since the Resurrection, Rene was not able to prepare the church and sacristy for the ceremonies of Holy Week, and believe me, we were like "sheep without a shep-
herd." Rene is now recuperating from several infections and hopes to enter
an assisted living facility, from where, no doubt, she will continue to serve as
a part-time consultant.

Actually, I write more to use Rene as an example than to praise her.
Because of her years working at Lourdes, she probably serves as the best
example of what this and any parish so much needs—the volunteer. Another
example, and one I choose because it is so very recent, is the golf outing we
held last Monday. Apart from raw winds and late-day rain, the event was
enormously successful. But no one knows better than I that the success of
the day came because a dozen or fifteen people worked and gave of themselves with extraordinary generosity. At the dinner following the golf, a
young non-Catholic guest who has reached the stage where she is doing
some serious reading about "the meaning of life" made the comment that
she never knew that Catholics could have such fun. I guess if all she knows
of Catholics comes from the daily press, such a comment makes sense; but
as grace would have it, she meets the Church "in person" at exactly the time
when she searches out deeper questions. Our joy at the Resurrection of
Christ (a joy, perhaps, of which we do not often think) takes on flesh for
someone outside the faith in the improbable setting of a parish cook-out
held indoors because of pouring rain.

My point, of course, is this: the person who gives time in support of
parish efforts—no matter how far afield they might seem to be from an
explicit preaching or teaching mission—works at something with wider
dimensions than they appreciate. Every gift of self, from S.O.M.E., to orga-
nizing a school fund-raiser, to reading at Mass, adds to a mosaic of faith that
presents something of the person of Jesus to the world. Such giving costs

much in terms of time, effort and energy; because that giving is a bit like the self-giving of the Lord, it, like His, bears much fruit.

A Sad Day for OLOL
and Our Spanish Community

June 16, 1996

Bad news is bad enough; but when bad news comes suddenly, it seems even worse. Last weekend we received news that Fr. Louis Hoffman has been reassigned by his religious community, the Sons of the Holy Family. Father had told me that there was a very real possibility of his being moved, but our expectation was that the first of July was a realistic estimate of when this might take place. However, the provincial council of the Sons of the Holy Family met during the first week of June and they and the Superior General of the Congregation not only asked him to take a new assignment in one of their parishes, but they also offered him the opportunity to take a thirty day retreat which began during this week we have just completed. So, in more of a rush than anyone had expected, Father was on his way. As many know, Father Hoffman's ninety-six year old mother lives outside of Phoenix, Arizona. Likewise, most of the parishes of his religious community are located in the Southwest. So, very likely, as of July first, this is where Fr. Hoffman will be stationed.

While there is a wonderful unity between the Spanish and English parts of the parish, it is inevitable that most English speakers are not aware of all that goes on among the Spanish speaking in Our Lady of Lourdes. This year, for example, almost one hundred and twenty-five were enrolled in English classes, with eight or ten teachers involved. In addition, there is an active religious education program for children for whom English is still a second language. Weekly, also, the Spanish community prepares a meal after Mass that allows the development of a sense of community so far away from their homes. These meals are also a source of significant income for the parish. All who have heard the Spanish choir know what a marvelous contribution they make to worship. All of these activities Fr. Hoffman encouraged, facilitated and built up. One of his great gifts was his ability to enable people to use and develop their own gifts. While all of us deeply regret his transfer, his great ability to challenge people to stand on their own, means that his work will continue in his absence. This, indeed, may be the great attribute to his priestly work at Our Lady of Lourdes.

Since Father's opportunity to make a thirty day retreat meant his leaving so quickly, a replacement for him will not be with us until, probably, the first of July. Spanish Masses will be covered until then by help from student priests from Catholic University. We will pass on Fr. Hoffman's new address as soon as we receive it.

God speed, Fr. Hoffman, and thank you!

Our Growing Church

I read in the paper that some propose a twelve month school year and I shudder in dread. Part of this, I suppose, is what remains of my youth and the joy of anticipation that looked forward to summer vacation. However, even today that anticipation of the summer is with me because I hope it will mean that life in the parish will take a bit of a breather during these ten weeks. At every level of education at this time of year students are evaluated according to their performance. In that spirit, perhaps such a year-end look at Our Lady of Lourdes might be helpful.

First of all, a good Catholic parish is one where the baptized regularly worship God at Mass and acknowledge their need for mercy in the Sacrament of Penance. Let us never forget that, according to those terms, this parish comes up very short. There are, I am sure, thousands who live in our boundaries who no longer fully practice the faith and this reality forces us to admit that things could be much better in the parish. However, there are indications of growth that should give us hope. Most importantly, our Mass attendance is growing. Each October, every parish in the Archdiocese must count every person at every Mass. In 1997, we were up about three or four percent. Happily, what was true here, seemed to be true throughout the Archdiocese. Also encouraging is the very good number of people at daily Mass. The numbers at Confession are hard to judge. (In the old days, some priests used to use counters: not here!) But, I think there are fewer times during Confession hours when no one is at Confession. Especially is this true when we hear them before the noon Mass.

Our school and religious education programs are coming to the end of successful years. The Sunday morning CCD classes serve more children each year and they are taught by a wonderful group of faith-filled men and women. Mr. Patrick Serra is finishing his first year as principal at the school. Attendance continues to grow and he has done a fine job coping with the crises that arise when trying to lead and educate a large group of children on a daily basis. He is the first to admit that his job is made easier because of the wonderful faculty that was in place when he joined us. While on the subject of education, the number of people who take advantage of adult education offerings continues to grow. Since the Catholic faith is so rich in intellectual content, there is no question that the more one knows about the faith, the more likely he or she is to live the faith.

The Church must be a servant Church if it is to be faithful to the Gospel. So, we must be grateful for those who bring that dimension into the community. Close to 100 are involved in feeding the homeless on Sunday evenings; others assist in Helping Hand or at Bethesda Cares or in preparing food for SOME; our Hispanic young adults are becoming more active at Waverly House and others from the parish assist the bereaved at times of funerals or in other service projects throughout the area.

Thanks be to God, there has been growth in the parish. May God grant that it continue.

Parish Life Goes On in the Summer
July 24, 1994

The Our Lady of Lourdes Summer Institute of Advanced Biblical Studies has completed its first annual week-long session. Scripture students from all over the Bethesda metropolitan area have gathered to discuss and debate various ideas of spirituality and daily living based on the teachings of the Old and New Testaments. The students ranged from ages four to eight. Yes, our first Summer Bible School was a great success and, while many of the thirty or so students show some weakness in grasping the Biblical languages of Hebrew and Greek, no one would question their expertise in arts and crafts. Thanks to the adults who taught and supervised during July days that must have been something like those of ancient Israel.

Yes, there is more going on in the parish during these hot days than you might expect. Our first session with those who are interested in joining the Church through the Rite of Christian Initiation of Adults (RCIA) has been held. Thank God, a number have called the rectory expressing interest, but we can accept new people until later in the fall. If you can say that you derive strength and hope from your Catholic faith, then why not ask yourself if there is a friend or a neighbor whom you could invite to our next preliminary meeting on August 16, at 7:30 p.m., in the rectory. Of course, you can come with the person. We Catholics have a well-deserved reputation for being very private about our faith. My mother used to say that if a Catholic brought just one person into the faith, they would go automatically into heaven. (Of course, her husband was a convert.) I am not sure about my mom's theology, but imagine if each Catholic was responsible for bringing just one person to Christ and the Church.

We have also begun some much-needed repair work around the parish. Work is well underway on a new ceiling for the school cafeteria. The tiles, dented by forty years of basketballs and well-aimed crutches, and greasy from two generations' hot lunches, are being replaced. Also, although many have fallen in love with the orange cone on the church walkway, we will be replacing concrete both there and in front of the school and other places where wear and tear have done to concrete what they do to people.

So, while many of us are vacationing, life still goes on in the parish and, needless to say, we appreciate your support.

Taking Your Parish Seriously

June 4, 1995

The weeks between Ash Wednesday and the first of June are the busiest of the year for a priest, for reasons that even a casual observer of a parish can imagine. From the parish devotions of Lent and Holy Week, we move into the season of weddings, graduations, First Communions, Confirmations and all other activities associated with spring. However, over the Memorial Day Holiday, I could see on the horizon the end of all this activity and could begin to anticipate the quiet weeks of summer. However, I also spent a little time trying to evaluate where Lourdes is as we come to the end of another year of parish activity.

It is hard to measure the spiritual pulse of a parish because, after all, a parish is a group of individuals, each at his own point on the road to heaven. Certainly, the number of people at daily Mass has to be a good sign, as is the number who stop daily for prayer before the Blessed Sacrament. The response to the number of offerings during the year of a spiritual and educational nature also seems to indicate that there is a real desire to grow spiritually. One of the best indications of spiritual health in a parish, the number going to Confession, points in the wrong direction. My suspicion is that roughly half of our people go to Confession rarely, if ever. This is particularly, and tragically, true of our young. Few things scare me more as a priest, than to contemplate the trouble our youth will get into without the grace of Penance.

From a very positive perspective, I sense that more people are willing to commit some serious time to parish activities. This weekend's parish picnic, for example, came off only because of the work of many. The parish survey indicated that quite a few people are willing to give of themselves for Our Lady of Lourdes. The RCIA, which we initiated this year, involved a large number in the important work of drawing new members into the Church. Financially, too, we seem to be on solid footing. Little by little, our offertory increases, to the point where we will end the fiscal year having collected about $30,000 more than the previous year. That, pray God, is a sign of greater commitment on the part of our people to the parish.

The greatest challenge at Lourdes is one that the Church faces through-out our country. The attitude towards Confession is one symptom towards what some call "cafeteria Catholicism." The Church is regarded affectionately by her members, but also regarded as something like a kindly social service agency: she gives advice that can be taken or rejected. Lourdes, like the whole Church, can never be all she is meant to be until we recognize that we owe to the Church the obedience, loyalty and love that we give to Christ Himself.

I Shudder to Think. . .

October 5, 1997

Every so often, one of those little tremors of fear will shoot up my spine: the kind one feels when, half way through a project, there is a question about whether there is enough material left to finish it. This happened a couple of weeks ago when I looked at the August financial report. Now, of course, no month is less indicative than August of parish finances since so many are out of town. On the other hand, since we can compare with August of the year previous, something can be learned. One thing I saw did not surprise me: expenses are up. What did cause that little tremor of which I spoke was the realization that offertory giving was down for the month and, in fact, down since the start of the fiscal year on July 1.

That little shiver quickly passed. Who can muster a real shiver in August? However, I was reminded that an essay on giving is not out of place. Or, to put it another way, the projects are underway; we cannot turn back.

It was so nice to make it through the summer with no problems or complaints about air conditioning—aside from those who said it was too cool or too warm (equal numbers of each!). However, I was never able to forget that this happiness was purchased at a cost of $75,000.00. Now, of course, this theoretically came from last year's budget; in fact, we are still digesting the cost. Now, after accepting the wise advice of the school community and the finance council to purchase new windows for school, rectory and convent, we are faced with the little chore of paying for them: again, at a cost of about $75,000.00. There will be a rebate from PEPCO because of energy savings, but this will not much change the burden.

I could go on: the electrician is afraid of the wiring in the church; the boilers in the church and the rectory were inspected by the State and were found deficient at a cost of a few thousands of dollars; even a failed fan in a stove in the school kitchen will cost over a thousand dollars to replace for reasons too complicated for this young mind to contemplate. Oh yes, new padding for kneelers in the church are coming. I'm afraid I will be using them to beg the Lord for the money to pay for them.

Of course, we are not in crisis, but, we will be if things do not turn around. I hate to vex people with parish fundraisers; offertory giving should be more than able to support a parish like ours. Personally, I suspect it may be time for me to reevaluate how much I give to the parish. I offer the same question for all: how faithfully do I fulfill my obligation to support the church?

The Spirit, a Window and Renewal

May 31, 1998

Today's celebration of Pentecost recalls the gift of the Holy Spirit to the Church. Despite the weakness and sin so obvious in the humanity of believers, faith confesses that, somehow, the Spirit continues to guide the Church toward the end of time. Even though individuals, even communities, can and have abandoned the Church, somehow the Spirit works through the events of history to make the Church more aware of who she is as Bride of Christ. As we as a parish look ahead, we have to be aware that unless we seek to be guided by the Spirit, we will not see what really is the will of God for us.

I suppose the most obvious thing the future holds in store for Our Lady of Lourdes is our Millennium Window. The generosity of our parishioners over the last six months to the Millennium Window Appeal has made possible not only the installation of the window, but also the new lighting around the exterior of the church, the new kneelers, the extensive repair work to air conditioning vents on the roof and all the unseen, but expensive, work in the boiler room this past winter. Work on the window should begin very shortly and, despite the change in appearance it will make, should not take more than about three weeks. We regret that, during the time of construction, we will cancel the daily Mass at noon. Incidentally, a group of our parish council went with me one day last week to Shenandoah Studios in Front Royal, Virginia to see the window being constructed. Fascinating!

Our second major upcoming project concerns our parish involvement in RENEW 2000. I believe it was during the years 1985-87 that the Archdiocese last was involved in RENEW. Its effects in the parish still continue because groups that are much involved in parish service today emerged from the small groups formed during those years. RENEW 2000 is about forming small groups of ten or so persons who wish to participate in a well-prepared program of faith discussion. These groups will meet for only six weeks, beginning in the fall, but they will meet again each spring and fall until the Millennium year 2000. Experience may not have taught me much as a priest, but it has taught me at least these two contradictory things. First, Catholics tend to be very private about their faith, both to fellow Catholics and to non-believers. Secondly, when we do share our faith, we realize how strong is the faith of others and how much we have in common with them. Our own faith and our commitment to live the faith grows stronger. Jesus founded a Church, a community of faith; He never intended us to follow Him in isolation.

Already, volunteers throughout the parish are involved in committees who are planning our participation in RENEW 2000. Much will be said and written about it in the next months. Plan to make the commitment to be a part of this great work of the Spirit over the next few years.

The Story of Our Millennium Window

July 12, 1998

The wraps will soon be off, perhaps even as you read this article. The scaffolding and the green plastic have preserved the church from the dust and dirt associated with construction, but now that the final touch-up of painting is finished, we can see our new window. I am delighted to say that Cardinal Hickey will join us on the evening of September 13th to bless the window, but I do not want to wait until he is with us to acknowledge those who have contributed to this project.

First, my friend Joanne Morrow, who on coming to see my new parish three or four years ago said, "Tommy (her husband and I go back to grade school), what are you going to do with that space over the altar?" In a million years, it never would have occurred to me that the space should be filled. Shenandoah Studios of Front Royal, Virginia, designed and built the window. We chose them because Mr. Peter van Rossen, who designed the original windows, now works for them. If you ever need a stained glass window in your family room, they are the people to see: every dimension of their operation is professional and friendly, efficient and warm. Their love of their art and the family spirit of their company touch the whole operation.

Of course, a number of sub-contractors are involved in such a project. The painting and touch-up were done by Occupied Spaces, Inc.; the wooden framing around the window was done by Park Woodworking; the steel shoring that held up the building while the hole was in the wall, was done by Steele Foundations, and the structural steel work that gives additional strength to the wall was done by Bethesda Iron Works. The scaffolding, both inside and outside the church, was done by the Millstone Corporation.

I am guessing, but I suspect final costs for the project may be 20 percent lower than expected because of donated services. Great thanks are given to Mr. Chris Stark, an old friend, who donated hours of design time to solve structural engineering problems. He also made three or four visits from his home in Carroll County to check on the project. Wells and Associates, my brother's brick contracting company, first tore out the hole for the window and then did the brick work around the window after it was finished. For their week's worth of labor we have also received no bill. And, finally, Dave Eason, a parishioner, who works as a project manager for The Keystone Group here in Bethesda. Foolishly, Dave gave me the "Anything I can do" line when I first came to Lourdes—and he meant it. Imagine if I had had to coordinate this project! The contractors were briefed on the work; they were scheduled so that one could start after the other had finished and they knew where to turn with any questions or problems that came up after they arrived on the scene. Almost daily for the last month, Dave has been on site to coordinate. Dave, of course, grew up in the parish and so I know he sees this as work for his family, but that does not affect in any way my debt of gratitude to him for the hours, effort and love given to this work.

The people of the parish deserve the last word of thanks. Over $100,000, in large and small donations, have been given thus far. The window, our new outdoor lighting, the kneelers, and new vents on the roof of the church: your loyalty to Lourdes has made these possible. Thank God for the faith and love of those who have given so generously.

Enduring Symbols in the Millennium Window

July 19, 1998

My thought had been that people would be looking at our new window for some few years to come, so it would be nice to let them gradually learn to read it. However, I am already getting tired of explaining this or that feature, so perhaps a bit of an explanation might be in order.

The first thing to remember is that the new window seeks to complete the theme of those installed in the 1960's. There is a page of explanations which help to read those individual windows, but taken together, they represent the parts of the Mass. Our new window then, seeks to summarize what is our faith in the sacrifice of the Mass as we enter the third millennium of the birth of the Lord. The window moves, as does the Mass, both from earth to heaven, and from heaven to earth. So, the green panel represents the earth; the hands, of course, represent both the priest and the people who offer the Lamb of sacrifice to God the Father. The lamb represents Jesus, the Lamb of God who takes away the sins of the world. To go just a bit more deeply into the tradition, we recall that the Passover for Jews represents the Chosen People's passing over from slavery in Egypt to freedom in the Promised Land. The lamb sacrificed at Passover represented the union between God and His Chosen People. Jesus, then, is our Passover Lamb, whose life is offered to God so that we might be freed from slavery to sin. Jesus, our Passover sacrifice, is an acceptable gift to the Father and so the Father shares the offered victim, Jesus, with us in a sacrificial meal. This we see symbolized in the window by the blood flowing from the side of the lamb into our hands.

The glorious yellows and reds at the top of the window represent the holiness of God. You notice that one shaft of yellow passes through the center of the window, through the lamb and again, into our hands. This represents the gift of the Holy Spirit of God which is given to us through Christ. That gift of the Spirit is the Father's response to the sacrifice of Jesus on our behalf and so, fittingly, the window portrays the Spirit as intimately connected with the sacrifice and the Eucharist. A nice touch of the artist, I thought, was that the yellow in the window is used only for God: at the top of the window, in the halo around the head of Jesus the Lamb of God and in the shaft representing the Holy Spirit.

All have commented on how much light our new window lets into the church. My prayer is that the window may be an instrument whereby the light of faith in the Eucharist may shine ever more brilliantly in our parish.

Prayer:
Pick Your Spot and Chat with God

November 6, 1994

A number of people (well, actually two of them) have asked me to share some thoughts on how to pray. I often mention the importance of prayer in living the Christian life, so perhaps it might be useful for some to give at least a few suggestions on how to pray.

I begin with two notes of caution. In a society that craves instant gratification, prayer—like most really important activities—goes against the current. Prayer is the principle means for drawing close to God, but that drawing close takes place over the course of a lifetime, and, most often, we do not notice it as it happens. Secondly, there is no "right" way to pray. Because each of us has a different personality, each relates to God differently. For any Catholic, of course, there can be no authentic prayer life where the Mass is not at the center, because in the Mass, in a perfect way, we pray with Christ who leads us to the Father. As for prayer outside of the Mass, what I suggest are only basic principles that, I believe, have served me well over the years.

First, prayer is like brushing your teeth: do it each day and at a regular time and it will become a habit. God is Spirit; we are active in the material world and, therefore, most of us are not inclined to turn off the obvious material world in favor of listening to the much less obvious spiritual. In addition to a regular time, try to find a place for prayer, perhaps before a Crucifix or favorite religious image. The reason for this, of course, is simply to put ourselves into a prayerful frame of mind. Russian Orthodox homes, for example, have a special corner where an icon is placed and before which a candle is lit at time for prayer. Obviously, at Lourdes, the adoration chapel in the church is an ideal place for prayer. However, if it is not practical to come daily, why not schedule a period each week to come before the Blessed Sacrament?

Finally, the heart of prayer is listening to God. Obviously, what He has to say in prayer is more important than what I say. Equally obvious is the insight that I cannot hear God as I hear another person. That is why I recommend praying with Scripture. Each day, the Church selects passages from the Bible for use at daily Mass; but, even if I cannot get to Mass, I can still use the readings as a way to hear God's Word each day. No, if I give the Lord five or ten minutes each day and quietly try to hear what He is saying in these passages, I probably will not "hear" anything. But, if I make this listening a daily habit, I guarantee that over time His Word will sink into my life and I will find it gradually shaping the way I live. God may be subtle; but He most certainly is powerful in those who listen to Him!

Seeing the World Through Jesus' Eyes

June 23, 1996

I was reading, recently, a small book that someone gave me years ago, *Rule for a New Brother*, written for a religious community in Holland. As the title indicates, it seeks to train new religious in living in community. But, since all of us live in community of some sort, the wisdom of the book has wider applications. For example, in describing the following of Jesus, the author says, "It means following the path He took and seeing things as He saw them."

St. Paul said much the same thing when he said we must put on "the mind of Christ." A friend of mine is a music director in a parish. She told me the story recently of a Sunday Mass where she ran a music practice with the congregation until two minutes after Mass should have started. The celebrant was so frustrated that he simply told the servers to start down the aisle, even though she was still practicing some other song. The next day, she received a call where he blasted her once again. This person is quite capable of blasting back, but as she said, "I just had this sense that there was something going on in his life." Now, of course, neither she nor I knows if she is right, but I know her to be a prayerful person who really seeks the wisdom of God in her life. She really believes that it is possible to at least begin to see things as Jesus sees them.

There are many reasons why people do not pray. One of them, of course, is what has been called "practical atheism," acting as if God does not exist, no matter what a person might say he believes. But, believers too, often give up on prayer. Their problem, though, concerns what they expect to get out of prayer. In a society that is so preoccupied with feelings, many expect that prayer will result in feeling close to God. In fact, though, the great fruit of prayer is virtue. Putting ourselves into the presence of God opens us to the power of the Spirit that orders our priorities to see as Jesus sees and to desire what He desires. It is not just that God gave my friend patience (which he certainly did), but perhaps He also allowed her, in some small way, to see this good priest as God sees him. Prayer gives us the grace to move beyond preoccupation with self and, little by little, to put on the mind of Christ.

Achieving Strength in Our Weakness

February 26, 1995

I always await the coming of Lent with a sense of foreboding. I know that it is a season of enormous grace, but the grace comes as I respond to the difficult call of the Church to prayer, fasting and almsgiving. Lent invites me to go with the Lord for forty days into the desert where I can reflect on how weak is my attachment to Him and how strongly I am attracted to the world. The little habits of self-indulgence, whether as simple as the TV on as background noise while dressing in the morning or the drink before dinner each night become surprisingly important when, all of a sudden, I resolve to give them up.

Many can remember when the Church mandated fasting for the days of Lent. Whether dropping the rules of fasting was a wise move or not can be debated, but the change in the rule certainly did not mean that we are discouraged from this ancient form of self-denial. What the Church was after, I believe, was to encourage people to freely choose forms of mortification rather than have them simply obey an imposed Church law. Whether people have so responded is a question that, I am sure, cannot be clearly answered; but surely, the life of faith that has no fasting or self-denial is impoverished. Saying no, for the love of God, to the cravings of the flesh is a form of prayer that is both difficult and powerful.

While Jesus did fast when He was in the desert, His primary aim during those days was to be in communion with the Father in prayer. This second practice of Lent, prayer, should always be a part of the Christian life, but Lent calls us to more disciplined attention to our personal relationship with God. I am sure prayer has never been easy for most people, but I am also sure it must be more difficult for a society so beset by noise and outside distraction. Many, especially if they have never tried to develop a serious life of prayer, find silence intimidating; there is a kind of fear that if I stop to listen for the Lord, I will hear nothing. Ultimately, in some small way, we must try the silence of the desert where no human distraction stands between us and God.

Looking Inward, Then Upward

June 30, 1996

One of the most vivid memories of my life is that of the first Friday night I spent in the seminary. Since we had Saturday classes, Friday was just another study evening. The first week really had not been as bad as I had expected (probably could not have been), but now it was Friday and I obediently sat at my desk. I remember perfectly how the lamp's light showed the creamy institutional yellow of the wall, and then it hit me, "What am I doing in this place on a Friday night?" I remembered the Friday evenings of a few months earlier when I had been a senior in college and the comparison was not helpful. Well, I got through the first Friday night and the first year in the seminary. That first year was really the last of the "old style" seminary education where, as much as possible, the administration tried to have the seminarian's every waking minute occupied. During that first year, though, I was exposed to one valuable spiritual practice that, only recently, I have begun to understand and appreciate—that of the daily examination of conscience.

In those days, I saw examination of conscience as that which I did before confession: trying to discover my sins; and, of course, that is probably the most important aspect. However, I am starting to realize that the greatest natural gift that God gave to us is the gift of freedom, the gift that allows us to make choices. The daily examen, as it is sometimes called, invites us to focus on the choices that we make; and especially, it allows us to see our habitual choices. For example, as I began to look at what I was going to do for Lent this year, I discovered that I was gradually watching more and more television. It was not that I was neglecting my work so much that I was using free time in front of the TV instead of reading, something I have always loved to do. This is no sin, but I had to face the fact that I was not choosing the best use of my time. Likewise, the daily examen might reveal that a person is often in the situation where he is sought out for a listening ear. God might want a person to understand a gift that has been given so that the gift can be used for others.

The daily examen need not take five minutes a day. I simply put myself in the presence of God and ask for wisdom to see the day I spent as God sees that day. I thank Him for the good choices I have made and ask His forgiveness for the ways I have fallen short. The daily examen, taken seriously for a period of time, begins to reveal how the gift of freedom is being used.

Our Lady of the Beltway Traffic

October 13, 1996

There are a lot of good things about being a parish priest. One of the best is that we live where we work. Actually, since people always know where to catch us, maybe it is not always so good; but today at least, having a commute that involves going downstairs seems wonderful, because today it is pouring outside. The Beltway, I hear, is an obstacle course of jack-knifed trucks and the forecast tells us that the evening will be worse. Some people, no doubt, get used to it; but I know how frustrated I would be.

This, of course, is a strange introduction to a discussion of the rosary. Stay with me: I think I can tie up the daily grind of the commute with the praying of the rosary. The origins of the rosary as we know it are not exactly clear, but the number of Hail Mary's in the devotion, one hundred and fifty, give a good clue as to how it got started. "One hundred and fifty," some might be thinking, "there are only fifty Hail Mary's." Remember, the whole rosary contains all three sets of Mysteries, the joyful, the sorrowful and the glorious. Originally, the recitation of one hundred and fifty prayers, usually Our Fathers, was for monks and laity who could not read but who wanted to be a part of the daily recitation of the one hundred and fifty psalms in the monasteries. By the time of the early Middle Ages, there was the custom of stringing beads together to count the prayers. The custom of focusing both on Our Lady, with the praying of the Hail Mary, and on the mysteries of the Lord's life, death and resurrection, evolved over two or three centuries; but by 1500, the rosary was much as we find the devotion today.

Note though, that the origin of the rosary was in the desire of illiterate Christians who could not pray the psalms to sanctify the day. Our challenge is not illiteracy, of course, but time. The days of most, especially commuters, are over filled. However, I submit, that most have one period of enforced isolation, the daily commute. Will a rosary said on the Beltway be a prayer of sublime communion with God? I doubt it, there are too many distractions. But, for the many whose daily prayer is almost non existent, taking these fifteen minutes, with the radio off, to be in the presence of God and Our Lady, is a wonderful sign to the Lord that we share the desire of our spiritual ancestors to give each day to Him.

Bumper-To-Bumper Holy Rosary

October 11, 1998

October is the month of the Holy Rosary where the Church reminds us of the value of this beautiful method of prayer. I know that I find the rosary an ever greater gift in my life: not because I pray so well, but because I pray so poorly. Some historians speculate that the origins of the rosary go back to efforts, even before the Middle Ages, to help illiterate lay brothers in monasteries and laity in the fields to pray. The monks could pray the psalms and read the Gospels and in them, find fruit for prayer, but those who could not read had little on which to fall back for spiritual inspiration. (Incidentally, the stained glass windows in the great cathedrals served the same purpose. They could be "read" by the illiterate in such a way that the truths the windows depicted were taught to those who could not read.) At first, apparently, the people were encouraged to pray, for example, fifty Our Fathers. Interestingly, the Hail Mary, as we know it today, was not known before about the twelfth century. Incidentally, the repetition of prayers, which we sometimes find difficult, is a practice known throughout world religions. Strangely enough, the repetition can free the mind from having to find things to say to God and allow the person to hear what God might be saying. Beads strung together to help in the counting of prayers is also a very ancient practice.

The development of the decades of ten Hail Mary's separated by the Our Father and the meditation on particular mysteries of the life of Christ and Our Lady gradually came about as more effort was given to teaching the laity to pray.

The rosary is such a gift for our day because, while we have the ability to read, and thus use Scripture or other spiritual aids in trying to pray, many feel they have not the time. The rosary solves the problem. I know people who pray the rosary on the subway, who say it while commuting, or while going through the torture of running for exercise. Probably they will never become mystics in their prayer, but at least they give time to the Lord each day and ask the prayers of His Mother on behalf of themselves and those they love.

Every car should have a rosary in it. There should never be a long ride in the car with the family without the family rosary being said. It should become habit that when there is a stretch of free time, at least some of that time should be given to God in this wonderful exercise of prayer. No matter when we say it, whether alone or with others, whether in the quiet of the evening or in the chaos of the Beltway, let us use this month of the Rosary to join countless millions who have gone before us in this prayer with Our Lady to the glory of God.

A Grateful Priest

February 18, 1996

In one of those happy "God-incidences" with which life is filled, just a couple of weeks before I celebrated my twenty-fifth anniversary as a priest, I made my annual retreat at Loyola Retreat House. It was an ideal opportunity for me to look at myself as a priest after what I hope might be a little less than half of my life in that vocation.

First of all, there is the sense of gratitude. I cannot imagine myself as anything other than a parish priest. I delight in the marriages and families of my brother and sisters; I cannot begin to imagine my life without the friendship and support of countless married couples. Working with young people continues to be a source of joy and exhilaration for me. And yet, I know well that God could not have given me a way of life more suited to me than priesthood.

One of the other things that came to me was a renewed sense of wonder at the Mystery of Catholic Christianity. All who profess Christ recognize the gap between God and sinful humanity that was closed through the death and resurrection of Jesus. We are truly His adopted brothers and sisters. And yet, it is only in Him that we can approach the Father; consequently, the closer our union with Jesus, the more able we are to give the Father the glory that is His due. I believe that God hears my prayer because I pray in the Spirit of Jesus in which I was immersed in Baptism. And yet, because of all the weakness to which I am subject as a result of the sin of Adam, I am incapable of giving God the glory that is His due. But Jesus, the sinless one, has not these limitations. The genius of Catholicism is that it remembers that, in the sacraments, and most perfectly in the Mass, God is offered perfect praise because Jesus is the great high priest.

Priesthood, then, is first and foremost, to stand as "alter Christus," another Christ, who sacramentally represents Him who calls His people to be a part of that one perfect act of praise which is His sacrificial death and resurrection presented in an unbloody way on the altar at Mass. This priest of only twenty-five years thanks God for his call and begs for prayer that I might become more and more like Him in whose place I stand; that I might, in the way I serve, lead God's people to Him I represent as priest.

Need for Others

As can be easily imagined, one studying to be a priest gives some little bit of thought to the subject of celibacy. Especially for me, this was the case in the months before I was ordained a sub-deacon when, in those days, a man made the promise to remain celibate. The funny thing is that I can remember thinking during those decision-making sessions, "Well, I think I would enjoy being a priest. Now, if I just pray hard enough, I'm sure that God will help me to make it on my own. He'll help me not to need anyone."

Well, two out of three is not all bad, I guess. Indeed, I do love being a priest and for sure, I believe as strongly as ever in the need for prayer. However, one thing the good Lord has not done is to help me not to need people. Indeed, while I have come to understand that celibacy certainly means not having that one person with whom life can be shared; I have also come to see that celibacy is given so that one can be more involved with God's people. My seminary meditations where I thought the ideal was to be the great independent who can operate in a splendid isolation was, however, not too far from much in contemporary relationships. I apologize, but again I go back to the example I mentioned a few weeks ago where the large number of one of our second grade classes, when I asked them in a class last year, had eaten the dinner the previous night by themselves in front of a television. I even saw an ad the other day for some kind of microwave dessert "perfect for the busy family who must grab dinner on their own." Maybe it sounds corny, but how many husbands and wives would list their spouses as best—even one of their best—friends? As a priest, I worry that many seem not to take their relationship with God seriously enough; I suspect that as good a question is how seriously we take our relationships with those around us.

These thoughts are not written as some sort of first venture into "pop psychology." Marriages, families and larger communities increasingly are disaster zones. Could it be that we do not take each other seriously enough? The Bible says that we are made in the image and likeness of God; that means, first of all, that each of us reflects the Mystery who is God and cannot be taken for granted. It also means that, like God, each of us is endlessly fascinating and lovable. We need each other, much as we need God Himself. The interdependence between God, self and others gives lie to the notion that, "I can make it on my own."

Sin of a Priest

February 12, 1995

When I heard and read the stories of sexual abuse of a teenager in the seventies that involved four priests of our Archdiocese, one of the thoughts that came to me was that these things were going on just as I was starting my priesthood and also, that I attended a couple of meetings in the rectory where, at the time, these crimes were being committed. And yet, even so few years ago, the vast number of priests—young, naive and newly ordained, as I was then, or experienced and older—would have been horrified and uncomprehending at the manner of activities taking place at other times in that same home. Men ordained to stand before God's people in the place of His Son were, at the same time, abusing that trust in ways that disgust the healthy imagination. I am ashamed and, on behalf of this Archdiocese, I can only repent for the terrible scandal that has been given; for the numbers who, perhaps, will cease to live as Catholics, because of their disillusionment.

Am I sorry that this has become public? Certainly it was easier to operate in the atmosphere in which I was ordained: but that is the atmosphere, perhaps, that allowed such actions to go undetected. No, for all the horror and anger these disclosures bring forth, it is better that the truth be known. The Church is certainly divine because it is filled with the Spirit; but, it is also a Church of sinners, and the better we know the power of sin, the better we can fight against it. The Church, which learns more and more about the phenomenon of pedophilia, becomes ever more able to treat those who suffer from it; and, more importantly, she begins to be able to spot people in whom the condition may exist.

I have had the joy of working fairly closely with the vocations office of the Archdiocese over the years. I often laugh at the twenty minute interview that preceded my acceptance as a candidate for the priesthood. Today, the process of interviews, of psychological evaluations, and of conversations with those who know the candidate well are geared, of course, toward discerning proper spiritual motivation and maturity, but also, they are tools that allow the Church to, pray God, spot psychological problems of which we scarcely dreamed when I was ordained. Everyone knows that the numbers in the seminary are down; not everyone recognizes how many, today, are rejected even before entering.

Pray for your priests. Sin in any of us is horrible and has horrible consequences; but the sin of a priest—especially when so repulsive—can have especially terrible consequences. Pray for those who suffer from such sin and pray for the Body of Christ, so wounded by such actions, that it will allow, somehow, the grace of God to bring good out of such evil.

Cardinal Hickey: Church-Man

September 15, 1996

Last Sunday afternoon, I was part of a large crowd that filled the Shrine to celebrate Mass with Cardinal Hickey as he commemorates fifty years of priesthood. This year is also the Holy Father's fiftieth anniversary. The Cardinal, as is required under current Church law, has submitted his resignation to the Holy Father, though he professes to have no idea when it will be accepted. While we may pray that God give to each of them continued long years of service, I must confess that my thoughts turned to what each of these men, and especially Cardinal Hickey, has given to the Church in their half century of priesthood.

For a few years in the eighties, not too long after Cardinal Hickey came to Washington, I served in the Pastoral Center as the Director of the Permanent Diaconate. While I have thanked God every day since for a return to parish work, the job did give me the chance to learn a little about how the Archdiocese works at the administrative level. Among the important lessons was the insight of an older priest working there. While discussing the Archbishop one day, this priest remarked that, "He is a church-man in every sense of the word." Cardinal Hickey and, obviously, the Pope have given their whole lives to serving Christ in the Church. For example, within a year of his ordination in Saginaw, Michigan, the young Fr. Hickey was taken out of parish work and sent to Rome to begin graduate work. While, certainly, the Cardinal has had many of the pastoral satisfactions that are the daily lot of the parish priest, it is also true that his life has been given to administrative duties that many priests would not trade for the personal interaction and friendships of parish life. I am not saying that I would not have that same devotion to the Church as institution (I pray I would), but I surely can say that I stand in awe of a self-giving that must have so few personal satisfactions.

The service of both the Pope and Cardinal Hickey reminds us that Catholic Christianity celebrates and makes Christ Jesus present in the context of Church community. Yes, community is people; but community is also organization and structure and, when the structure is focused on the mission of the Church, the whole community benefits. This priest, who so enjoys the pastoral dimension of my vocation, thanks God for Cardinal Hickey, who has given himself so generously to the institutional Church. His work has made and makes my work much easier. God bless you, Your Eminence, and thank you for being the "church-man" that you are.

Journey of Two Holy Pastors

January 24, 1999

At the very core of my spiritual life, at the center of who I am as a spiritual being, is the profound prayer that I utter prostrated before the living God: THANK GOD FOR CELIBACY! For what seems like months now, I have been getting boxes together, I have been discovering pin-striped pajamas from Christmases long past and putting them into new Germantown cubbyholes and I have decided once again to keep books given by kind parishioners from four parishes ago in the expectation that I will sometime have seven or eight months with nothing to do but to read books "that I really think you'll like, Father." But, as that moment when I near the choice to close the door, put plywood over it and paint it so that Fr. Meyers will not even know the space is there and I can leave the stuff forever, I think to myself, "Suppose, Wells, you were married with five kids and got transferred to Dallas." (Well, actually I'd quit the job if I had to live in Cowboy's territory.) At such moments, I lift my head and heart to the Lord and say, "THANK GOD FOR CELIBACY!"

These days, of course, have also been filled with gratitude and more than a bit of sadness. The gratitude I tried to express at Mass last Sunday; but, I must say, that the notes I received at the reception after the 9:00 o'clock Mass filled me with a thanks that comes close to awe. That God could ever use me to touch peoples' lives in some of the ways described shows not only how hard up He must get sometimes, but also the gift of being called by Him to proclaim the Good News. The sadness comes from leaving, of course, but also from the news of that same Sunday of the death of Msgr. Adam Kostick.

As many remember, Msgr. served here as pastor for a few years in the early eighties. I did not know Msgr. Kostick well since he was quite a bit older than I, but I clearly remember (and identify with) his disappointment when he was transferred from Lourdes after too short a time because of some need the Cardinal must have perceived at St. Mary's in Rockville. I know also that he was one of those priests, so characteristic of his generation, who always put the Church as his first priority. He served in World War II, and the discipline and awareness of the need to put yourself at the disposal of the greater good were qualities he brought to the priesthood. The story in the Post tells us that Msgr. Kostick died after the consecration of the Sunday Mass. Could God give to any priest a greater gift than to be with his people doing that which makes his priesthood most worthwhile, at the moment when he is called to the full experience of the heavenly banquet? May God grant Monsignor Adam Kostick life eternal.

A Concise History of the Sacrament of Penance

October 23, 1994

I have been reading, for the last few weeks, Thomas Bokenkotter's, *A Concise History of the Catholic Church* and, of course, have read again, a bit of the history of the development of the Sacrament of Penance. While the Church never questioned that Christ had given her the power to forgive sin, the way in which the power was to be exercised evolved through the first one thousand years of the Christian era. In the early centuries, when the examples of the martyrs and hermits going into the desert to do battle with the devil were so much a part of Christian life, there was a high expectation of spiritual rigor on the part of the believer, and when there was serious sin, there was very serious penance before reconciliation. The expression, "sackcloth and ashes," comes from this period and refers to what was worn during long periods of public penance before absolution was granted.

Alas, human nature being what it is, the average Catholic fell short of the ideal of spiritual perfection; also, recognizing the fierceness of penances demanded before reconciliation, the custom developed of putting off confession until just before death. Not until the Irish monks virtually reconverted Europe after the barbarian invasions, did the practice begin of Penance as we would recognize it. It was the Irish who encouraged regular confession that was followed by private penances—still strict by our standards, but which could be performed in a short period of time. For well over a thousand years, the Church has built upon the Irish practice and has seen frequent confession as important in spiritual development. In the last thirty years or so, many Catholics seem to be reverting to the earlier practice of confession only in extreme situations. Is this a promising development?

This week and next, I would like to give my answer to this question based on my experiences as confessor. Especially I want to look at the sacrament from the perspectives of honesty, growth and focus. Grace perfects nature, as the Church has taught throughout history. A culture that preaches human perfectibility finds it hard to accept human moral limitation and so begins to pretend that what cannot be overcome by human effort is, therefore, OK. Perhaps nowhere does the Church challenge the pessimistic attitude of the world more than in her celebration of reconciliation after sin. Tune in next week.

The Gift of the Sacrament of Penance
January 15, 1995

As a boy, the custom in our neighborhood on Saturdays was often to go to the Avalon Theatre on Connecticut Avenue for the movies. Since it was only about a mile and a half from there to home, we would, of course, walk or ride our bikes. Also, since we had to walk right by the church, we would usually stop for confession on the way home. One Saturday, I guess my mother must have asked if I planned to go to confession and I must have said I did not want to go that day. Her response was, "He only made seven sacraments, so go to confession." I guess I went.

Unlike my father, my mother was not interested in deep thinking about religion, but she had the kind of faith that said, roughly, it is a sacrament and if Jesus gave it to us, it is kind of dumb not to use it. But so many of us do not use it. Yes, on a Saturday we are busy hearing confessions; but usually only one priest is hearing. Yes, at Christmas and Easter we hear hundreds of confessions, but I can tell you that these confessions represent only a small fraction of our Catholics and, here I am really guessing, only one half of those who go to Mass weekly. I have some ideas why folks do not go to confession, but would rather dwell on the grace that flows from worthily celebrating the Sacrament.

Grace, of course, is precisely the point. Was not the definition of the Baltimore Catechism that "grace is a supernatural gift from God that enlightens the mind and strengthens the soul to do good and avoid evil?" The sacraments are the primary ways in which we have the opportunity to encounter God and to grow in His life within us. In addition, each of the sacraments confers a particular grace that is unique to that sacrament. Open up the paper in the morning. Who would question that we live in an era of moral laxity and in a time where truth, civil behavior and honesty are less than taken for granted? In the face of these declining standards, is it not interesting that two of the sacramental graces of Penance are strength in the fight against sin and the inner vision that allows us to see sin at work within ourselves?

It is not that most of us are evil in some classical sense of that word. Rather, I think the Catholic population is, to a great extent, morally retarded, not really aware of the battle between good and evil in which we are involved, whether we like it or not. On the other hand, I have seen it happen too many times for it to be simply coincidental: when a person begins to take confession seriously, he grows, for God is not a liar. When we ask for forgiveness, He gives it; when we ask for strength against temptation, He gives it; when we ask for insight to know our moral weakness, He gives it. This is what the Sacrament of Penance is all about; how stupid of us not to accept the gift.

A Gift to Be Used

December 4, 1994

I had time over Thanksgiving to spend some time with a family with whom I have been close since the early years of my priesthood. One of their older sons has gotten a pretty good job in Atlanta and was visiting for the holiday. We had the opportunity to talk and, shy though I am, I nailed him about his spiritual life, especially since the early glow of being away from home and making pretty big money has begun to fade. "Do you get to Mass every Sunday?" I asked, only to receive the not surprising, "Probably not as often as I should." However, to my next question, "When was the last time you went to confession?" I was happily surprised to hear that he had been to the Shrine that weekend and that he usually goes when he is in the area. I assured him that he is allowed to go to confession even when he is in Atlanta, but I have to admit that his answer reassured me. I am not saying that Penance is as important as the Eucharist, of course, but I do believe that, very often, it is the foundation on which God builds a solid spiritual life. The person who will face his sinfulness and who recognizes God as the source of forgiveness and growth eventually will experience the increasing spiritual strength.

I know that people have hang-ups about confession and that each of them must be dealt with individually. Theological questions can be answered, usually fairly easily, but it is tough to answer a question that is never asked. I have said and written this before but, since I still believe it, I will write it again: the saddest aspect of contemporary Catholicism is the abandonment by so many, and with so little apparent thought, of the Sacrament of Penance. That God would say, in so many words, "I know that your biggest problem is sin; I know you cannot overcome it by yourself; but I will give you a special gift that, in a personal way, allows you to overcome this problem," and that we, in turn, say, "I do not need it," is not only arrogant, but unspeakably sad. The good Lord is in the business of giving mercy, strength and forgiveness, but He will not force us out of the mediocrity and vague unhappiness that comes from sin. He offers the grace in Penance. We must accept it.

Lourdes is participating in the "Come Home for Christmas" program with a number of other parishes near metro stations. It seeks, primarily, to invite those who have been away from the sacraments to come home to the Church. Believe me, though, when I tell you that there are many whose spirituality is incomplete because they are not dealing regularly with the realities of sin and reconciliation and they may be at Mass every week. They too are encouraged, during this wonderful season of homecomings, to be renewed and reconciled through the Sacrament of Penance.

Grace Through Confession

October 30, 1994

Isn't it funny the things that stick with you? I was thinking today of something one of the nuns said in some religion class when I was in grade school. "You're either getting better or you're getting worse. You can't stay the same." Even today, that kind of frightens me. While I probably do not feel a great passion to be a saint, I also most surely do not want to grow worse in my relationship with God. Hence, one of the reasons I am most grateful for frequent confession: it is an aid in the daily growth away from sin and toward the Lord.

Theologians tell us that grace perfects nature, but most of us are probably willing to concede that any kind of important human growth takes place very slowly and is often impossible to notice. Honesty with self, for example, sometimes grows only gradually with the grace of conversion. Often a penitent will begin to confront a troubled relationship by, virtually, giving the confession of the other. But it is amazing how, with frequent confession and submission to grace, he or she gradually begins to see within, the force and power of sin. One of the strongest of these powers is that of self-deception where, without fully recognizing what I do, I can slyly change the focus of my conscience, so that dishonesty within seems fully justified. How gentle, and yet how persistent and strong is the grace of frequent confession, that challenges me to see myself as God sees me and allows me to stop blaming others for problems for which I bear much responsibility.

The same is true with establishing and clarifying a focus for life. One thing about the Lord is that He is quiet and will stay in the background unless we invite Him to come forward. Achieve this; your children need that; work is everything; pleasure brings happiness; money talks: who can blame anyone for losing focus, or worse, being focused on a hundred different things—some of them contradicting each other and contradicting the demands of the Gospel. Grace, the life of God within us, is indeed quiet; but again, the grace of frequently confronting my tendency toward sin in confession is one that allows me to sift through the conflicting calls of the world around me and to focus on what is the authentic call of God. That grace is, I guess partly, the grace of humility. I am neither smart enough nor wise enough to keep my eye on the goal which is, "life on high." Thank God for the grace of Penance that will forgive me for focusing, so often, on the creature instead of the Creator and which will take the scales from my eyes so that I can see, ever more clearly, the things of God.

Grace of Frequent Confession

June 21, 1998

During a period of about four or five years, I served as a confessor to a convent of about twenty sisters. This meant that every two weeks, I would go across town for a couple of hours to hear the confessions of those who chose to take advantage of the sacrament on that particular day. How does one put this politely? Well, let me say only that these women took their vocations very seriously and, happily, they had little "serious matter" to confess. In other words, on more than a few afternoons, with the sun shining warmly into the room where he sat, Father had to be gently called back to full awareness of what he was doing. Boy, was I bored! And then, as God would have it, something happened. Since I was there for four or five years and, therefore, heard the same sisters' confessions regularly over that time, I began to notice changes in the sisters. Without even their fully noticing, these individuals, in ways unique to their spiritual journeys, showed the graces of the sacrament in their lives. Impatience with this or that sister began to fade; stubbornness in the face of authority became a bit less challenging, or frustration with the girls in the school showed itself only after just a bit more provocation.

I had always heard that the sacramental grace of confession is that we are gradually given the help to turn away from habitual sin. These sisters, already close to God, showed me how grace, over time, gently turns us away from all that is not of God. What is true for religious women can, of course, be true for any of us; and interestingly, I also see it here at Lourdes. As you know, we hear confessions daily from 11:30 to noon. Because confession is so available, we get many people from the offices nearby. Most go behind the screen, so, in one sense, I have no idea who they are; but as with those sisters, it is fascinating (and inspiring) to hear the spiritual journeys of individuals. And unlike the sisters, some begin that journey after years away from confession. Habits of sin, I have come to believe, are addictive in some ways and, therefore, are hard to break. One of the reasons I have come to love hearing confessions is that it is such a thrill to hear of the gradual victory over the addiction to habits of sin. We are tough and stubborn—almost like sidewalk concrete—but given an opening in ourselves, grace can gradually destroy the hardness of sin.

St. Paul says that faith is the ability to believe in things unseen. So many Catholics seem to have lost faith in the Sacrament of Penance. The act of confessing sins can be, of course, tough. It is true, certainly, that venial sins are forgiven through receiving communion, for example; and therefore, there is no obligation, in the strict sense, to celebrate the Sacrament of Penance unless there is serious sin. Obligation is one thing; opportunity is another. What a tremendous gift that promises that, in time and with God's grace, we can gradually move away from those petty habits of sin that so impede us from living the life of Christ. May God continue to draw people back to regular use of this wonderful Sacrament of Reconciliation.

Corporate Penance

February 16, 1997

Where there is sin, there has to be sorrow for sin. There, as simply as it can be put, is the reason for penance. We have signs, the sacraments are examples, that point to the sources of our joy. What are the signs that point to our sorrow for, and rejection of, sin? Jonah preached repentance to the people of Nineveh and their reformation was shown by their wearing sackcloth and ashes. The penance performed after confession is supposed to be a sign on our part not only of our gratitude for absolution, but also of our sorrow for the sins we have committed. But, how powerful a sign is this penance? The former practices of Lent made obligatory daily fasting during the season. When these laws were dispensed, the thought was that individuals would choose their own form of Lenten observance. The fact that many people did, in fact, not choose such practices is one unfortunate thing; also unfortunate, I believe, is that we lost a sense of corporate penance. We perhaps have lost a sense that, as a Church, we fall short of what we are called to be as God's people. The reality of sin in the community should cause sorrow in us as a people, and the sign of corporate penance and fasting was probably a good thing.

Tradition speaks of the world, the flesh and the devil as the sources of temptation. Another justification for penance and mortification is the battle against the flesh. It is a false spirituality that speaks only of union with God in prayer and love of neighbor without considering that the being with such exalted aspirations (namely, me) comes clothed in flesh that makes demands both subtle and powerfully obvious. Just as the out-of-shape body is not prepared for hockey and will quickly retire from the game, so the body used to catering to every physical and sensual desire, to every craving for warmth, food or pleasure will be quickly and surely distracted when the impulse to serious prayer or service comes its way. Look at how many impulses to do good cross our minds; see also how often they slip by because of supposed fatigue or the desire to satisfy some superficial desire for entertainment. We do no battle with even the simplest desires of the flesh and, consequently, the flesh exerts enormous control over our lives.

So often I deal with individuals addicted to sins, often of the flesh. They find it impossible to contemplate living without the vice. It is a very long way, I admit, between that kind of sinful addiction and living a Christian life without penance and mortification; but they are on the same continuum. Over and over Scripture calls us to prayer and fasting. Any Lenten observance lacking the battle against the flesh is incomplete.

The Grace of Seeing Who We Really Are

September 27, 1998

It is while celebrating Mass that I sometimes have the strongest impression of personal sinfulness in my life. For example, at the words in the consecration where the priest, taking the place of Jesus, says to God the Father, "He gave you thanks and praise...," I will sometimes try to imagine the praise and gratitude of Jesus, the purity of His prayer, even though this was the night before He was to offer Himself in sacrifice for our sins. But, just as I try to imagine His self-giving and love, I remember some aspect of how impure is my thanks and praise to the Father. It might be some failure of this particular day or a continuing temptation in my life or—and this is always a tough one—the impurity of my motives, where maybe I do the right thing, but with motives that are both good and not so good. It is very like the image Jesus Himself uses of the cup that looks okay on the outside, but is full of impurities within.

The way I have this experience is perhaps unique to me because I am a priest, but it is a grace that is often given to each according to his state in life. Yes, as much as I hate to be reminded of my tendency toward sin and of how far I am from being what my priesthood calls me to be, the experience is a grace. A married friend knows the same feeling: he knows how good is his wife, how wonderful she is as wife and mother, and he hates how poorly he responds to that love. Yes, he knows it is a great marriage, but he clearly sees the reality of sin that threatens even something so good.

What is being experienced is the "tension and struggle of the human heart," as the Holy Father describes it in "Dominum et Vivificantem," his encyclical on the Holy Spirit; or as St. Paul put it first (Gal 5:17), "The desires of the flesh are against the Spirit, and the desires of the Spirit are against the flesh." As we open ourselves to the Spirit, we become aware of how far we are from living fully the life of that Spirit.

As a ballplayer, I suspect Cal Ripkin has never assumed he was good enough; he is known for his training and for looking for his weaknesses. In the spiritual life, if we do not allow the Lord to show us the ugliness of sin within us—ugliness as compared to Him, not to some obviously evil scapegoat who lives down the street—we will never grow. One of the graces of frequent confession is that the Lord gradually reveals to us who we really are and what we are called to be. It is not a happy revelation, but it is surely hard to grow without it.

Confession: Antidote for Self Deception

March 2, 1997

You have probably noticed that a little landscaping had to be done on the side of the property next to Waverly House. During the last (we hope) sleet storm, a huge branch fell off one of the tall maples and blocked the driveway and broke one of the windows at Waverly House. A friend who is in the tree business gave me a good price, but he also said that three of the trees were seriously diseased and in danger of coming down. Most of the work is now done and, as a matter of fact, I told them to leave the wood for any who might want to take it for home fireplaces. It will need splitting, though; these were big trees.

But I got to thinking about those trees. They looked, at least to me, great; but they were rotten inside and ready to collapse. I am sure you can see where I am headed—the difference between appearance and reality. We know we are not supposed to be judgmental, but let us be honest. Most of us know people who appear to be in fine shape, but who, we suspect, have values and opinions very different than what they seek to convey. In fact, many of us are very perceptive at noticing the difference between appearance and reality in other people.

Self-deception is something else again. I often think of the woman who came in to see me early in my years in Bowie. She did not go to church; she did not agree with the Church about this or that and, especially, she saw no sense in the whole question of Confession. Somehow, I began sharing with her some thoughts on the Parable of the Prodigal Son and how the self-righteous second son who never did anything wrong was actually the great sinner in the story. All of a sudden, she almost yelled out, "You mean I'm a sinner!" She said it two or three times, each time with greater amazement. For some reason, listening to that story, she allowed her defenses to drop and let the Lord show her just a bit of who she really was, as compared to the person she wanted to appear to herself.

Probably the saddest phenomenon of the "new Church," is the near disuse of the Sacrament of Penance. Sad because I suspect any confessor has experienced that one of the great fruits of this sacrament is the grace that allows us to see the reality in our lives. In frequent confession I open myself to the healing light of Christ which gradually illuminates the dark rot of sin from which, because it is so unflattering, I understandably try to hide.

I am not by nature a pessimist, but, my friends, I suspect that more than a few of us appear far better to ourselves than we really are. Regular confession should be part of any Catholic life. If it is not, beware of that self-deception.

The Prodigal Son

June 7, 1998

"You mean I'm a sinner!" the woman exclaimed. Two or three times she said the same thing, "You mean I'm a sinner!" She had come into the rectory on a Saturday morning, outraged because we insisted on preparing her child for confession before Communion. (Happily, this is not a recent story.) A child could not sin; a child needed to know the joy of Christianity, not guilt; a child could be damaged by trying to find the negative in her life. And so it went until, as she had become a bit more calm, I asked her about her own use of the Sacrament of Penance and about the reality of sin in her life. Finally, we read together the story of the Prodigal Son (Luke 15) and discussed the figure of the second son in that story. You may remember him as the son who stayed at home, never did anything wrong in terms of actions, but who had a heart that was fixed on himself rather than either his father (God) or others (his brother). It was as I was talking about the older brother's self-righteousness and judgmental attitude that, out of the blue, she cried out her question. Shortly thereafter, she went to confession; I guess the child soon did the same; and I have no clue about what became of either mother or daughter.

Read over the story of the Prodigal Son if you are not familiar with it. While we focus on the colorful younger son who spends all his money on loose women, it seems that Jesus was primarily focused on that older son. One of the many lessons of the story is that, while the younger son was most certainly a sinner and most certainly had to pay the consequences of his sin, his realization of his need for his father's forgiveness gives him a nobility when compared to the older brother who really believes that doing all that he has done around the farm entitles him to happiness. Because he focuses on actions and things, rather than on his hard heart, he completely misses the Father's love that calls to him as surely as it called to the Prodigal Son.

When an individual says, in actions if not in words, that he does not need the Sacrament of Penance, could he not be imitating the older son? Can any of us listen to Jesus as He says, "Come, follow me," and really believe that selfishness, fear or lack of faith have not kept us from really obeying? Sin is not so much a stain on our souls, I believe, as a disease which we must always fight. Is it possible on the one hand, to believe in the damaging power of that disease, and on the other, not to take advantage of the antidote, the Sacrament of Penance?

Be Reconciled with Your Brother

March 20, 1994

Several weeks ago, as I was walking from rectory to school, a woman walking a dog approached me on the sidewalk. I greeted her, but was not prepared for her response: "Don't talk to me, you are an evil person." To which, hoping I had misheard, I responded, "Excuse me?" She said, "You priests are the worst people in the world." At that point, I confess I laughed and asked, "Even worse than Stalin, Hitler and Pol Pot?" She huffed, perhaps agreeing that priests are, indeed, worse than these figures and continued on her way.

Of course, it was not too long after this that the Gospel reading at Mass told us, "If you bring your gift to the altar and remember your brother has something against you, leave your gift at the altar and go and be reconciled with your brother." (Mt.5.23) The most important thing about the command of the Lord is that He does not say that my brother has to be right in having something against me. In other words, it is possible that priests are not the most evil people in the world; it is even possible that I am not entirely evil. In short, my acquaintance may be wrong in her evaluation of the world ranking of priests. However, she does have something against me, and although things I may have felt like saying were not said before we parted, we surely were not reconciled, nor had I made an attempt at reconciliation. Whether it was bad experiences or life-long prejudice or simply the frustration of a bad hair day that motivated her remarks, she quite clearly was in need of the reconciling power of God in her life.

Have no fear, I am not consumed by guilt over the incident. The encounter, however, does remind me of something very important. Jesus lived His life entirely focused on the good of the other. It took me God knows how long before I could get over the stupidity of her remarks and my defensiveness about them and begin to ask what would have made her say what she said. Jesus wants us to be reconciled with those who have something against us, not because we are guilty of something wrong (though sometimes we probably are), but because any unreconciled person runs the danger of being outside the community of God's life and love. Surely, that woman is wrong and surely her anger is abrasive: but surely too, she is loved by God and He wants her to be reconciled with His love, mercy and truth. "Father, forgive them; they know not what they do."

We must constantly pray for the Holy Spirit to take over our lives because, by ourselves, we will most often react to situations from the perspective of self rather than the good of the other. In fact, to see things from the perspective of the other's good will seem absurd. It is precisely the absurdity of a God who loves us enough to die for us even though we are His killers. It is to that absurdity to which we are called as followers of Jesus.

A Balm for Guilt

March 10, 1996

I am a great believer in guilt; but I am an even greater believer in forgiveness. I do not know if psychology gives a precise meaning of the word guilt; for me, it is the voice of conscience that confronts me with the reality of sinful choices I have made. By way of small example, I look at the battlefield map that is my desk and I am confronted with letters not yet answered. They may not be answered because of an overwhelming desire to communicate with the writers, but they will be answered because of a conscience that challenges my laziness and selfishness. For me, that is an aspect of what I call "good old Catholic guilt."

Believer though I am in guilt, I am even more of a believer in God's forgiveness. The focal point of my celebration of that forgiveness is the National Shrine, in the little chapel off the Crypt where confessions are heard daily for five or six hours. Thanks be to God, mortal sin at least for now, is not a problem in my life, but there are still those times when I see a choice or failing of mine in such a way that I am disgusted with my willingness to sin. Surely I believe that venial, lesser sins, can be forgiven just by saying an act of contrition or, for that matter, by receiving Communion; but for me, there is power in the words of absolution spoken by the Church. Also, especially when confronting habits of sin, I also rely on the power of the sacramental grace to gradually give me the strength to overcome habitual weakness.

At the Shrine, when the line is long (as it often is), impatient me will often shorten the line by going into another box and starting to hear confessions. Because the Shrine is so anonymous, a confessor gets a beautiful insight into the power of the sacrament. This is where people with the "biggies" often come, rather than their parish. What a beautiful experience, there or anywhere, to be a part of a person's being able to make that crucial step in a journey back to God. What a beautiful thing to say, in the power of Jesus' Name, "your sins are forgiven," and to allow a person to shed the gloom and pain of guilt.

It is tragic that so many have given up Confession: tragic, because, they lack the insight-giving grace of the sacrament. But, before it is tragic, it is sad. How sad that the dear Lord would give us so healing a balm for the guilt that is the result of our sin and we should turn away from that gift in pretense that we have no need of it.

We Are Most Like God When We Forgive

August 7, 1994

I guess if experience is the best teacher it is no surprise that some of the wisest things that I have ever heard have been spoken by elderly people to whom I have taken communion over the years. At any rate, I often think of the woman who, for reasons I can no longer remember, said one day, "Father, I think we are most like God when we forgive."

Obviously, as a priest, I have the opportunity to do a bit of spiritual direction and counseling. One of the things I am confronted with is the real abuse that some people suffer, often at the hands of those who should be the most supportive and loving in a person's life. I think of the call I received just last night from a young person now living in another part of the country, who has to contend with belittling remarks from parents about choice of job, girlfriend and dreams for a lifetime. This person has been told that he is not worth the money spent raising him. Let me assure you, both job and girlfriend would bring joy to most parents. Of course, he keeps calling his parents because he so much wants their approval and some sign of their love for him and, of course, he almost certainly will not get them. So eventually, because we can take only so much putting down, he will probably be tempted to give in to resentment, anger and even hatred against the source of so much pain.

No one, I hope, will be surprised when I say that when I sit and listen to some of these tales of unrelieved pain and of the resentment that so often is the result, I often feel like saying, "Right on." As when we watch the pictures of the starving in Rwanda, there is understandable anger at those who inflict such suffering and the desire to inflict revenge. The problem is that when we give in to these temptations we often choose that which we would most hate: to pass on to another generation what we have suffered. Revenge and anger seem so understandable; they are so destructive.

No, the only alternative is, in that marvelous phrase of St. Paul, "to put on Christ." From God's perspective, forgiving us must seem absurd. After all, here we go again, with the same old sins; but because God is love, forgiveness flows from the heart of that love. The prayer to see those who have hurt us as God sees them is a very hard prayer, but as God answers it, we gradually receive the power to forgive as God forgives. Make no mistake, the alternative to forgiveness is bitterness and, like any inner quality, bitterness cannot be limited toward just this or that person. It spreads. Of course forgiveness is hard; it comes from the heart of Christ Himself. But, just as He will forgive us, He will give us the grace to forgive those who trespass against us.

Gratitude for the Sacrament of Penance

November 10, 1996

I answered the doorbell one recent afternoon to find a young Hispanic man who wanted to go to confession. Since Fr. Roman was not available, I told him that somehow we would make it through the language problem. (After all, was it not always our dream as kids to confess to a priest who was deaf?) At any rate, since many of our words for sin come from Latin and are similar in Spanish and English, we had little problem. Soon he was on his way. As it turns out, I too was soon on my way. He had knocked at the door just as I was about to go out for a run; so, when he left, I did too. Consequently, I had time to think about the attitude of this young man; something I probably never would have thought of if I had not had those few free minutes.

You see, what struck me about him was his gratitude. Happily, I am often humbled by the gratitude of people who express appreciation for the way I perform some priestly task. Because I do try to do things as the Lord would have me, of course I appreciate the thanks of people. But the gratitude of this young man was different. He was thankful not for how I did something, but for what I did. It was obvious that he was grateful for my priesthood. I do not think that it mattered that I could not fully understand him, that I could not listen with compassion and sensitivity to his story. I had what he needed: the power to impart the forgiveness of God for his sins. He was, with probably not too much education, thoroughly Catholic.

Protestantism, to a great extent, rejected the Catholic understanding of sacraments: that they are effective not because of the goodness of either the minister or the recipient, but because of the power of God's Spirit working through physical signs and human words. Much affected by our culture, many American Catholics seek experience rather than sacrament. They choose this parish because of its music; reject another because of its preaching and the philosophy of a third sends shivers up the spine. I am sure my penitent likes some priests better than others; I'll bet he has had some experience with the weak humanity of some priests; but somehow, he communicated to me, through his attitude and gestures, that he had grasped the heart of the Catholic faith: that God, in Christ, has given us a Church, so very human, but also divine, that makes present the saving actions of the Lord until the end of time.

God's Love Gives Us Dignity

April 2, 1995

It is so nice to see something work the way it should. Last June, I received a phone call from former parishioners concerned about a teen-age son whom, they feared, was heading quickly into chaos. In school, his marks, discipline, and attitude were such that they were facing his expulsion. Often, I have found, it is easy for people to run from a problem—only to find that, when we stop running, the problem is still with us. On the other hand, sometimes a new beginning can be just that: a chance to go back to step one and let experience teach a person to take a different second step. And so, I offered to call a high school principal about accepting this young person as a transfer student.

What impressed me was how well the new school handled the young man. Administrators welcomed him, students showed him around the facilities, some whom he had known from grade school "hung out" with him on the day he looked around and teachers promised him extra help in subjects in which he was weak. Then, after he had been made to feel like a million dollars, the principal took him aside, without his parents, and told him that the behavior that had gotten him in trouble in his previous school would be forgotten by both the student and the administration—but, that it would not be repeated. Three quarters of the way through the next school year, the young man is passing everything and has become, in so many ways, a new man.

The wonderful Gospel story of the woman caught in adultery from today's Mass, reminded me of this story. Jesus, by the way He confronted the Pharisees, and by the way He treated the young woman, reminded her of her dignity and of the infinite value she had in the eyes of God. Only after He had given her this essential message of her worth, does He command her, "Go, and commit this sin no more." Like my young friend, she had to be reminded of the glory that was hers as a dearly loved daughter of God before she had the courage to face life without sin. She and my friend two thousand years later, both know their sins—and neither was proud of what they knew about themselves. What they needed to be reminded of is the dignity that is ours because we are loved by God.

So it must be in the Sacrament of Penance. Of course we are sinners: foolish is the person who denies it. My sinfulness, though, is as nothing compared to the love of God and His desire to immerse me in His forgiveness. The woman caught in adultery and my young friend were able to change their lives not because they were so strong, but because, in their weakness, they discovered the power that comes from being loved by God.

Return to the Sacrament of Penance
February 23, 1997

First confessions are this weekend. Experience tells the seasoned confessor to prepare for the worst; but first confessions are always sobering reminders of a world gone wrong. I violate no seal when I relate that there is an awful lot of disobedience around and far too many hit brothers and sisters.

Are our children ready for confession at age seven? Certainly they could have no better preparation than they do in our CCD and school. From that point of view, they are surely ready. But are they ready, too, from the perspective of maturity? Particularly where parents have played a role in preparing children for the sacrament, I find that children can show real insight into sin as the conscious decision to do something that affects relationship with God or neighbor. They may not be too concerned with the details of past sins, but invariably, I will hear confessed something like, "This morning I got mad at my brother and I hit him real hard." There is a consciousness of making a choice that hurts another person.

But what of the parents of these children and, for that matter, what of so many of the adults who seem to have abandoned the use of the sacrament? One cannot read the Scriptures without being confronted with the celebration of Jesus as victor over sin. From the story of Eden to Good Friday, Scripture makes plain that we are a part of a battle between good and evil: a battle that, apart from the grace of God, we are bound to lose. How is it that so many Catholics, given the gift in the Sacrament of Penance, of forgiveness and growth in the battle against sin, seem to have abandoned use of the sacrament? Can they see the disorder in society and think it unrelated to sin; or can anyone think that he or she has no individual part in the sin that is around us? Or rather, will people accept the Protestant objection that says we have only to confess to God and that there is no need of a human intermediary? Of course they have forgotten that the humanity of the priest is at the heart of his role. He represents the Church, our brothers and sisters, and thereby, all whom our sin has hurt. Surely, we should daily confess to God, but confession to a fellow human helps us to realize that it is our fellow humans who are affected by sin. How great the blessing that the Church, torn by our sin, can also reconcile us through our ordained brother.

Despite appearances, I believe that these are happy times for the Church. Many have strayed, often very far away, in recent decades; but I believe many are gradually coming home again. I truly believe though, that for that process to be complete, there must be a return to the Sacrament of Penance. Then can we say, with our young second graders, that we truly are reconciled with God and His Church.

Know the Peace of Christmas and Confession

December 14, 1997

The last words of the Bible (Revelations 22:20) are, "Come, Lord Jesus." They remind us that Christians look forward to the second coming of Jesus when He will come as judge of the living and the dead. Consequently, since Advent not only remembers the coming of Jesus in history on the first Christmas, but also looks forward to His coming at the end of history, that prayer, "Come, Lord Jesus," is particularly associated with Advent. But, of course, it is not only at that time when the world will be no more that we look forward to Jesus' coming, but also now, in the events of daily life do we seek Him.

I am sure there is no hope at Christmas that more touches us than for the peace associated with the holiday. Whether the creche itself, or a snowy scene with smoke rising from a decorated farm house, or a favorite Madonna and Child: so many of our images of the upcoming days call forth our desire for the sense of being at one with God and those around us. The heart of the Christmas story, of course, is that Jesus brings the "peace that the world cannot give," and that, apart from Him, there is no real peace As the bumper sticker (one of the great sources of theology!) says, "No Jesus, no peace. Know Jesus, know peace." Because the principal reason our experience of peace is so limited is the reality of sin in our lives, Catholics thank God that Jesus comes into our lives through the Sacrament of Penance.

More and more, my experience tells me that, while we are—and should be—confessing sins when we go to confession, God's agenda is somewhat different. I believe the Good Lord wants to heal the attitudes and fears deep within us that cause us to commit the sins that so to speak, catch our attention. I may, for example, confess getting angry at another driver. That sin, certainly, is forgiven; but I believe that the grace of frequent confession (what we call the sacramental grace) is that, little by little, that deep-seated anger is overcome.

The Lord really does want to come into our lives; He wants to come as healer and as one who reconciles us to Himself, to others and even to ourselves. In love, He offers us the Sacrament of Penance as that way of coming into our lives; but all the love in the world cannot force us to take advantage of it. May one of the graces of this Christmas be that He leads us back to His gift of Confession.

The March For Life—Why I Go

January 22, 1995

From a political or purely human point of view, the past year was both very good and very bad for the pro-life movement in the United States. Even though it has not been too widely reported, the recent elections brought dozens of new pro-life senators and members of Congress to Washington and, most wonderfully, not one pro-life national legislator or governor lost in the entire country. The bad news, of course, involves the murders by two fanatics at abortion clinics in Florida and Boston. While both killers seem to be somewhat unbalanced, their crimes remind us of the danger of violence begetting violence and that we cannot assume that hating the sin but not the sinner is always easy to do.

Monday's Right to Life March, then, will be held in an atmosphere that is both hopeful and sober. Hopeful because, against all that media wisdom had told us, the American people seem to be saying something important about the value of human life; but there is a sadness as we reflect that some who may have marched with us in earlier years have resorted to evil comparable to that which we protest.

Such reflections aside, the March for Life is one of my favorite events of the year. Of course, I know how important it is that the pro-life community demonstrate against what is the great evil in our society. I truly believe that any complaint by this country against supposed human rights abuses in other nations smacks of hypocritical cynicism as long as we as a nation allow—even encourage—the killing of the unborn. To be honest, though, I have to confess that these reasons of high principle are probably not the main reasons I go year after year to the March.

Do you remember reading about the joyful and enthusiastic crowd that greeted the Pope in Denver? That is the same type of people that come each year, from all over this country and Canada, to the March. It is wonderful to get off our convenient subway and to run into high school students from Scranton, young families from the South and members of parishes who have been on buses for twenty-four straight hours from God-knows-where in the Mid-West and who get back on those buses immediately after the March to return home. Frankly, it is also a wonderful time to see people from this area whom I have known over the years from previous parishes; people who are, really, the heart of the Catholic communities from which they come.

Yes, I go to the Right to Life March to protest abortion; of course, I do. However, I go primarily for myself. I need the encouragement and hope, the joy and the laughs that come from spending an afternoon with people of faith who love life at every stage and who, quite simply, want the unborn to have the same chance to love and live as they have had. See you at the March for Life.

Marching for Unborn Mozarts

January 28, 1996

The Father Wells version of the Right to Life March is one that is all march and no talk. As March veterans know, there is a rally on the Ellipse before the March with speakers from Church, politics and the pro-life movement. I am sure the rally is essential to set focus and all, but, to be honest, standing on the cold, wet Monument grounds for an hour or so does not uplift this marcher. So, generally, I eat lunch at the rectory (an army cannot march on an empty stomach), get on the subway and arrive at Constitution Avenue just as the hard work of trudging those ten or twelve blocks is beginning. Pro-life principles aside, those next two hours are possibly the most uplifting of the year.

This year, as I walked down Thirteenth Street from Metro Center, I stopped a befuddled group of twenty or so resolutely marching up Pennsylvania Avenue, away from the March route. Hoping they were not leaving because of lost principles, I asked if they were lost. It turns out they were from Boston and were disoriented because their bus had been forbidden to bring them downtown because of the floods. They had contended with the subway and, God help them, with add-fare, and were by this time, on the March to nowhere. Soon they were redirected. I had met a priest with them who also went to Boston College; blizzard stories had been exchanged (they exaggerated better than I) and we had gone our separate ways as we joined the March. And so it happens all day long: old friends from high school or other parishes are met, new acquaintances from all over the country and Canada are made and, in general, there is the opportunity to delight in being with thousands of people with whom all the important things are held in common.

Even one abortion is criminal. How many Mozarts have been slaughtered for the sake of convenience? But, the providence of God is wondrous indeed. The realization that this country we have thought to be so good could allow this obscenity has jolted millions of fine people—most of them of faith—into calling out for reform. It will probably take a long time to outlaw abortion, because evil can be easy to live with, but those thousands of people at the March have discovered each other and they represent other thousands from their communities all over the country; and, ultimately, because light conquers darkness and good is stronger than evil and joy is more wonderful than despair, those people will prevail.

One last thought: thank God for the role of the Catholic Church in the pro-life movement. Surely, the Church could do no more; surely, many

Catholics have sold out for various reasons. The Right to Life March, though, with all those from so many religions, demonstrates that, were it not for the Catholic Church, the movement might not exist.

The Absolute Significance of Life
January 18, 1998

The Washington Post reported last week the results of a survey that should bring hope to any who recognize that the twenty-second of January is the twenty-fifth anniversary of Roe vs. Wade: the decision of the Supreme Court in which that body invented and decreed the right to abortion. I am sure that many saw the Post article and so a detailed review is unnecessary. What most gave cheer to me is that the number of college freshmen (the group surveyed) who expressed support for abortion declined for the fifth straight year. A still depressingly high 54% of this group supports abortion rights, but this is down from the 65% support expressed in 1990. Remember, this group (at least in public schools) has been exposed to sex education; they probably have never seen a movie or heard a pop song expressing a pro-life message and their parents were the product of the era of the sexual revolution. What is happening?

The only answer I can put forward with certainty is that God is answering our prayers. So often, though, His answers come in apparently natural ways and I have a guess—no more than a guess—at part of what might be going on. This generation is the first that could have been aborted. Now, I know there have always been abortions; but, until 1973, the vast number of civilized people—not to mention Christians—saw abortion as the gross obscenity that it is. Of my generation, virtually no one could even conceive of his or her mother even thinking of having an abortion. (Even saying this now gives me chills.) This generation is the first that knows it could have been aborted! If their parents are really liberated, perhaps they have even been told they had aborted siblings. Now, for sure, that is not how parents would put it; but children have an uncanny way of seeing truth through foggy words. In other words, perhaps these college freshmen have an intuitive understanding that they were only conditionally wanted and accepted; that, if conditions were different, they would never have been college freshmen! The Post also bemoans the apathy of many of these young people. Who can blame them?

The March for Life began immediately after the Supreme Court decision in 1973. Annually, on the anniversary of the decision, January 22nd, hundreds of thousands have met on the Mall and marched to the Supreme Court. The weather, so often cold and bleak, seems to match the chances to overturn this ruling. Even now, legal remedies seem far away; but hearts are being changed. Taking an afternoon and walking down Constitution Avenue may seem a small gesture against so great an evil; but that gesture is a sign and, who knows, that sign may say something about another attitude toward life that could give encouragement to a college freshman in need of assurance about the absolute significance of life.

True Discipleship: Rocking the Boat

July 3, 1994

I know fairly well, a family who is extremely involved in the pro-life movement. Not only have they contributed financially on behalf of the unborn, they have been involved in marches and other demonstrations, some have been arrested for short periods and they have done everything possible to get their church involved in what they believe to be the paramount moral issue of our time. Their reasoning is that if the weakest in our society can be disposed of for the sake of convenience, then all are, ultimately, threatened. Perhaps you will not be surprised to hear that many see this family as rather extreme. To many who wish to lead quiet, moral lives, this family appears somewhat fanatic. They say and believe the right things, but say them too loudly and perhaps, believe them too deeply.

Last week, while I was on vacation, I saw infinitely more television than I usually do. In addition to being swept up by the USA's performance in soccer, I also watched a man, who was by many regarded as a hero, exposed as something quite different. He always appeared to be nearly the perfect ideal of the American male: he is athletic, he dresses impeccably, he is glib of speech and never used that speech to say, publicly, anything that would make anyone feel uncomfortable. For many, this man's sophistication, style and physical grace were the unattainable goals to be sought by the American male.

Why is it that, for so many Catholics, it is not the pro-life family but the telegenic athlete who is the source of inspiration? Why are we embarrassed when we see people who are so in love with God and their neighbor that they will put their lives on the line for that love? Look nice, dress well, act politely, believe what you will—but do not rock the boat. Last week, perhaps we got just a hint of that while the boat looks fine, a lot of the wood is pretty rotten and the boat needs a thorough overhaul. One thing also is for sure: if the Gospel, especially as it is proclaimed and celebrated by the Church, is not the source of society's overhaul, the work will not be done.

Land of the Free, Except for the Unborn
July 2, 1995

So little is simple anymore. We are in the midst of Independence Day weekend; and, while most of us are not very demonstrative, it is the time of year when we are most prone to feelings of patriotism. Truly, there is so much reason to give thanks for being citizens of the "land of the free and the home of the brave;" and yet. . . The abortion reality is a cancer on our whole national character. Only slavery, I suppose, has provided us as a people with a dilemma with so little opportunity for political compromise. I love my country and yet, if I believe there is any way that we are responsible to and for each other, I have to recognize that all of us are deeply stained by the permission we give to kill the least powerful in the country. We can be proud of progress in space exploration; we salute the work of many to conquer sickness; all benefit as the economy expands. But, like a black cloud, there is the dull awareness that, all around us, abortions are being performed. How does the Christian respond?

The prophet Hosea was one of the earliest in the prophetic tradition of Israel. While little is known of the details of his life, the text of the Book of Hosea leads us to believe that he had suffered the agony of an unfaithful wife. His prayer and the inspiration of the Spirit led him to recognize that Israel, at that time filled with all sorts of immorality and corruption, was like an unfaithful wife. Hosea recognized that, despite her infidelity, God would remain faithful but that God demanded that Israel return to her former faithfulness. The role of Hosea was to say to Israel, "Come, let us return to the Lord," and to remind them that God desires, "steadfast love," and not love that is "like the morning cloud, like the dew that goes away early." The main role of the prophets, contrary to our picture of them as visionaries, was to call God's people back to their covenant relationship with Him.

Many Catholics would love to see the abortion issue go away. They would never commit one or encourage one, but they are willing to let the issue die away on the political level. They recognize that the Church is more and more seen as out-of-step and as intransigent; holding on where others have resigned themselves to the inevitable. As with prophets denouncing the abuses of a corrupt Israel, the Church seems a jarring, discordant voice; continuing to carp when many would like to declare the issue settled. But the Church must maintain its prophetic voice. These fetuses are as human as you or I; if they are in danger, all are in danger. I love my country; I know that the original ideals of my country make us capable of so much more; I believe that, in the Spirit, we can reform; but Christ, through His prophetic

Church, must remind us of the evil in our midst.

Twenty-five hundred years after the prophets wrote, it is quite clear who were the great lovers of Israel and it was not those who "went along to get along." I thank God this Independence Day for being an American; but, for love of country, I pray for the grace to do what I can to cure this enormous evil in our national character.

Crusade Against Chaos: World Population Council

September 11, 1994

Probably not since Pope Pius XII so publicly and so strongly denounced Communism in the years after World War II has any pope taken so firm and so aggressive a position in the political realm as is being taken by Pope John Paul II in the deliberations surrounding the World Population Conference in Cairo, Egypt. As one commentator remarked, the Holy Father seems interested not in compromise but in confrontation. Others, even some who are usually sympathetic to the Church, have watched his inflexibility and have hinted that, perhaps, the effects of age are weakening his judgment. Perhaps.

Another columnist bemoaned the fact that practical problems, such as how to cope with the teaming populations of cities like Cairo itself and Mexico City, are not being dealt with because the Vatican seems to want to do battle with Western "cultural imperialism." However unintentionally, I think this writer came close to what motivates Pope John Paul II. The Holy Father knows, probably as well as anyone in the U.N., of the problems and sufferings of the poor of the earth; but he also knows the moral and philosophical principles upon which solutions are built have a greater lasting effect than any particular solution.

Family planning, child bearing, abortion and many of the issues being debated in Cairo are questions of morality, and as such, they touch upon humanity's relationship with God, the author of life. The West, and alas, particularly the United States, sees these questions and answers in a purely secular framework, one that assumes that the world is answerable only to itself. Therefore, if population is seen to be the problem, any solution that limits population, whether it be abortion or whatever, is seen to be open for discussion. Practicality is the criterion for judgment.

A Papal spokesman, in an article in the Wall Street Journal, reminded his readers that ours is a nation founded on the principle that it is "self-evident," that each person has the right to life. When that fundamental principle is denied, even if the goal seems good, chaos must surely follow. That, I believe, is what the Holy Father is crusading against. A purely secular world view is one, ultimately, that pits powerful against weak and rich against poor; it is a world where only the fittest survive. The Holy Father is making himself quite unpopular with his uncompromising message. May God grant to him long years and loving passion to speak his unpopular, but Godly, message.

Truth Cannot Be Compromised

October 2, 1994

Some have said that John Kennedy's speech before a convention of Baptist ministers in Dallas in 1960 was key to his election as president that year. In an atmosphere of traditional anti-Catholicism, that feared that the pope wanted to control all countries where Catholics had political influence, Kennedy went before this audience and told them that, if elected president, he would place his responsibilities as president before his personal religious faith. I suppose this "moment" symbolized, as much as any, that Catholics had finally been assimilated into the American society. In a huge percentage, we were children and grandchildren of immigrants who admired and aspired to all that was American. Of course, much that was American was based on a Protestantism that rejects the claim of the Catholic Church to be the "one, true Church founded by Jesus Christ" in favor of a generalized religion that says, basically, that one religion is as good as another. It was also an America that, in politics, revered the art of compromise and give-and-take. It is important to note that, in those more innocent days, few of Kennedy's fellow Catholics disagreed with what he said in Dallas. We could not imagine national policy ever being at odds with Catholic moral principles.

All of this serves as background for what may be the great long term lesson for Catholics out of the recent Cairo Conference on Population and Development. So much of the world, especially the Western world, has adopted the American attitude that all things can be worked out by simply changing words or fudging on this or that phrase or idea. The Holy Father, through his representatives at Cairo, stood and reminded us that truth cannot be compromised. Life is what life is; abortion is what abortion is: end of discussion. Politicians can fudge with words regarding much of political life; but, sometimes, the art of politics breaks down when the distinction between truth and compromise is forgotten. Let us be honest, the fear of losing one's job not infrequently leads people to back away from standing for the truth.

The American bishops have designated October as Respect Life Month and have invited us to focus on abortion and other life issues. Happily, we have in the parish a respect life committee that will help us to cooperate with the vision of the bishops. But, underlying all of the discussions, I think, is a very real sadness that John Kennedy may have been wrong. Ultimate truth comes from God and is taught most perfectly by His Church. It may well be that the great contribution of the American Church to our country will be our standing—alone, if necessary—without compromise in the defense of life. May God give us the necessary love and courage.

God—Created in Our Image

For the last few weeks we have been praying the "Prayer for the Nation," after all the Masses. Perhaps for that reason, I have given some thought as to why the bishops have thought that there is a need for such a prayer. The initial reason, of course, is that we pray that somehow the veto of President Clinton of the partial birth abortion ban will be overridden by the houses of Congress. To that end, last Sunday we were encouraged to call the offices of our national legislators to ask their vote on behalf of the unborn. Two of those individuals are at least baptized Catholics and will, apart from a miracle of grace, vote for this even most obviously brutal form of baby killing. Until one of these individuals was dropped from the position by her pastor, she was a lector at Sunday Mass, which fact at least indicates that she may have taken her faith seriously at one point. How can a Catholic live with such a total disconnect between faith and life? An article from *Faith, Moral Reasoning and Contemporary American Life*, edited by Sr. Madonna Murphy, C.S.C. (1995) at least points to an answer.

The article, "Atheistic Catholics," is by Paul Mankowski, S.J. Fr. Mankowski maintains that while liturgies, manners of prayer and rituals remain intact, many church-going Catholics no longer believe in God. His is an awful prospect, but perhaps there is truth in what Father writes. As I read the article, the essential question concerns the content of Christian revelation. As Father Mankowski writes, "Is the revelation of God to man ultimately God's work, or man's work?"

I am sure that a Catholic legislator who is pro-abortion does not intend evil, for example. However, when the fairly obvious argument is used that says, "Thou shall not kill," how often will one hear a response like, "God would never intend a woman to suffer." On the one hand there is the tradition that reveals what God says about killing; on the other, a sentiment about what God should intend; a presumption that God thinks as we think. In other words, without giving up the comforting rituals and traditions of religion, we simply invent a God created in our own image. If I think (or feel) God should say this, then God does say this.

Prayer for the nation is most appropriate, particularly if we are becoming a nation who worships a God that is, essentially, a projection of our hopes and aspirations. The God of Israel, the God of our Lord Jesus Christ, is the fullness of truth. Apart from that truth, there is chaos.

Postcards for Life

September 1, 1996

Some will remember the decades immediately following World War II and the first analyses of the Holocaust. At that time, to the scandal of many, Pope Pius XII and the Catholic Church as a whole were criticized for not doing enough to save European Jewry. The debate raged for awhile and, as is the manner in such things, positions quickly became fixed. While, on the other hand, the statements and the courageous decisions of the Holy Father certainly seem to make his place in history secure, it is also true that, with thousands of exceptions, individual Catholics probably were more caught up in personal concerns than in giving support to neighbors taken unjustly by the Nazis. Certainly, there were Catholics who actively cooperated in the evil; but, here, the distinction must be made between being baptized Catholic and those taking faith seriously.

I mention this partly from a bit of shame. Next Sunday, the bishops of Maryland are asking the Catholics of the state to participate in a post card blitz to ask our senators and congressional representatives to override President Clinton's veto of the ban on partial birth abortions. I am ashamed to admit that my first reaction was, "What's the use?" Both of our senators and our representatives are militantly pro-abortion and there is no way that they care what these post cards represent. Even though all three belong to Churches (Catholic and Orthodox) that are unambiguous about the sanctity of life, it looks as if they believe—and they may well be right—that standing up for life might mean political death to them.

Ultimately, of course, the abortion question for Americans is as starkly one of good and evil as that of slavery. I really believe that, ultimately, we will decide for life. Hearts must be changed; prayer must be unceasing; progress will be in tiny steps (like a ban on partial-birth abortions); but, ultimately, truth and life will prevail. But, history must be clear about the role, the teaching and the commitment of the Catholic Church. History, obviously, will not remember these post cards. History will remember that, time after time, in marches, in petitions, at clinic entrances, in prayer and in a thousand other ways, men and women of faith would not submit to evil. Fill out a post card next weekend. No, it is not much; but, it will say that we will not grow tired; that we will not pretend that evil is good; that we really do believe that the weak ones of the earth will confound the mighty.

Why the Church Stays in the Battle
October 6, 1996

I received a visit recently from a member of the parish, newly back to the sacraments, who wished to discuss a matter of concern to her. She is delighted to have discovered a personal relationship with Christ; she looks forward to receiving Him in Communion and particularly appreciates the Sacrament of Penance. What surprises her and distressed her enough to bring her in was an involvement in politics by the Church that she did not expect and did not remember from her younger years as a practicing Catholic. She was referring to the various efforts in parishes and on the national level in recent months that were aimed at overturning the President's veto of the partial birth abortion ban. Because these efforts have been extensive, it occurs to me that this woman's questions may reflect the questions of others.

In investing ourselves so deeply into the abortion issue, the Church does risk seeming to involve itself, in a partisan way, in a political issue. While I have no right to speak for the Church as a whole, I believe the involvement is justified for three reasons. First of all, someone must speak on behalf of truth. Great numbers of Catholics might well be deceived by talk of women's rights; not to speak the truth about what abortion is allows people to form their opinions on the basis of faulty premises. People of good will, who see things as they are, generally try to choose in favor of the good.

More importantly, the Church is a community of love. "Whatever you do for the least of these, you do for me," the Lord tells us. Not to speak for the unborn babies would be as serious a moral failure as the Church could commit. Love for these children and love for the country that allows their abortions impels us who believe to call for political changes. We know that, for many, the fact that something is legal can make it seem moral. Laws must reflect the moral.

Finally, we must be involved because of what the legalization of abortion says about each individual in the country. Our courts have said that unborn individuals have value only if the mother chooses to give it to him or her. By this standard, the right to life is conditional. If the right to life of the unborn is conditional, whose is absolute? If the child is born with defects, can I then kill it because of quality of life? If the auto accident victim is in a coma, can I kill him because of the cost of maintenance of life? The right to abort an unwanted child establishes a principle that the strong have power over the weak. Of course, the Church must involve itself in the political struggle to reestablish the principle that "all men are created equal." This battle will be long and frustrating because it is over the soul of our nation. What a privilege is ours to be part of a struggle where the stakes are so enormous. May God give us the grace to persevere.

Political Double Standard

August 23, 1998

Clarence Thomas nearly was deprived of a seat on the Supreme Court not too many years ago because one person alleged, with no supportive corroboration, that Thomas had made lewd and harassing comments to his accuser while she was an employee of his. Last night I watched President Clinton as he admitted to an inappropriate relationship with an intern in the White House who was in her early twenties when the relationship began; and I watched as he admitted that he had misled both his wife and the country about the matter. I think there is little question that if those who had been so loud in condemnation of Justice Thomas were similarly loud in denouncing acts that, today, are no longer in question, Mr. Clinton's position would be far less secure than it now is. Why the difference in reaction from the very same people?

American Catholics wisely prefer their priests stay away from political stances. Some may fear that I violate that principle in these comments. Believe me, my intention is to comment on the great moral issue of our day, not on a passing political crisis—as painful as it is for the nation. You see, while I have seen only one brief remark in the press, and that was several weeks ago, that would agree with my point, I believe that the abortion issue underlies so much of what we are going through during these awful months. I believe that Clarence Thomas is hated by the pro-abortion segment of our society because it was clear from the beginning that he stands in favor of life. It has been said by more than a few political commentators that the one group of supporters that President Clinton has not let down in the years of his administration is that same pro-abortion lobby. On virtually the first day of his administration, on the day of the annual March for Life, he revoked various anti-abortion restrictions on military facilities that had been imposed by Presidents Reagan and Bush. From that day to this, he has always taken the position most antithetical to the rights of the unborn. I believe that those who strongly objected to Clarence Thomas because of supposed sexual harassment are so quiet today because of their gratitude to the President for his pro-abortion stance.

In a sophisticated city like ours, Catholics can feel ill at ease by the Church's uncompromising stance in favor of human life. Those who form opinion and who meet in the right places assume enlightened consensus, especially where "personal freedom" is concerned. Punishment can be harsh where the consensus is violated; and going along with it can lead to toleration even of some pretty sordid stuff. We as Catholics may want to avoid the messy and uncomfortable consequences of seeing things as they are, but, believe me, those who oppose life see exactly what is at stake.

I truly have no desire to speak on politics. I do believe, however, that beneath all the politics, something else is being contended, and that is the great moral issue of life and death that is abortion.

The Tragedy of Euthanasia

October 16, 1994

Not too many months ago, a dear and good man, who had become, I think, a friend, died after a fairly long bout with a terminal illness. After doctors had done all they could do, and after it had become clear he was now to be homebound, he called and asked to see a priest. Now that he faced the imminence of death (in fact, he lived almost two years from this time), he discovered that he had to deal with whether or not he really believed in God. The whole process of his final preparation for death—or better, being a part of the last stage of his life here on earth—was both a privilege for me and the source of an awful lot of meditation.

This man's story comes to mind because I read recently an article about the euthanasia in Holland. This country, whose Catholics at one time had the highest rate of religious vocations in the world, is now, for some reason, a pitifully sad meditation on what happens when a people loses its faith. The culture of euthanasia is so entrenched that the killing of patients without their consent, on only the determination of a physician that the patient's life is no longer worthwhile, is fairly commonplace. The Dutch Pediatric Association is drawing up guidelines for killing infants thought not to be worthy of living; these guidelines are thought necessary because of the frequency of infant euthanasia.

The tragedy of euthanasia is that, in presuming either that there is no God or in acting in such a way, the dying, and those associated with them, are deprived of what might be life's final—and ultimate—chapter. My friend grew from being a man who had never really confronted whether he believed in God, to one for whom prayer was as natural as breathing. One of the great things he discovered about God is that, while he and the world may have thought growth was over, the Good Lord still had a lot of things He wanted to teach. Perhaps not until the end of life could God catch my friend's full attention.

I surely am not looking forward to suffering, and especially, not looking forward to getting ready to die. But, I really do thank God for the people I have known who have gone through this last stage of life. God has allowed them to teach me that He will be there and, in fact, that He may have some pretty wonderful things to teach me before He brings me to Himself.

With His Help I Can Do Anything
August 4, 1996

For several years back in the eighties I served as Director of the Permanent Diaconate for the Archdiocese. In that capacity, I was responsible for the training of deacon candidates and personnel matters for the ordained deacons. I mention this because one of the things that surprised me in this job was the number and quality of deacons who had in common their membership in Alcoholics Anonymous.

It has been said that Alcoholics Anonymous and the various "twelve step" programs that have sprung from A.A. comprise the greatest spiritual movement of the twentieth century. Its principles are deliberately non-religious in the sense that A.A. espouses no specific creed, but many commentators have remarked on the similarity of its principles with various Catholic spiritual traditions. Most parish priests work closely with people active in A.A. - and not a few are active in priesthood because of the help they find in twelve step programs.

Put into Christian or Catholic terms, what A.A. recognizes is the inability of a person to survive without the help of God and community. While the program speaks of a "higher power," a Catholic recognizes Jesus in the principle that says that a person "came to believe in a power higher than myself who could restore me to sanity" and twelve step literature continually speaks of fellowship of people who band together to help each other to sobriety. Only a fool would under-play the hell that is alcoholism or drug addiction, but it is also true that like any other cross, these can be the routes whereby individuals recognize their need of salvation.

As concerns those wonderful deacons who are members of A.A. I began to understand that it was their experience that God really will save us that led them to seek a way to share the Good News. And because they also had experienced that they could not begin to recover from addictions without the help of God as they found Him in others, they recognized a call to serve in the community of faith.

Twelve step programs have recognized what the Church has always known: we cannot grow, apart from God and community. Sin leads us to believe we can "stand alone." Ultimately, life, God or experience will teach us that by ourselves we can do nothing of lasting value.

Christian Love

March 15, 1998

St. Ireneaus said, "The glory of God is man fully alive" and Jesus tells us that the greatest of His followers will be, "the last one of all and the servant of all." I guess I thought when I was younger that knowing the glory of God would be feelings of intense joy or perhaps, like Peter, James and John at the Transfiguration, getting a glimpse of the divinity of the Lord. A story about my Dad I remembered not too long ago gives me a better sense of what God's love is all about.

At about ten years of age, nothing gave me greater joy than going to Griffith Stadium to see the Washington Senators get blasted by whomever was in town. Night after summer night I would beg my father, who had left home by 6:00 am, to return at least twelve hours later, to take me to a game. (Obtaining tickets, as some remember, was never a problem.) On more than a few nights, he would relent. What I remembered recently was one time looking over at him during a game and being shocked that he was asleep! I am shocked no more.

I see this kind of serving love in parents all the time. I see them give the countless hours to the one child who just does not "get it" academically; I hear their children complain that at the dinner table parents will not stop talking about religion or morality; and I think of the countless second jobs I have seen fathers take so that children can go to Catholic high schools. And those who are being served have no clue that anything unusual is going on!

Of course, it is not only parents. How I thank God for the religious sisters who taught me. Now I marvel at what kind of love motivated them to go back into a classroom of fifty or so children year after year; now I know that often they would go back to the convent and do a day's chores before even thinking about preparations for the classes of the next day. Thank God, I see the same serving love today as I meet spouses who watch and serve; who bathe and feed; who pray and wait as a companion of half a century prepares to meet the Lord. Here, of course,—and thank God—the service is usually recognized as the miracle of grace that it is.

The gift of Lent is to be reminded both of our call to serving love and of the deep-rooted selfishness that is within us. Serving love costs plenty and it often hurts. It is so easy to turn in to self and to abandon the never-ending call to be poured out like Jesus. May God grant that our prayer, our acts of Lenten service and our self-denial during these weeks will make us just a bit like Him who has served us even to death on a Cross.

Call To Love

June 2, 1996

Why is it that if someone criticizes the length or organization of one of my sermons I will brood on it for hours afterwards; but if I hear someone on TV express contempt for Christ or the Church my regret passes quickly? Why is it I can go back over and over again to a bad golf stroke but quickly dismiss from my mind a family who has lost a place to live because there is no work? As St. Augustine says, "As for the other things of this life, the less they deserve tears, the more likely they will be lamented; and the more they deserve tears, the less likely will men sorrow for them." Why is this?

One of the things that I say to couples preparing for marriage is that if they have not yet seen themselves as prone to selfishness, then they do not know themselves well enough yet to get married. In more traditional terms, I am trying to remind them of one of the principle effects of the original sin, that we are prone to put ourselves at the center of our existence. This tendency, known as concupiscence, is not identical with sin; but unchecked, it certainly opens the way to sin. A quote by a mother of eight that I often use describes concupiscence best, "Anyone who does not believe in original sin never raised a three year old." The whole process of Christian moral formation involves our denying that tendency to put ourselves first and choosing to give priority to God and neighbor. Not, God knows, that I am an expert in childraising, but this battle against concupiscence is being fought even when parents win the struggle over when the two year old will go to bed. Will the child live by his feelings or his parents' standards? The basic training involved in table manners, picking up a bedroom, doing chores, using hand-me-down clothes and all the other parts of family life, hopefully begin to form a will that understands that the greater good is served when self-centeredness gives way to the good of the other.

Any culture, of course, recognizes the importance of surrender of self for the good of family and community. For the Christian, the stakes are greater. Our vocation is to live the life of Jesus who "came not to be served, but to serve." Our call is to love not only those whom we know, but the stranger and even those who hate us. Why do I brood over an unkind comment? Because I am a son of Adam and Eve—prone to focus on myself, but I have also been given a share in the life of Jesus. I can move beyond that self-centeredness and live the redeeming life of God's love.

Reawakening the Need for the Presence of Christ in Russia

October 27, 1996

Perhaps it is an early indication of the Christmas spirit, but a couple of people recently have asked me for suggestions on what I considered worthwhile charities. They seemed to be looking for charities to give to where even a modest gift might really affect the work being done. I hope everyone has a favorite charity, but for those who do not, here are a couple of my favorites.

Writing these thoughts makes me realize how many years it has been since the day I was reading a Catholic magazine in the seminary library. Way in the back of the magazine, in the classified ads, I found a tiny ad advocating my giving to Nevett Fund to support the work of a Fr. Nevett, S.J., in India. The ad was so pitifully small that I said to myself, "Maybe, they'll appreciate my $5.00." I sent it off to the address in Chicago, and before long, I received a thank you letter that made me think they had thought the check was for five thousand dollars. Over the years, I have corresponded with Fr. Nevett, who I came to recognize as a saintly missionary, very much in the tradition of the earlier Jesuit, St. Francis Xavier. Father's work was mainly in the North of India and as I understand it, was largely devoted to educating children of the lowest classes. Fr. Nevett died several years ago, but his work goes on, and a wonderful woman in Chicago, Rita Anton, continues to administer money sent to this work: Nevett Fund, 3431 North Ashland Avenue, Chicago, IL, 60657.

A friend from my first parish in Bowie who later moved to Anchorage, Alaska, has gotten me involved in the second work of charity. The Catholic Church in Vladivostok, Russia, is in that part of Russia closest to Alaska. An American priest is working there, in a diocese that is twice the size of the United States! The descriptions of their efforts are as inspiring as their obstacles are daunting. Most of the Catholics in the region were sent there by the Soviets either as prisoners or as labor for various projects of the Soviet government. The priest speaks of giving First Communion to people who were baptized seventy years ago and who persevered in the faith throughout those years. But they have, almost literally, nothing with which to work. Heat, books, medical care for the poor, real estate on which to build churches: everything needed to build up the church—except dynamic faith in the Gospel message—seems to be in short supply. If you want to be a part of the effort to bring Catholicism to this bleak part of Far Eastern Russia, donations can be sent to Vladivostok Mission, 225 Cordova Street, Anchorage, Alaska, 99501.

Finally, I know of a wonderful parish in Bethesda, Maryland, but more of this charity another time. . .

Making a Difference with a Donation
December 3, 1995

As Fr. Myron Effing spoke at the 7:30 Mass last Sunday, he said at one point, "I hope to have the time to speak with the pastor privately about how Our Lady of Lourdes can share in the work of Most Holy Mother of God Church in Vladivostok." Because I am so great a sinner, my reaction was, "Uh-oh, here we go." However, after we had our meeting, my reaction was quite different. What Father is proposing is that a Sister Parish Committee for the Most Holy Mother of God Catholic Church be established among members of the Parish of Our Lady of Lourdes.

My impression is that, while Fr. Effing spoke at all our Masses last week, he said different things at the different liturgies. Perhaps at your Mass, you did not hear him speak of the history of his parish. Because Vladivostok is the chief Russian port on the Pacific coast, it attracts a diverse population. For that reason, the church was founded in the early part of this century (before the revolution) for Catholics who have settled in the area. The Communists, of course, closed the church and for years it was used as some kind of warehouse. Fr. Effing, who is an American, got permission after the fall of Communism, to serve in Vladivostok. He lives with one other American priest and they serve a territory that I think he said is as large as the Forty-eight States. He speaks of three hundred mile journeys by train and car to anoint individuals who have not seen a priest since before the Communist Revolution. Most of the work is in serving Catholic survivors of Communist concentration camps and their descendants. Especially among the young, however, there are converts and there are even two men from his parish ("pure Russians," he told me) who are studying for priesthood.

The Sister Parish Committees have started in parishes throughout the United States. Their three purposes are to pray for the sister parishes (in our case, Lourdes and the parish in Vladivostok), to foster vocations and to develop projects, unique to each parish, to support Most Holy Mother of God. For example, a group in Minnesota raised money to refurbish an organ no longer used by a church and they paid for shipping to Russia. An organist in the parish even arranged to extend a business trip to Japan so that she could spend a few days training pianists in Vladivostok to play the organ. It is the only organ in Russia east of Lake Biakal. Another group coordinates fund-raising mailings throughout the United States.

If there are individuals interested in aiding the work of reestablishing the Catholic Church in Russia, please leave your name and phone number at the rectory. I would be glad to facilitate your gathering together in support of this good work.

Support Exodus Youth Ministries

November 12, 1995

One does not have to be a scholar of the political scene to recognize that the elections of November, 1994 changed dramatically the American scene. Not only did the Republicans take over both houses of Congress, but the battle over budget, Medicare and welfare demonstrates that they seek to place their imprint on the course of government policy. I suppose this is how it should be, but all these proposals come amidst great controversy.

Advocates of the present welfare system decry stringent requirements that, it is feared, will drive people off the system and, therefore, out of housing and into greater destitution. Some Catholics fear that capping benefits for successive illegitimate children will even encourage abortions. On the other hand, conservatives argue that the Great Society, as it was called in the 1960's, clearly does not work. Family life in the cities has been virtually destroyed; education, despite billions of federal dollars, is a disgrace; and stories of the victims of crime are apt to be part of any conversation. Where lies the truth?

As a Christian, I believe the debate shows the emptiness of a society without Christ. That is why I am so enthusiastic about our Thanksgiving project of collaboration with Exodus Youth Ministries. Begun about a dozen years ago by an Episcopal priest and his wife, both of whom converted to Catholicism before his death from Lou Gehrig's disease, this group is composed mostly of volunteers in their twenties and goes weekly into different areas of the most devastated parts of the city. They have a recreational vehicle set up as a classroom and they park it at the same corner each week and make themselves available to teach the young about Jesus. Through this outreach, they are invited into homes and even, despite their obvious Catholic beliefs, have been invited to set up outside individual city Protestant churches. It is the families affected by Exodus Youth Ministries, as well as members of Assumption Parish with whom Lourdes has had a relationship over the years, that will be served by your Thanksgiving generosity.

The problems of our society are so vast; the response of a group like Exodus, while beautiful, seems so small. The Roman Empire, as the Church began, was both vast and interiorly rotten. The Church, empowered by the Spirit, conquered that civilization; only Christ can save us. Let us support even the smallest beginnings.

The Church Serves
Through the Cardinal's Appeal

March 1, 1998

It was about five years ago when a woman came to see me in the rectory. While she was often at daily Mass, I did not know her except to greet her when coming in or out of Church. I came to find out that she was an immigrant from the West Indies and stopped at the parish because it was on the bus line to her job as a housekeeper. She came to see me as a last resort after having found out about a diagnosis of breast cancer. Of course, she had no benefits and she had no savings and so, as sometimes happens, she dumped the mess into my capable hands! That was the morning that I discovered the Health Care Network developed by Catholic Charities. I know I should have already known about it, but to be honest, if I carefully read all that the Archdiocese sends me, I would have to stop saying Mass it would take so much time. At any rate, I discovered that dozens, perhaps hundreds, of doctors in the region agree to give free service to those recommended by pastors or Catholic Charities. In addition, services such as x-rays are often supplied by Charities. This woman, within weeks, was back at daily Mass, I suspect somewhat more grateful to God than she had previously been.

As a pastor of somewhat limited organizational skills, it is all that I can do to react to the daily challenges of phone and door; so it does not surprise me that I did not know this program. Likewise, as a member of the parish, full of love for God and neighbor, but also full of responsibilities in many different areas, you are probably only dimly aware of all whom the Church serves through the Cardinal's Appeal. If we hear about them, we are happy that three Holy Cross Sisters serve at Mary's Song, a program in Southern Maryland for family support and health care. We take satisfaction, I am sure, that the Church supports eight Pregnancy Aid Centers throughout Maryland and DC. Likewise, most are delighted that over two thousand young Catholic students receive financial aid that allows them the opportunity to experience the Catholic education many of us took for granted. To be honest, the Cardinal's Appeal operates mostly (but not entirely) in areas of the Archdiocese not familiar to many of us.

Thanks be to God, this parish has a strong tradition of support for the Cardinal's Appeal. First of all, I suspect this tradition reflects a deep Catholic loyalty to the call of the Archbishop for help in serving those in need. Last year, we gave a bit over $250,000, which was a jump of some $30,000 over the previous year. More importantly, our number of donors increased as about 60% of those registered responded to the Appeal.

Either through the mail or next weekend through the in-pew campaign, I pray that we at Lourdes continue our tradition of support for the Cardinal's Appeal. We in the Archdiocese are one Church; we are one in the Spirit of Jesus. May that unity in Christ inspire us to serve the materially weaker members of our family.

Catholic Giving: The Cardinal's Appeal
March 12, 1995

There was a time when giving to the poor seemed, somehow, easier. We may chuckle about giving money to ransom the pagan babies that Catholic school classes of the fifties collected for and named by the thousands, but we knew that dedicated missionaries were giving their lives to bring the Good News to needy people. Or closer to home, most Catholics were near enough to their own immigrant roots that they could identify with families, often fleeing from Communism, who needed help to get started in a new country with its strange language and economic demands. Likewise, when we saw the poverty of Appalachia, the memories of the Depression and its devastation sparked a willingness to try to help. These were our kind of people, in the sense that we perceived that they shared our goals of family, hard work and self-reliance. It is so different now.

The twin curses of drugs and the sexual revolution have brought about a poverty that is no different than the hard but understandable press of economic hard times. In addition, we see some of its effects in the street people who are apt to be in any neighborhood, and often, the way they press for money makes anyone question how effective is anything given to the poor. Even immigrants seem so different than we knew in earlier times (though to be certain, anti-immigrant sentiment is not new to this country).

In this environment, the Cardinal's Appeal is taken up this Sunday. The Church reminds us, through the collection, that we are not allowed to isolate ourselves from the weakest of the Lord's brothers and sisters, no matter how unattractive they seem. The Church must be involved with the homeless, especially when we recognize that so many of them would formerly have been institutionalized because of mental and emotional disorders. The Church must continue to try to make Catholic education available to the poor; parish schools cannot become slightly less expensive private schools for the middle class. The Church must try to make marriage and other types of counseling available to those of modest means: their lives are as stressed as those who can afford expensive help. The Church must seek to serve the rural poor who, because they are isolated and without political clout, can be ridden. All these things and so many more the Church tries to do with what we contribute to the Cardinal's Stewardship Appeal.

Accepting God's Wisdom

March 27, 1994

I am just finishing what has become a classic in modern Christian literature, *A Severe Mercy*, by Sheldon Vanauken. Vanauken, incidentally, recently converted to Catholicism, one of a fairly large and quite influential group of Evangelical writers and ministers, who have "come to Rome" in recent years as they both search the Scriptures and examine the moral stands of the Church. At any rate, this book, written long before his conversion, tells the story of his romance and marriage, the death of his wife and his struggle to find the hand of God in the loss of so beautiful and faith-filled a woman who was only in her thirties. I highly recommend the book, especially, I suppose, for widows and widowers, though I guess I am proof one need not have been married to profit from it.

Without going into detail into Vanauken's faith journey, he finally came to believe (with the help of his good friend C.S. Lewis, whom he met while studying at Oxford) that the loss of his wife, whose faith he feels to have been much stronger than his, was a mercy for him because, if she had lived, he would have given in to a jealousy of the God who had become first in his wife's life.

In other words, he had prayed for a good (the recovery of a dearly loved and young wife) that he later came to see, in the light of prayer and faith, was not the highest good. Strangely enough, the celebration of Palm Sunday is what brings this story to mind. Did you ever ask yourself why, on this visit to Jerusalem, the crowds wanted to acclaim Jesus as king? He had, no doubt, been in the city many times before. The answer seems to be tied up with the raising of Lazarus from the dead. As you can read in John's Gospel, many were coming to Jesus on account of Lazarus. Why? Because, at least for some who so resented occupation by the pagan Romans, Jesus, with the power to raise the dead to life (not to mention multiply loaves and fishes), seemed the fulfillment of the Messianic longing of Israel. Even today, we would acknowledge the right of nations to fight for their freedom, so we should not just laugh off the Jews who thought they recognized in Jesus the long awaited military leader who would be the new David.

He could never have explained on that Palm Sunday, the incompleteness of their hope. Even the Apostles did not understand. The challenge of the Twelve, that of Sheldon Vanauken and that of any who claim to believe, is to continue to trust in the Providence of God in the face of defeat, suffering and even death. His destiny for us, as for His Son, is eternal and only in the light of that inheritance does his will for us here on earth make sense.

Suffering: The Effects of Sin

March 5, 1995

Several weeks ago, in speaking about the Cardinal's Appeal, I mentioned, in some detail, my feelings about the priests arrested in the child abuse case. In addition, I wrote on the subject in this column. With relief, I thought to leave the subject—at least in public comment. However, I find that I must say one thing further, concerning a dimension of the story that I had not anticipated.

Perhaps selfishly, I spoke that day of the abuse priests might have to take because of those events. This may be the case, though most priests with whom I have spoken tell mainly of the wonderful support they have found among their people. What I did not think of is the reactions with which our laity would have to deal. This has been one of the tough dimensions of the story. Over and over again, I have listened as people have told me of the comments and snide remarks they hear at coffee breaks, on the sidelines of little league basketball games or wherever folks gather who know that a practicing Catholic is present. It seems to have put a prominent murder trial temporarily out of peoples' minds.

I just think that our people deserve a pat on the back and a word of credit for their loyalty to the Church during a time when the evil that a few men have done has given the Church such a bad name. I wonder if the sly laughter and the jokes do not indicate that anti-Catholicism is not as dead as we might hope it to be. Also do I wonder if the weakness and failings of these few are not being used, in a perverse form of nonreasoning, to ridicule the moral positions that, almost alone, the Church continues to uphold.

I hate the suffering that was caused to individuals and families by the actions of these men. It is exactly that way with sin, so I should not be surprised, but I also hate how the effects of the evil spread ever farther, touching ever more innocent people, even people who want nothing more than to live their Catholic life in peace. In this, though, as in all things, we must not forget to put all in the hands of God. Somehow, through His grace, as so many times before, He will bring good out of this evil. The loyalty of so many of our people will, no doubt, touch many, even those who ask the hardest questions and who make the most snide remarks.

Mary—Model for Suffering and Dying

May 14, 1995

Our theology stresses the isolation of Jesus on the Cross. Abandoned by His followers, He cries out, in seeming isolation, "My God, my God, why have you abandoned me?" Granted the loneliness that is the most awful effect of sin, I have often wondered why the Lord allowed the presence of Our Lady at the foot of the Cross. Was it because He could not have "taken it" had He been deprived of even her, His purest disciple? I think not. Mary's presence at the foot of the Cross has far more to do with us, the Church, than it does with her giving comfort to the dying Jesus.

Remember always that Mary is, as Vatican II called her, Mother of the Church; she is the model, in her faith, obedience, love and sinlessness, of what the Church is to be. At the foot of her Son's Cross, she reminds us that the followers of Jesus cannot be spared participation in His suffering. It is Flannery O'Connor, the great southern Catholic writer, who reminds us: "In the presence of this faith now, we govern by tenderness." (from "*A Memory of Mary Ann*," 1961). Faith tells us that suffering with the Lord leads to a share in His resurrection; the absence of faith leads to the avoidance of suffering, especially when suffering rips at the most tender of emotions. The so-called doctor in Michigan attends the so-called minister who commits suicide because of the undeniable intensity of his physical pain. Would even the least tender of hearts object? Yes, especially if that heart understands that perhaps in final suffering a rebellious soul might finally surrender to God; or if, perhaps, the suffering of a relative or spouse might allow a last opportunity for reconciliation or healing of broken relationships. The person of faith even believes, as difficult as it is for us to accept, that our choosing to join our sufferings with those of the Lord is the most powerful of prayers.

And so, Mary stands at the foot of the Cross. Certainly, as a mother, she stands there to comfort Him; but, as the model for all believers she draws as close as she can to His Cross, recognizing that union with Him in His suffering means union with Him in His work, which is the salvation of the world.

Why Purgatory? Understanding What Christ Has Done for Us

November 3, 1996

Scholars have argued since the Reformation about whether the Catholic doctrine of purgatory is found in the Scriptures, but I, for one, think our belief in purgatory is one of the most common sense things taught by the Church. Like all that the Church teaches, this doctrine is linked with the rest of the fabric of faith. So often today we hear at the time of death, "We need not pray for this person; we will only remember their goodness." I am not so sure.

First of all, God does not treat us like children. He has given us the dignity of being brothers and sisters of His Son, the Lord Jesus, and He expects us to take that dignity seriously. So, for example, Jesus says the two great commandments are to love God with our whole being and to love our neighbor as we love ourselves. I think it is safe to say these are not throwaway lines; He means them. Yet who can say, "Oh sure, I have obeyed those two commandments 100%." I am not interested in generating feelings of guilt, but when I have free time and I give it to TV rather than trying to pray, for example, am I not violating that commandment? When I say that God will not treat us like children, I mean that at some point He will confront us with how lightly we took our responsibility to love Him and our neighbor. He will want us to know, at the deepest possible level, how our sinful choices affected others. As a priest, for example, I pray that, when I am in purgatory, I will not be shown a soul in hell, who, had I treated that person differently, might have made different choices with his life. Pray God, I do not have to face such a vision, but can I pretend that God would want to spare me knowledge of the consequences of my selfishness?

Purgatory then, is not God punishing our sins. It will be intensely painful, I am sure, but the pain will come as I experience, on the one hand, the depth of God's love for me, and on the other hand, how badly I responded to that love with my life. In a certain sense, the pain of purgatory is the pain of honest self-knowledge. I would not want to be in heaven unless my self-deception (for example, "It's been two years since my last confession, but I've been a good person, Father") had been purged away. In His great mercy, God has long since forgiven my sins; but because He respects me so much, He wants me to understand just what He has done for me.

The practice of praying for the faithful departed is valid because ultimately, we will go to heaven when we obey those two great commandments.

The soul in purgatory will experience pain in self-knowledge; but the focus cannot remain on me the sinner, but must turn to God, who loves me despite my sin. Because my prayer for the soul in purgatory comes from my love for that person, I believe it is somehow united with the Holy Spirit of God's love and it is that which ultimately draws the soul from purgatory into bliss of heaven.

The Price of Loving

January 26, 1997

If I know the widow or widower of a recently deceased spouse well enough, I will sometimes say to them, in the midst of their grief, "That's what you get for falling in love." What the probably inappropriate use of humor intends, of course, is to remind the person that their loneliness and grief are the other side of love. Similarly, it is often said that Christmas is a time of depression for many people. Part of this comes, I suppose, from investing too many hopes in what a season of the year can do for mood; but for others, the recollection of the joyful memories of Christmas past evokes a painful longing for what time or distance will not allow to be recaptured. Homesickness, too, is a pain of loneliness that comes from the experience of being away from those with whom goodness in life has been experienced.

My point is that the pain of loneliness very often exists only because we have loved and been loved. I suppose one sure way to avoid such pain is not to give of self wholeheartedly; but the widow grieving after fifty years of marriage would never give up the lifetime of love to avoid the pain of separation. Likewise, a friend was screaming about the long-distance phone bills of his freshman in college who calls home three or more times a week. Cynic that I can be, I was thinking of the reaction when she stops calling because she has adjusted to life away from home.

I do not mean to diminish the pain of grief; but as horrible as it can be, it does point out a couple of important things. First of all, we are made for others. John Wayne or other screen stars (John Wayne! Am I dating myself?) may evoke an ideal of the individual standing alone and conquering all, but our experience is that the "rugged individual" usually becomes self-centered and bitter. Secondly, not only are we made for others, we are fundamentally made for the Other, for God. The pain of the loss of a spouse or a dear friend reminds us, certainly, of their goodness and of what they have shown us of the good things of God; but their loss also reminds us of the longing for love and union that can be filled only by God. We experience hints of our destiny here on earth; but as wonderful as these hints can be, they are as nothing compared to what awaits us when we are at one with God.

Ash Wednesday

February 9, 1997

Why do they want those ashes on their foreheads? Every year I ask myself that question as people pour through the doors on Ash Wednesday. There are lots of jokes about "ashes and palms" Catholics, of course, but the jokes do not explain why, on Ash Wednesday especially, churches will be jammed with people. I think it has to do with death.

Happily, we live in a society where no one has to die. Oh yes, a few people each month in our parish have not yet gotten the message, but it will only be a matter of time before we are all 'beautiful people" (with full heads of hair). We eat right, we exercise faithfully; we get plenty of sun (whoops! not plenty of sun), and the practice of preventive medicine prepares us for. . . who knows what. A man I received into the church about twenty years ago died recently at ninety-one. I was told that he died because he ate the wrong kinds of food! Yes, I believe that Ash Wednesday draws so many people because it is one time when society says it is okay to refer to "the certain, sad sentence of death," and all that it implies.

Let us start at the beginning. As children of Adam and Eve, we are marked with the stain of their original disobedience and with the punishment for that sin, which is eternal damnation. It may not seem "fair", from our perspective, but there is a sense that our parents, at the moment of their sin, were the entire human race, and as such, they chose for us. We are marked with a corruption that does not change God's love for us, but which makes us unworthy of Him. We are utterly in need of salvation. Made in the image and likeness of God, we want to be like Him—to be in control—but our constant experience, which culminates in death, is that we reach for a perfection that we cannot obtain. Frankly, the sooner we embrace our sentence of death, the sooner we can begin to live.

And so, Ash Wednesday is about my death. How many had ashes imposed on their heads last Ash Wednesday whose bodies, this Ash Wednesday, are becoming ashes themselves? May Jesus lead us during this Lenten Season to recognize that only in Him is there victory over the greatest enemy—death.

Living—Preparation for Death

February 22, 1998

In the days before Vatican II, certain of the more austere religious orders used to observe silence during meals. Now this rule certainly still holds in contemplative houses, but without a feature of former days: that is, eating the meal with a skull on the table, as an invitation to the monks to remember, "the certain, sad sentence of death," that is in store for us. Indeed, while in a more subdued way, it is that same reminder the Church seeks to make as we have ashes imposed on our heads this Wednesday. The same old jokes will be made this week about "A and P Catholics", who come only on Ash Wednesday and Palm Sunday when the Church gives away something for nothing, but it is nevertheless true that churches will be jammed on Ash Wednesday; and I believe, jokes notwithstanding, that something deep within folks—even those who barely practice Christianity—is troubled by the ashed reminder of the reality and inevitability of death.

Certainly, there is something both horrible and frightening about death; but it is also true, that for the believer in the Resurrection, the concern is more about life than death. Someone once made the wonderful analogy that the soul is like a radio battery, except that the battery outlives the radio. The life of the soul is undiminished by death; death is simply the acceptance by God of our lifetime of decisions on whether or not to live fully His life. Of course there is a hell—as surely as there is a heaven—because God respects us too much to force us to reverse the patterns and decisions of our life.

Lent then, invites us to examine more our way of life rather than to brood over the inevitability of death. After all, does not the person who has loved the Lord and sought to serve Him throughout life have reason to see death as victory? Most of us, though, recognize the persistent inclination toward selfishness which is the rejection of God. And, let us be honest, more than a few of us have experienced the addictive power of sin, that if not overcome by God's grace and constantly kept in check by that same grace, could easily lead us to eternal death. Fasting and self-denial have their essential place in the Lenten regime because they remind us how easily our lives can be focused on other than God and His will.

As always, the Catholic focuses first on the grace of God; but that Catholic never forgets the human freedom that cooperates with grace. The practices of Lent so often remind us that we must choose to die to self so that we can more open ourselves to the grace of Him who died for us. Yes, we most surely must be reminded of death; but more surely, we must be reminded that it is the living that prepares us for that death.

Possessions—A Transitory Gift

July 26, 1998

A classmate of mine from the seminary died a few years ago. While his story is, in many ways, not unusual because of his age (and mine), it is one of those events that pulled me up short. Fr. Pat was bright, very bright. He had a wonderful quick wit, and in the seminary, had an enviable way of being able to integrate the branches of theology with practical pastoral situations. After ordination, he was put into education, and by forty, he was in charge of Catholic education in his diocese. And then, with bewildering quickness, he was diagnosed with cancer and was dead. I am told his death was beautiful; that his faith sustained him, his family and his friends, and that his wit was brilliant until the end.

I think about Fr. Pat's death in connection with the first beatitude, "Blessed are the poor in spirit." I guess anyone who has begun to take Christianity seriously realizes that possessions can possess us. That, until we are wise and extremely careful, the things that money can buy can come to seem essential to life. The person who is not troubled by an attachment to things has probably not yet reflected seriously about the reality and subtlety of false gods in life.

The thing that so struck me about my friend's death had to do with what seemed to be his intellectual possessions. He seemed to have everything a priest could want: faith, certainly; but, I speak more of the natural talents. His intellect was superior; he related easily with people and he had a seemingly effortless ability to be on top of every situation. What so struck me about his sickness and death is the realization that, in reality, he possessed nothing. I can remember thinking, at what appeared to be the prime of my life, that I could have a stroke or be hit by a falling tree or whatever. His going from strength to death in what seemed no time really shook me.

Poverty of spirit is the grace that allows me to understand that (as Archbishop Bloom, in *Living Prayer*, reminds us) "nothing that is mine is really mine." Everything is gift and all that I have signifies God's love. I am sure my friend realized this: that what was taken from him was only preparation for infinitely greater gifts. May God grant us the grace to recognize that all that is good comes from Him and that His gifts, whether physical or of the mind or spirit, are given to lead us to Him and not to a false sense of our own power or security.

Virtue: Temper, Humility, Courage

June 19, 1994

An individual that I saw in a recent traffic jam on the Beltway is the inspiration for these thoughts. We were reduced to the usual 15 mph crawl and I could not help but notice the man in the car next to mine who was consumed with rage at the state of affairs. He was banging on the steering wheel, cussing at the top of his lungs and in other ways indicating his lack of pleasure. On the other hand, I need not travel on the Beltway to encounter anger: there are, for example, children in the school who fly off the handle at the slightest provocation and who teachers and fellow students are able to set off on an almost weekly basis. As I work with people, I come to see anger as one of the most common emotions and, possibly, the one that can cause us the greatest trouble. By anger, of course, I do not mean the garden variety: "Mom's in the kitchen at five o'clock and the children are fighting and she loses it because it has been raining for three straight days." I suspect that response is more healthy than dangerous (as well as being something that rolls off the backs of children). Rather, I refer to the volcano that seethes underneath a surprising number of people.

I do not pretend to know what to do with the problem of temper. First, I suppose, one needs to recognize that it even exists within me. It is easy to deny it and blame work, family, traffic or whatever for my constant loss of temper. Facing the fact that I am always upset with the way I find the world may lead me to seek help—maybe even professional help; very possibly it will also lead me to ask some important questions about what I expect out of life. If I expect the world to march to my tune, if I make myself the center of my universe, I may very well be surprised and angry when all others don't agree with my assessment of myself. Spouse, children or fellow worker may care about me very much, but they should not confuse me with the center of their existence. If I become angry when all do not respond as I think they should, perhaps I should ask some questions of myself about whether God's will or mine is what I am looking for in life.

These are a few thoughts about a profoundly important subject. Pray God that the humility to see anger in myself will be accompanied by the courage to do whatever is necessary to overcome it.

Mortification Word Check

September 21, 1997

This week it's green tea! Drink green tea and some wonderful thing will happen: maybe it counteracts the effects of Pocomoke River fish. Anyway, I wish I had stock in green tea; it might be just the place to invest since stock in tofu seems to be dropping. The word "puritanical" was once a terrible insult especially when applied to constraints upon behavior for a shared moral purpose. Puritanical blue laws closed doors on Sunday and meant that families actually had to spend a day together. The phrase, "banned in Boston," referred to puritanical judgments on the moral character of movies or books that prevented folks from openly and honestly exploring various kinds of deviant activities with which we should all be acquainted.

Thank God, puritanism is dead. Or is it? I saw a woman of mature age cringing behind a tree at a cook-out recently. In a parish bulletin, I will not write what she was putting in her mouth, but the more worldly among readers will know. Likewise, at a restaurant, someone at the next table ordered cheesecake (not my table, I assure you). Even the waitress (oops, wait staff) shuddered. All turned out well, however: the cheesecake lover assured companions that it was the first and only dessert for the week. The new puritanism, with its shunning of immorality, is alive. It is merely directed to goals the Pilgrims may not have understood.

But what of believers? Where those in the world will change habits of a lifetime to add six months to that life, what are followers of Christ willing to do in the battle against eternal death? Our Catholic tradition speaks of mortification (a word now so unfamiliar my computer word check does not recognize it); Scripture speaks of prayer and fasting as being essential in the battle against evil. Oh yes, many of us pray, at least in some habitual and half-conscious way; and for sure, prayer is of the spirit and self-denial is of the flesh. Is there, however, in most of our lives, any recognition that the desires of the flesh must be disciplined; is there any recognition that there is a battle between the world, the flesh and the devil on the one hand and the power of God on the other?

As Catholics, we glory in the things of creation, whether music, good food, the glories of nature or whatever. However, we also recognize that, because we are weak and easily deceived, we can confuse creature with Creator. To deny ourselves, both for love of God and to keep ourselves on our toes spiritually, is not puritanism; it is simply to be reminded Who is the ultimate source of every good.

Cheerfulness in Giving

November 16, 1997

Every so often, when I find myself in need of a late morning boost of spirit, I will take ten minutes to pass through the cafeteria as the school children are having lunch. Especially the little ones, I will tell them how hungry I am and ask if anyone has any snacks to share. What I much enjoy (apart from cheese doodles, my favorite snack) is the different reactions of the children. While some will see me coming and slyly try to hide their goodies, others will run up and offer something. Most wait—probably hoping against hope that I will go another direction—and offer when directly challenged (as in, "Wow, do I love garlic-flavored chips!") As I say, I enjoy both the snacks and watching the responses. More than once I have walked away marveling at how different can be the responses of a group of five of six year old children. I guess what I am really wondering is how the grace of generosity develops within us.

"The Lord loves a cheerful giver," we are told. I am beginning to see why He has that love, because cheerful giving is tough and probably not that common. Most of us strive for justice, thank God. We want to pay for what we receive; we feel we should repay acts of kindness; and in terms of our relationship with God, we recognize the justice of, for example, getting to Mass each week. We are big on duty, thank God, like the child who gives when directly asked; but cheerful giving is something else again. We sense that, in giving, especially of time, talent or energy, we will be sucked dry and that fear makes cheerfulness in giving a real challenge. I look at myself, for example. Duty is pretty much fulfilled, I hope, but I am far from that cheerfulness in giving that sees a need and tries to meet it, whether or not I am asked. I am far too prone to count the cost of giving.

Counting the cost is, I suspect, the heart of the problem. Giving at its best will focus on the one receiving; but when I count the cost, I am focusing on myself. The saints all have different personalities and focuses to their works, but they all have in common their desire to give of themselves for God and neighbor. They somehow break out of the self-limitation that cannot give without counting the cost. The result of their generosity is that others are blessed and they—the saints—are happy people.

Finally, of course, that happiness is the point. Because we are one in Christ, we are made to give. Surely, we must fight against selfishness and fear, but our happiness can only come insofar as we live the life of God; the life of total self-giving; the life of Him in whose image we are made.

Responding to Grace; Overcoming Isolation
March 22, 1998

In one of the ceremonies that lead our catechumens into the Church in the next several weeks, they will be presented with the Our Father. They will be given a handsome text of the prayer, but of course, this is only a symbol of something far greater. I sometimes believe that the most important word in the prayer is the first: "Our." Since these thoughts are written on St. Patrick's Day, I am reminded of the day about fifteen years ago when I and three friends were invited by some folks we had met in a pub on Achill Island to come the next day and help bring in the turf (or peat) from the bog. This turf would be used for heat the next winter, and it must be first brought from the bog where it had been cut from the ground the previous February. The man who asked us saw three "Yank" suckers from a distance from whom he could get a day's work for nothing as part of our Irish experience, but it was still one of the great days of my life. At any rate, at the end of this day's work—filled with laughs and mud enough for a detergent ad—he asked us if we would like to stop at the pub for some refreshment. I, of course, said, "no"; alas, my friends said the opposite, so in we went.

The point of the story is that, at one point, while our friend was at the bar picking up some pints, he mentioned to the publican that he had brought in John's turf that day. When I asked him who John was, he told me that he was an old man in the village who could no longer go to the bog because he was so old. In other words, our friend had given his day (and ours!) to serving an old man who could not help himself—and he never even bothered to mention the act of charity to us. Thus, we pray, "Our Father."

The effect of sin is always isolation; that of grace is always union with our Father and all of His children. I know (and regret) that often at Mass we seem anonymous to each other; the reality is that we are united with our brother, the Lord Jesus, as He offers Himself to the Father on our behalf. In response, the Father shares with us the life of Jesus in Communion. That bond establishes between us and the Father a union that is as holy as God Himself. If we do not attempt to live out that unity in our daily lives, St. Paul says that we eat and drink condemnation unto ourselves. God truly is our Father and we, just as truly, are united in a bond far more intense than that of blood.

Dr. Alfred Delp, S.J. was martyred by the Nazis. In his *Prison Meditations*, he speaks of the isolation as he awaited execution. Allowed communion with no other prisoners, he experienced from other humans only hatred. He writes: "I would so love to shout across to another cliff where a friend sits equally isolated. But the words do not carry. . . But then—Our Father—and all at once the chasm is spanned. Suddenly we see the truth that in God, through God, we have always possessed the shortest route to reach our neighbor."

Retreat: Stop and Listen

September 18, 1994

When I was a boy, there was a priest living in the rectory at Blessed Sacrament who wrote a column for the *Catholic Standard*. I guess I must have thought that he was really important to have been published in such a prestigious journal, because I can still remember that the name of his weekly column was "View from the Rectory."

I can tell you that if that was a good title for a column written from a rectory on Western Avenue, it could not be surpassed from a view that overlooks the corner of East-West Highway and Pearl Street. There are exceptions, of course (such as the impressive number of people who stop for prayer before Our Lady's statue or who go into church for a moment) but for the most part, what I see from the rectory is action. Our parking lot begins to fill well before 6:00 a.m. and I doubt if the last of those who rent from us are gone before 10:00 p.m. at night. I see parents drop their children off in the morning and literally, run back to their cars. God help the person who is slow from the light at the corner or the pedestrian crossing too slowly from the "fast food" restaurant, because either of them is likely to get a blast from an auto horn that will move them into the next block. I see it in myself: my plan for the day is set and God forgive the thoughts that go through my head when someone "needs to talk to a priest" without a planned appointment.

These thoughts, strangely enough, come to mind because I note that the Annual Lourdes Retreat for Men will be held the weekend of October 7 - 9 at Loyola Retreat House. Sometime we have got to learn to stop, to go apart and to listen to God. The confusion, anger and lack of focus that exist all around us are not because we are not doing enough, but because we so rarely make the attempt to find out what the Lord would have us do. I know two things well. First, that the majority of men who hear about the retreat and who make an excuse not to go will use the excuse of not having enough time. Secondly, I know that anyone who gives that weekend's time to God will find it an investment of tremendous worth.

St. Thomas More: Enemies of Christ Are Wide-Awake

March 17, 1996

The children of our religious education program gave me a copy of Gerard Wegemer's, *Thomas More: A Portrait of Courage*, for my twenty-fifth anniversary, a book which, with great profit, I have recently finished. Most people I hope, recognize More as the subject of the marvelous movie of 1966, *A Man for All Seasons*. Incidentally, showing that movie in the family with discussion could be a great Lenten lesson, especially for teenagers. Courage in standing up for faith is not a frequently treated subject in movies today.

Reading his story again, I have been struck by the writing that he did in the last year of his life, as he was imprisoned in the Tower of London, knowing that, inevitably, the law that he had practiced with such honor all his life, would be twisted so that he might be executed for his fidelity to the Catholic faith.

As St. Thomas faced his own death, it is no surprise that much of his prayer focused on the passion and death of Christ, but his meditations were not only personal. He saw how the players in the drama of Christ's death were present in his day—and ours. I was particularly struck by his meditation on the sleep of the Apostles while the Lord was in agony in the garden. He contrasts the sleep of Peter, James and John with the zeal of Judas who was scurrying about in his efforts to betray Christ. As More says, "For very many are sleepy and apathetic in sowing virtues among the people and maintaining the truth, while the enemies of Christ in order to sow vices and uproot the faith, are wide awake."

It becomes difficult to ignore the real hatred of the message of Christianity, and especially the Catholic Church. As a priest, I must examine how hard I work to teach and preach the good, but confrontational news, which is the Gospel. Thomas More recognized how easily fear can influence our living of the faith. He wrote, for example, of Jesus' fear and dread in the Garden as He contemplated His death. He recognized that fear is, first, a temptation, but like all temptations, can be overcome especially with prayer. Those who oppose the message of Christ are wide awake, just as they were in Thomas' time. Pray God that those who have the gift of faith will give in neither to sloth nor fear as they are challenged to live fully the Christian life.

St. Francis of Assisi: Awesome Joy

September 29, 1996

Francis of Assisi lived only forty-four years. As we reflect on the heroic virtues that make him one of the awesome ones of the followers of the Lord, let us never forget that Francis lived a life that was filled with joy and happiness that was widely recognized even during his lifetime. Few have taken the call of the Lord more seriously than St. Francis and few have experienced more profoundly than he how wonderfully the Lord keeps His word.

Study Francis' father, Pietro Bernadone. The Middle Ages gave way to modernity first in Italy and this man was among the first who would be at home in our day. First of all, he was in France when his son was born—on a business trip buying and selling cloth. He insisted, upon his return, that the name given the boy, John, be changed to Francesco, the little Frenchman, so that this son might be a growing advertisement for the father's business connections. There is no reason to think that the father did not go to Mass on Sunday. In a small city like Assisi, he would have socialized with the bishop (and the monsignori!), but he had no clue as to the growing faith that overcame his son. Pietro recognized, despite the nod of affection and respect given to religion, that the middle class of which he was one of the very early representatives, was dependent upon hard work and money as the sources of its power. I think the anger and public abuse of his son—even after Francis had begun his new life—come from the son's implicit rejection of the father's way of life and values. Francis held the Gospel up to his father as an invitation from the Lord and the father had not the faith or courage to accept the invitation.

In looking at the life of Francis, it is so easy to focus on what he gave up; on how he turned away from the world. Francis himself would focus on Whom he chose to follow, not on what he left behind. When Jesus told him, "Sell all you have and follow me," Francis paid attention to the following not the selling. When in a vision, the Lord told him to, "rebuild my church," Francis began immediately to put stone upon stone in the ruined chapel in which he prayed. So overwhelmed was he with joy in the experience of God's love, that following the Lord was all that mattered. Let God take care of practical details of what was required.

So far as I know, Pietro and Francis never made peace. There is not even mention of the mother, which indicates she was forbidden to see her son. Perhaps the father could not reconcile himself to finding God and joy through poverty, but thousands of others, even while Francis lived his short life, could. And we, living in a world the father helped to create, continue to be challenged to choose between the faith of the father and the faith of the son.

St. Elizabeth Seton: Zeal for God's Work

January 25, 1998

Every commentator of Jesus says the same thing, but saying it once again makes it no less true: He really had His eyes open as He wandered the land of Israel. There is, for example, the parable in Luke (16:1-8) where Jesus talks about the manager of property who had taken a financial bath with the owner's resources. The manager comes up with this scheme that recovers most of the owner's money. Jesus sees this imagination and ingenuity and makes the observation that "the worldly take more initiative than the other-worldly when it comes to dealing with their own kind."

Perhaps I read too much into the story, but I can almost see the Lord looking at His band of Apostles and the others who follow Him. While the worldly work themselves sick trying to build up their fortunes, His followers often seem quite willing to put so much before picking up their crosses and following their Master. Why, He seems to be asking, do not we who have been given the greatest of all opportunities, imitate the zeal of the worldly. My nephew spoke this Christmas of a legal case in Texas of which he is a tiny part and of the millions of dollars and (carefully counted) hours being spent in the pursuit of billions.

The difference between ourselves and the saints is that they really let God be the supreme influence in their lives. Maryland's own St. Elizabeth Seton, for example, let God lead her into the Catholic Church despite the horror of her wealthy family; she let God lead her into religious life after the early death of her husband and trusted that the God who so called her would help her care for her children; and, against all odds, she moved to Emmitsburg and in effect founded the American Catholic school system.

We can begin by asking: "Use me, Lord, to be Your hands and to be Your voice in my world. Use me to announce Your presence to those who do not believe, Your mercy to those who despair and Your power to those who are weak. Let me, Lord, be a sign to all whom I meet of the joy that comes from letting Your Son, Jesus, be Lord of my life. AMEN."

The North American Martyrs' Faith
October 18, 1998

In October the Church honors some of the most wonderful saints on the calendar. Since I grew up in the age before blood, guts and violence on TV, I suppose some of my boyhood fascination for that dimension of life was satisfied by the descriptions of the martyrdoms of some of these saints. Especially did I love to hear about the deaths of the North American Martyrs, Jesuits of the late 17th century who were killed by Iroquois Indians in upstate New York and Ontario, and whose feast is celebrated on October 19th. Make no mistake about it: hearing of their tongues being cut out of their mouths, the gauntlets through which they would have to run and all of the bloody tortures were enough in a more innocent time to stimulate my imagination.

I still am in awe of John de Brebeuf, Isaac Jogues and the other martyrs, but for slightly different reasons. Now, I find that how they died is not as fascinating as why they lived. These men (one was a layman, the others were priests and brothers) came from what would today be seen as a middle class environment. I suppose their entering the Jesuits was not seen as extraordinary, but then they volunteered to go to the missions of French Canada to preach the Gospel to the natives of the region. What was it like to go from Paris to the small frontier village of Quebec and then to take virtually nothing but equipment to say Mass and head into virtually unexplored wilderness hundreds and hundreds of miles away from anything resembling civilization? Talk about motivation! Isaac Jogues at one point was rescued by the Dutch from the Iroquois. The Indians had chewed off some of his fingers so that, by Church law at the time, he was no longer allowed to celebrate Mass. Isaac Jogues returned to France, got a dispensation from Rome that allowed him to say Mass and then begged his superiors for permission to return to Canada. It was not long after this that God allowed him to give his life as a martyr.

St. Paul, in Galatians 5:6, says that all that matters is faith working through love. I think that what he means is that our faith is in a God who is love; who loves us enough to give His Son to be our brother and the sacrificial offering for our sins. Consequently, faith in God must be expressed through love. The North American martyrs, all saints, love God and neighbor so gloriously because they first believe in God's love for themselves. Probably first in the font of Christian love that the home should be and then through their religious formation, these men allowed themselves to be filled with the Spirit of the living God so that, in some sense, they had no choice but to go out with the Gospel of love to those who might kill them.

Over and over again, I ask myself why the 1,500 or so of us who come here each week for Mass attract so few to think of joining the Church through the RCIA. I have to speculate that perhaps we have not allowed the martyrs' faith to grow within ourselves and therefore the love of Jesus that flows from faith is not nearly as attractive in us as it should be.

St. Joseph: Male Role Model

December 20, 1998

I suppose it depends on the generation, but Hollywood seems always to have a strong, silent role model for moviegoers. Maybe John Wayne was not exactly silent, but he filled the role of one for whom words were second to action. Clint Eastwood, with the Dirty Harry movies and the series of spaghetti Westerns, filled the role for those of us in our forties and fifties. Not having been to a movie in a couple of years, I do not know if such male types are still politically correct or not, but I suspect the market is still out there.

I am no critic, but it is easy to know that the key to these roles is that the hero can overcome all obstacles—and get the girl—by means of his unaided strength, wit, and rough charm. Another TV series, no longer being produced, made the same point for an older set of viewers. The Equalizer features an utterly sophisticated hero in his sixties who can outwit any criminal by use of his CIA connections, his brain and steely determination. But, again, the strong individual can conquer all. Compare these fictional male roles with Scripture's example of the strong, silent type: St. Joseph.

It really is amazing when you look at him, because while he is present in quite a few stories—and in the background in several others—Joseph never says a word. Certainly his strength and leadership are not in question. Imagine taking your family out of the promised land of Israel into pagan Egypt, getting settled there, and then leading them back home again. Imagine the strength of his love in taking Mary as his wife when the expectation of the community would be that he would "put her aside", as Scripture delicately puts it. Yes, Joseph is both strong and silent, but what calls him forward as a model for us is his listening faith. There is no dimension of his life that we might call easy, but St. Joseph can live his tough life because he is constantly attentive to the voice of God.

Something in the male spirit seems to seek to develop strength and personal achievement, and I am sure this would not be there if it were not somehow part of God's plan. The potential flaw is to confuse strength with self-sufficiency. The greatest power is that which only God can give. Like St. Joseph, any father's greatest potential is developed as he humbly turns to the Father who is the source of the only strength that really matters.

St. Joseph, foster-father of the Son of God, pray for the men of our parish, that in their humble attention to God our Father, they may bring to perfection, for those whom they love, the gifts God has given to them.

At the Heart of Vocations Is Eucharist

April 24, 1994

"How did you know you wanted to be a priest?" How I dread hearing that question! I suppose it is sort of like asking someone, "How did you fall in love?" What does one say? It just happens; and in terms of priesthood or any religious vocation, each person's story is unique and individual. As I have thought about answering that question for myself, however, I think there are two important parts to the answer.

First of all, I confess that, by personality, I am a person who lives pretty much in the here and now. I am pretty good at responding to the crisis of today; much less good at planning for the future. I suppose no one has everything, so I'll have to live with who I am. At any rate, as I grew up, I pretty much lived day to day: from grade school to high school to college (never even got around to applying to college until February of my senior year). I was the type (I do not recommend this) who would get up at 5 a.m. to study for a test because I had put off studying until then. The point is that I never gave much thought to vocation until my last year of college: I just was not that worried about the future (plus college was a lot of fun). But I think deep down, I always kind of knew that I would end up a priest. I never talked about it to anyone, I never even thought that much about it, but I think it was always there. In other words, God knew my personality and He just waited until I was ready to pay attention to His call.

The second, and much more important thing, has to do with the Eucharist. In a variety of ways that space does not permit me to describe here, God led me, through influences at home, in parish and in Catholic schools, to a real faith in and love for Christ present in the Eucharist. I truly believe that perhaps the greatest spiritual gift of my life is that God has allowed me to deeply believe in the power and strength that are in the Mass. Therefore, since the celebration of the Mass is so central to priesthood, I suppose it did not knock me to the ground in shock when I came to face the possibility that God wanted me to live my life as a priest.

I cannot, of course, speak with any authority about the call to be a sister—though this call, too, is one of service to and for the Church—but I can say, that for me, at least, the Eucharist is at the heart of the matter. I really believe that if we are a people who are centered on the Eucharistic Sacrifice, there will be no shortage of those willing to give their lives to the Church. And so, perhaps, our prayers for vocations should begin with prayer that we become, ever more completely, a Eucharistic community.

Fostering Vocations

November 13, 1994

Priesthood is sacraments. Of course, priesthood is many other things, too: priesthood is preaching; priesthood is counseling; priesthood is working with children and young people; priesthood is parish administration; priesthood is teaching; priesthood is being with people in sickness and as they die; priesthood is serving the poor. The heart of priesthood though is the sacraments—especially the Eucharist.

There are certain predictable questions with which every priest must deal on a regular basis. Among the most frequently asked concerns the number of candidates for Holy Orders and especially, explanations for the relatively low number of seminarians today. Of course, the rule of celibacy is a factor. However, human nature does not change and, let me assure all who read this, the commitment to celibacy has never been an easily accepted thing. However, in earlier generations, there has been an abundance of our best seeking priesthood. A more important factor, I suspect, is a fear in our world of making and keeping any commitments. One need not look at the numbers entering priesthood or religious life to see the reality; the statistics concerning those entering marriage and sticking with that life-time commitment allow us to see that this is, for whatever reason, a time when many are reluctant to give their word and then to keep it.

As I wrote above, however, I think that the essence of priesthood itself places certain preconditions on a candidate. I do not question that God could call a man who has not yet fully begun to appreciate the Mass, but normally speaking, the person who has begun to sense the awesomeness of the Eucharist and what it makes present for God's people is the person who begins to consider any kind of call to priesthood or religious life. As a priest, I have been called to stand in the place of Christ Himself to offer His Body and Blood to the Father; I have been called to stand in His place to minister the forgiveness of God to sinners. If these and the other sacramental realities are not at the core of a Catholic's faith, why would a healthy person ever consider priesthood?

The fostering of vocations, in my opinion then, begins with a love of the sacraments and a recognition that they are the actions of Christ Himself. When that love is present in a community, I believe that there will be no shortage of qualified men who believe they may be called to fill the priestly role for another generation.

A Project of Love and Grace

May 3, 1998

My friend from seminary days returned my call early this morning. I say from the seminary, but of course he is a D.R.Q., a dirty rotten quitter, as we used to call those who left before ordination. At any rate, he is long since happily married and is now contemplating the cost of sending his oldest off to college. We laughed about her self-centered arrogance ("She thinks private college is a birthright"), but I did not have to look too deeply to detect his continuing joy and pride in fatherhood. From years of friendship I think I understand something of my friend's life as father and husband, but I am also grateful that he has real insight into my life as a priest. That shared insight comes not simply because he spent a few years in the seminary, but because, in so many important ways we look at life from similar perspectives.

In fact, I had left a call for this old friend, because I wanted to share something I had read recently that I suspected he would appreciate. This Sunday is World Day of Prayer for Vocations. Now, to be honest, I may not have given this day the attention it deserves, except that I happened to come across a brief talk given by the Holy Father on this annual call to prayer for vocations to the priesthood and religious life. Forgive the slang, but one of the Pope's lines "blew me away". He said that the Day of Prayer for Vocations is ideal for "announcing that the Holy Spirit of God writes in the heart and life of every baptized person a project of love and grace, which is the only way to give full meaning to existence." I obviously do a lot of Baptisms, but the Holy Father's insight has developed my way of looking at the sacrament. "A project of love and grace," he writes. In other words, the Holy Father invites parents to impress upon their children the wonderful challenge that, on the day on which God shares His life with us, He also gives to each of us a project that is uniquely and individually ours. And Pope John Paul continues, the attempt to fulfill that project is "the only way to give full meaning to existence."

I know this may sound naive, but suppose, as parents start to give moral and ethical formation to their children, they were to put that formation in the context of the child's attempt to discover the project that God has given to them for life. It is obvious in my life that God wanted me to be a priest; my friend, and I hope many who read this, would affirm that their God-given project involves marriage and family. *Man's Search for Meaning* was the title of Victor Frankl's book so many of us read in college. For the Christian, that search is not pointless and it is not conducted in a void. It is a search directed by the Holy Spirit for that project, to which I am called to give my life, that will be the source of blessings for those around me and which will give the fullest meaning to my existence.

God's Call Through Others

April 13, 1997

In Lebanon, I am told, where celibacy is not required of priests of the Maronite Catholic Rite, when the parish priest of a small mountain village dies, the people of the village will call another man from the village to become a priest. He, already married, will go down to the city for a few months, receive some theological and liturgical instruction and then be ordained. Our discipline in the Western Church is quite different—and even in Lebanon I am sure the scenario I describe is increasingly rare—but it does illustrate an important point about vocation. The man to be ordained often perceives God's call through other people.

I am almost embarrassed to admit this, but one of the first times anyone ever spoke to me about priesthood was when, out of the blue, a girl asked me, at a CYO dance when I was in high school, if I ever thought about being a priest. At that moment, I surely did not feel a call from God: I would hate to describe what I did feel; but isn't it funny that she had spotted something that seems to have had some validity. (Either that or she was seeking to spare the toes of a generation of women.)

At a time in our history when we more and more experience a shortage of priests, the Church is coming to rely on the wisdom of the people in calling men and women to vocations in priesthood or religious life. Particularly as the age of those responding to vocations increases, they are usually in work environments where they may have very little formal contact with the priests or sisters who, in the past, would have suggested religious life. Their fellow Catholics do know them, respect their faith, and perhaps, it is their fellow Catholics who might perceive them as possible priests, deacons or sisters.

If you have such a person in mind, whether they live in this parish or not, I suggest the "Called by Name" program which will be running for the next few weeks. Next weekend there will be postcards addressed to Cardinal Hickey in the vestibules of the church, on which you can share with him the names of men or women you believe to be possible suitable candidates. These individuals will be invited (only once, I assure you) to a meeting to find out more about life as a priest or religious, and perhaps, to begin a journey that will end in a life given to Christ and the Church. Previous use of this "Called by Name" program in the last five or six years in the Archdiocese has yielded the names of people who are now in formation, so your thoughts are valuable. Please pray for vocations daily, and, in the next weeks, ask the Lord to show you that individual who might well be called to serve us in the first years of the New Millennium.

Commitment in Vocations

July 6, 1997

Sometimes we should get credit for just getting up in the morning. Today, when I should have been setting goals for the new day, the radio alarm clock instead informed me that fewer households than ever are headed by married couples in the nineties. Tragic as is this statistic, it only serves to illustrate something I have felt for a long time. So often, in a discussion about vocations, people will speculate that if the Church would relax the requirements of celibacy, the problem of vocations would be solved. To be certain, I have known many men over the years who would have loved to be priests, but who felt that they could not live as celibates. So often, when these men would leave the seminary, it would seem that the best were leaving. Now of course, most of these men are husbands and fathers; though interestingly, some do later return to accept the call to priesthood.

Yes, superficially, the relaxation of celibacy might seem to be the answer. But, this morning's A.M. jolt on married households points, I think, to something more profound. We are increasingly a society that shuns commitment. People are reluctant to join organizations that formerly had millions of members; parishioners do not want to make commitments to chair activities; couples live in sin for years rather than commit to marriage; and even in sports, free agency means that contracts are signed that allow athletes to move from team to team after short numbers of years. These examples vary in importance, of course; they all point to a common fear of saying, "Yes" in a way that commits one in an open-ended way.

I believe that we are experiencing the fruits of either a massive loss of faith in God or of radical self-centeredness, really two sides of the same worthless coin. My parents got married in the Depression; many in the parish have grandparents who came to America in diseased boats; seminaries as recently as thirty years ago were filled with men who longed to give their lives for God's people. None of these people were perfect; many of them had colossal errors in their lives. But at least they believed that life is about commitment and about making things grow for the good of others. The reality of times being tough is never going to change; though from a purely economic point of view, we can ask if things have ever been better. Times tough or times easy, however, God is still God and He is still powerful in the lives of those who place their trust in Him. Let us beg Him to increase our own faith and the gift of faith in the lives of those whom we love.

There Is a Choice to Be Made

August 21, 1994

Sometimes I think so much like a priest that it scares me. However, I guess that is who I am, so bear with me. I am probably the only person in the world to make the comparison between last week's concert, Woodstock II, and the World Youth Day activities in Denver with Pope John Paul II, but I do think some interesting points can be made.

First of all, let us beware of over-simplifying. I know a number of young people who went to Denver last summer and some of them, at least, would gladly have been in New York State last weekend. I can easily imagine them sliding down some soaked hill, covered in mud. At every stage in life, but especially in youth, there are pulls toward alternative visions of living. Likewise, I am sure there were large numbers of concert-goers who take faith very seriously; and rightly, they understand that music and fun do not have to be unChristian. Where comparison between the two events is useful is in contrasting their fundamental goals.

Fun is great, and quite frankly, I often describe my priesthood with just that word. But, obviously, fun is not the point of my vocation. What Woodstock represents is a way of looking at life that puts fun or pleasure as one of the highest goods. I do not know enough to critique lyrics of songs in order to pick out any philosophical values, but I can tell you that (if news reports are correct) when one hundred thousand people cheerfully avoid paying a price of admission to an event, certainly some kind of message of self-centeredness is being given.

What the Holy Father called a similar number of young people to in Denver is to follow Jesus; in other words, He reminded us all that we are not the source of the happiness for which we yearn. His challenge was to break out of self in the Christian service of others, rather than to let life be focused on one experience after another. Life is about more than fun.

The two events portray clearly two utterly different visions of life. I do not fear the choice that will be made by our young people. What I fear is that they will not understand that a choice must be made.

Choosing the Fine Over the Flimsy

January 19, 1997

I picked up a book by Dom Hubert van Zeller recently entitled, *We Die Standing Up* that was written not long after World War II. I am sure it is out of print, and where I got it, I do not know, but it is a gem. In a chapter on goals, he has the line, "To distinguish between what is fine and the decision to follow the fine in an age when flimsiness is the fashion that costs us dear." Perfect example (to my shame): my sister-in-law called me this morning to ask if I would like to be at my nephew's Confirmation Mass. When I asked the date, my first thought on hearing the response was, "Oops, that's Super Bowl Sunday." Of course, I'll go to the Mass (which should be over in time), but I think you get my point. My first thought was about the flimsy.

There are few things I more enjoy about my life than the opportunity to hear confessions, especially on those occasions when a person is taking a significant step back toward the Lord. Every person is different, but often, a person comes to the sacrament after an experience of personal disgust at the realization of evil in their life. The disgust and the sorrow are real, the forgiveness by God is total, and reconciliation between the person, God and neighbor is absolute; but the journey has just begun. The thing that used to surprise me was how much, to use Fr. van Zeller's terms, the habit of sin teaches one to value flimsy over the fine. For example, after years of judging people on the basis of what they have or where they work, it is tough to begin to try to evaluate a person, especially a possible date, on the basis of who the person is or what he or she believes. Just as we must be trained to prefer vegetables over french fries, so spiritually, there is the process of choosing the deep over the superficial.

A lot of Catholics grow weary of Church harping on the pro-life message. Themselves anti-abortion, they feel the battle has been lost and that we seem crotchety and out-of-fashion to keep up the fight. Fight, however, we must, not only for the unborn, but for our nation and culture. In the most gruesome of ways we have chosen the flimsy over the fine, death over life. We are trying to pretend that the easy way out, even if antiseptic and quick, will not eventually poison us as a people. It has and it will. Recent statistics indicate however that, politicians notwithstanding, the word is having an effect. This is no time to turn away from speaking about the fine, just because those committed to the flimsy would wish it so.

The Pull of False Idols

August 28, 1994

The stories, especially the Bible stories from the Old Testament, were always the best part of grade school religion classes. What young boy cannot identify with David going against Goliath and even before *The Ten Commandments*, who had a problem imagining the Red Sea crashing down on the chariots of the Egyptians? Even as a boy, though, I never could understand the problem the people of Israel had with worshiping false gods. The authors of the Sacred Scripture pictured idol worship as foolish and I agreed. Worship a golden calf? You must be kidding!

Of course, nothing is ever quite so simple. Picture the Chosen People, actually a small group of former slaves trying to find a place to settle. Their God, Yahweh, has led them for forty years in the desert and they are grateful to Him. Now, however, they come into this new land where the people seem prosperous and strong. Looking back from our perspective of three or four thousand years of belief in one and only one God, we may think them foolish, but is it so great a surprise that many of the Israelites felt that such strong people must also have strong gods? They did not wish to reject Yahweh; they were going to worship Him and "the gods of the nations," as Scripture calls them.

We live in a land of tremendous natural resources. Politically, we formed ourselves at a time when individualism—as opposed to community—motivated decisions. Given such an environment, could we have avoided becoming a people for whom "wealth, strength, health (and therefore youth) and achievement were goals? While we never formally rejected Christianity (quite the contrary), we have become a people that to a great extent, evaluates ourselves according to external standards. Do not be surprised when I tell you that over the years, I have developed sympathy for the Chosen People as they struggled to avoid the worship of false gods. The worship of such false gods is a lot easier to fall into than I believed when I was a boy.

It is because idolatry is so tempting that we hear the words of Jesus, "None of you can be my disciple if he does not renounce all his possessions," with such dread. We want to believe that God alone is the source of our joy, but we fear the consequences that such a passage might have in our lives. Like the Jews, we continue to be torn between many gods. Wise is the person who has recognized the pull of false gods and who understands that one cannot be alive to God without being dead to the world.

The Foolishness of Pantheism

September 22, 1996

Last Sunday morning, a crowd of some five thousand people gathered to protest the logging of some dead redwood trees that are on the floor of the forest in an isolated area north of San Francisco. The concern of these people is that somehow, these dead trees are essential to the ecology of the forest. For all that I know, they may well be right. After reading the story on Monday morning, I asked one of the priests, "Since they were so far from a town, where do you suppose all these people went to Mass?" I received in answer to my question one of those looks that places me among the nearly brain dead. The point that I was trying to make was, of course, that those people did not have to worry about religious obligation: they were already fully engaged in the worship of nature.

Earlier this summer we saw another example of such devotion when a gorilla saved a small child who had fallen into a cage at the zoo in, I believe, Chicago. Buried deep within commentary, one expert on such animals did reveal that the gorilla's action was purely instinctual, but most commentary led us to believe this gorilla consciously chose, with maternal understanding, to reach out and save a suffering baby. I suppose the gorilla has since spent many a happy afternoon reading the notes and cards of gratitude she has received. You may have noted too, that Vancouver is closing its zoo because the city is no longer willing to tolerate the injustice to animals.

We are confronted with pantheism, a doctrine that says that the finite, changing reality that we experience did not come as a result of God's creation of a world outside Himself, but that creation is part of His being. If creation is part of divine being, then all of creation is equal. If all of creation is equal, then I have obligations to animals and trees that are comparable to what I owe to other humans. (In fact, if I can see unborn infants as a threat to the environment, then they become expendable for the good of the environment.)

The foolishness of pantheism is so dangerous because it tries to replace a divinely ordered universe, wherein humanity is at the summit of creation and wherein all of creation reflects the glory of the Creator, with a universe where, since all are part of the divine, all have equal status. But since all have equal status, each has equal standing in determining how the universe should be run. In such a world, the actor arrested trying to save the dead redwood trees senses no contradiction when it is revealed that the deck on his home is made of, yes, you guessed it—dead redwood.

The Demands of False Gods

November 1, 1998

Pick out a false god; any one will do. Let us take money for an example. If I worship money, I will do anything to be close to it, to have it in my life and to grow in appreciation of it and its blessings. My god is found powerfully in the markets; as nowhere else, it seems, my god is really present there. And so, with crowds of worshipers, I am present in the markets—and it is adoration, not obligation, that gets me there each day—seeking to appease them, to master them, to discern them and to know their mysterious ways, so that I can come closer to my god. How beautiful is my god; how wonderful its power; how able it is to give pleasure and to make me the source of envy. In my god is the source of security and a hedge against the future. My god comes into my life because I am bright, because I work slavishly for it and because I know its ways just a little better than most others who worship it.

As glorious as is my god, however, it has a side to it that is hard. I cannot take my eyes off of it for a moment lest it begin to slip away into the possession of one more faithful and loyal than I. While my heart is always set on my god, my god will tolerate no mistakes of judgment. And while my god cares not if I worship other gods, the pleasure, passion or joy they can give usually come at the cost of money. How much of this god can I sacrifice to obtain what another god can give? And yes, my god is also jealous. Ultimately, no person can come before it. The person next to me in the temple of the market is friendly; I have known him since my youth. But he can get in the way of me and the possession of my god and, therefore, he is my enemy. My god demands that I make a choice.

I want to control my god, to share its fruits with family, friends and those I want to impress, but how much energy is required and how demanding is this god. O that there was a God that cared about me; O that there could be a God before whom my weakness did not have to be hidden; O that there might be a God beyond what my wit and brains could control, but Who wanted me as child, friend and recipient of His blessings and love. Yes, I suppose I would have to be obedient to such a God, but would not the obedience of a dearly loved child before such a Father make an awful lot of sense?

Called to Be His Light
in a Secular World

November 27, 1994

"TBS gives thanks to Clint Eastwood. . . Parental discretion advised." I believe these lines faithfully quote part of a widely shown Thanksgiving week advertisement on TV and lets us know to whom the owners of Turner Broadcasting, at least, give thanks during this wonderful holiday weekend. In the days leading up to Thanksgiving you may have noticed the Postal Service announcement that either this year or next, they will cease to reproduce Nativity scenes on postage stamps at Christmas. This, I suppose, is because mail delivery has become so efficient that divine help is no longer necessary to enhance service. We have begun what offense avoiding merchants safely call, "the holiday season," and judging by the parking lot at Montgomery Mall this weekend, our response has been early and fervent. And, oh yes, this is the first Sunday of Advent.

Folks, ours is an increasingly and in some ways, militantly, secular age. TBS can announce an all-day barrage of Eastwood movies by confusing the movie star with God and probably not even realize their blasphemy. How many even spend any time at all asking the question, "Thank who?" as they celebrate the fourth Thursday of November? Let us not be naive: those who have given so much time to eliminating any reference to the birthday of the Lord from school holiday celebrations have been enormously successful. Many children of supposedly Christian heritage have no knowledge of any seasonal story beyond that of Santa.

In the first reading from the Mass of Friday of the first week of Advent, the Prophet Isaiah (Is 29:17-24) says, "Out of gloom and darkness, the eyes of the blind shall see." Certainly our age, as much as that of the prophet, is one of gloom and darkness, but the Advent message will not allow us to lose hope. For any who keep focused on Christ, there will be sureness of vision. But even more importantly, for those of us who have been baptized into Christ, there is a reminder that we—His Church, his people—are empowered by the Spirit to be His light that shines in the fog and gloom of secular unhappiness. It is not enough for us simply to protect ourselves from the darkness of unbelief, but also we must ask Him to use us to light the way for those lost in the darkness of the world's deceiving message.

The Confidence of Isaiah Relevant Today

December 11, 1994

Go look at some of the Christmas cards you have received. On some of them you will probably find the image of a baby lion peacefully sharing a manger with a helpless calf. For many, I suspect, that improbable picture is as close as they get to the prophecies of Isaiah. The Book of Isaiah is used so frequently during Advent that its author, with Our Lady and John the Baptist, is one of the three main persons of the season. While the long book of some 65 chapters was actually written during two different periods of the history of Israel and by at least two different authors, most of what we read during Advent comes from the first 39 chapters and is by the man whose name gives the title to the whole Old Testament book.

As was usual in the history of Israel, Isaiah wrote at a time of political crisis. The Israel of David had by this time, (around 720 B.C.) divided into two kingdoms, Israel (in the north) and Judah. Perhaps surprisingly, it is the southern kingdom, Judah, that continues the line of David and which is centered in Jerusalem. Isaiah was a major figure in Judah for about fifty years and this is not the time to summarize his career. However, two things can be said: he prophesied during a time of political corruption and external military threat and at the same time, he never lost hope in God's plan for His people. On the one hand, he blasts the corrupt who hold power—even those who reign in the line of David—but Isaiah never lets it be forgotten that "great in your midst is the holy one of Israel" (Is 12:6). As one becomes familiar with the corruption within his people and with impending threats from pagan nations, Isaiah's constant hope and joy seem more and more miraculous. At Christmas Mass, we will read again from Isaiah, "a child has been born for us, a son given to us" (Is 9:6). The prophet had no clear idea of how that prophecy would be fulfilled, but he believed with utter confidence, that Yahweh would not abandon his people.

Similarly, today, the Church lives in a world characterized by its political and moral corruption. As in the day of Isaiah, politicians called to faith, accept and celebrate the values of the world. Those values and those who accept them must be confronted by the Church as they were by Isaiah. But even more than did Isaiah, we have reason to speak to the world with joy and hope. We confront the world, we challenge those who have sold out and who should know far better; but we do so from a perspective that knows that, in Christ, the victory is already won. With Pope John Paul we say to believers, "Be not afraid," and "There are no grounds for losing hope."

Called to Stand Apart in a Secular World

August 13, 1995

David Knight, in his book, *His Way*, was the first I heard discuss what he called secular religion. He was referring to an attitude toward morality or religion that was defined more by the standards of society than by either Gospel or Church teaching. Our attitudes toward race unfortunately helped him to make his point. One local example: many in this area can remember a time when, without thinking, it was assumed that blacks would sit in the back of church or in the choir loft.

On the other hand, there was much about the secular religion that was based on Christian principles. Honesty was encouraged; marital fidelity was expected by society; neighbors took responsibility for neighbor's children. In regard to God Himself, few questioned the place of the "Protestant" Our Father in school prayer; presidents unashamedly thanked God for His providence at Thanksgiving; and priests, rabbis and ministers were routinely asked to offer generic prayers to open meetings or graduations. Religion was felt to play a stabilizing role in society.

Catholics were in a funny position as they gradually immersed themselves in American society. They came out of ethnic backgrounds where they were perceived as "different" by the Protestant majority (much as Hispanics are today, I suppose) and yet they really loved and appreciated their new country. They wanted to "fit in" and to be accepted. To a very great extent, Catholics, without really thinking about it, accepted the secular religion—what society accepted as right or wrong—while maintaining their Catholic religion and traditions. To a great extent, this "worked;" Catholics were accepted as American and remained Catholic.

Our attitudes toward race were probably a hint of what almost has to happen when society instead of the teachings of Jesus or His Church form our consciences. Without our fully recognizing what was happening, our secular religion has moved from being vaguely Christian to being utterly hedonistic. There are many reasons why we have "lost" so many from the Church in the last thirty years, but one of them most certainly is because, as the difference between secular and Catholic religions became more and more apparent, many chose the religion of the world. Until, in home, school and parish, we make it clear how a Catholic is called to stand apart from social norms—and not to fit in—we can expect the same losses in the future. Jesus is the Way and He is the only Way.

Combating Isolation in a Secular World
June 9, 1996

In the June, 1998 issue of *First Things, A Monthly Journal of Religion and Public Life*, the German theologian, Wolfhart Pannenberg, has an article entitled, "How to Think about Secularism," that I found immensely valuable. One of his observations about the cultural climate of secularism, sparked some thought that might be of help.

I was speaking with a woman recently who has worked for years in a government agency downtown. She goes to the noon Mass daily at St. Joseph's on Capitol Hill, much as so many from our neighborhood offices come to Lourdes each day. She was speaking about the environment in her office: about how many co-workers are divorced; about the official push for homosexual preference and especially, about the obsessive concern for money and the luxury that money can buy. Especially telling was the comment from a young clerical worker who remarked, last December, that she hoped to get "a lot for Christmas." The young woman had no clue that Christmas had anything to do with the birth of anyone. My friend, in speaking of her attempts to take Christ seriously, looks at the world in which she works and asks (as I have heard so many ask), "Am I crazy?"

As Pannenberg says, "A public climate of secularism undermines the confidence of Christians in the truth of what they believe." All of us have seen the eighteen year old from a Catholic family go off to college and come home at the end of a semester having ceased the practice of the faith. Surely the young person has responsibility, but without communal support (alas, even sometimes, in Catholic universities), is it realistic to expect the average young person to survive the onslaught of secularism? I have friends who live in one of those town house squares of fifty or so homes in the upper part of this county. They suspect they are the only people on that square who go to any church on Sunday. Jesus is still Lord, but to believe in Him and His counter-cultural Gospel, without the support of community, requires a faith that is heroic.

Two practical conclusions: first, families must work very hard at living, praying, and sharing the faith in the context of the home. Take for granted that each of you goes each day into a world hostile to your faith. We depend on each other; alone, the pressures may well be too much. Also, families must seek to form bonds with other families who believe as they do and the grace of extended family is one that cannot be over-estimated. I as a pastor, have as one of my most serious obligations, that of trying to lead a parish where people experience the community that we celebrate in the Eucharist; but you as members of the parish must recognize that simply fulfilling Sunday obligations will probably not be enough to combat isolation in a secular world. The human bonds you form through parish participation give you the wisdom to go into this world ready to stand alone holding the light that can lead others to God.

Msgr. Wells Says Goodbye

January 10, 1999

Apart from the few things that make up Christmas in a parish and as a member of a fairly large family, and apart from the packing of boxes, the notifications of address change and the other preparations for moving, these last weeks have been a time of quiet reflection for me. Since I am leaving a parish where the people are wonderful, where the clergy, sisters and staff seem to share a common vision of faith and service, where there are few money problems and where the parish is in the neighborhood in which I grew up and where many old friends still live, the quiet reflection has varied between kicking myself in the—well, you know—and the mystery of being called by God.

Ultimately—and this is true for any believer—it all comes down to making an act of faith. In the "new Church," I could have raised objections with the Cardinal and "gotten out" of a transfer. And sometimes I am sure, such objections have validity and the Cardinal listens. But in my case, other than "I don't want to," I could not think of any reason to say "no" to what His Eminence sees as a job he thinks I can do. But when I think of the couple who discovers that a baby is coming whom they had not expected, or when I see people drop long planned vacations because of a parent's sudden illness, or when I see someone work through the decision to leave a job because marriage and family are suffering, I am reminded that surrender to the will of God is at the heart of the Gospel. Either He loves me and will give me only what is for my good, or He does not.

The new Millennium Window makes the core statement of Catholic trust and submission to God's will. Jesus chose, knowing full well the horror of His choice, to love until death in the face of the world's sin. The blood that He shed as a result of His faith is the source of our life and our hope for eternity. And so it is with us; we believe that dying to ourselves for love of God or neighbor is, somehow, a sharing in the work of Jesus Himself. Most often, such dying is not very dramatic—and, really, accepting a transfer as a priest is not all that big a thing—but it is all of a piece. The more that each of us, in our not very dramatic ways, is willing to die to self, the more those around us experience faith and God's love.

I leave Our Lady of Lourdes for the second time. Sometimes all we can say is, "Thank you," and the words say nothing of what is in the heart. What could I ever say in response to what I have received from this parish family? I have been embraced, in you, by the very love of God. May that same God who has been so good to me in the parish of Our Lady of

Lourdes, allow me to share something of that goodness with the people whom I am now called to serve.

Bible Quotes

Book Quotes

Nouwen, Henri. *With Burning Hearts.* 15
Maryknoll NY: Orbis Books, 1994.

Pope John Paul II. *Crossing the Threshold of Hope* 16
New York: Alfred A. Knopf, Inc., 1994.

Quoist, Michael. *Christ is Alive.* 31
trans. J.F. Bernard. Garden City NY: Doubleday, 1971.

de Caussad, S.J., Jean-Pierre. *Abandonment to Divine Providence.* 103
trans. J. Beevers. Garden City NY: Image Books, 1993.

Powers, C.P., Isaias. *Quiet Places with Mary* 119
Mystic CT: Twenty-third Publications, 1987.

Bokenkotter, Thomas S. *A Concise History of the Catholic Church* 158
New York: Image Books, 1990.

Mankowski, S.J., Paul. "Atheistic Catholics." *Faith, Moral Reasoning and* 189
Contemporary American Life. ed. Sr. Madonna Murphy, C.S.C.
Brighton MA: Cambridge Center for Study of Faith and Culture, 1995.

Vanauken, Sheldon. *A Severe Mercy.* NY: Phoenix Press: Walker & Co.,1987 206

Our Lady of Perpetual Help Free Cancer Home, Atlanta. *A Memoir of Mary Ann* 208
Intro by Flannery O'Connor. New York: Farrar, Straus and Cudaly, 1961.

Bloom, Anthony. *Living Prayer.* London: Darton, Longman & Todd, 1966 214

Delp, S.J., Alfred. *Prison Meditations.* NY: Herder & Herder, 1963. 218

Wegemer, Gerard. *Thomas More: A Portrait of Courage.* Princeton: Sceptor, 1995. 221

Frankl, Victor. *Man's Search for Meaning.* Boston: Beacon Press, 1963. 229

Van Zeller, Dom Hubert, *We Die Standing Up* [Essays]. 234
New York: Sheed & Sheed, 1949.

Pannenberg, Wolfhart. "How to Think About Secularism," 241
First Things, A Monthly Journal of Religion and Public Life. June, 1995.

Spiritual Reflections of Interest to Special Groups